The Political Economy of Development

The Political Economy of Development

J. FAALAND
and
J. R. PARKINSON

Frances Pinter (Publishers), London

First published in Great Britain in 1986 by
Frances Pinter (Publishers) Limited
25 Floral Street, London WC2E 9DS

British Library Cataloguing in Publication Data

Faaland, Just
    The political economy of development.
    1. Developing countries–Economic conditions
    I. Title   II. Parkinson, J. R.
    330.9172'4   HC59.7

    ISBN 0-86187-605-9

Typeset by Joshua Associates Limited, Oxford
Printed and bound in Great Britain by
Biddles Ltd, Guildford and King's Lynn

Contents

Preface

Economic development may be seen from many different points of view: in terms of history, theory or empirical generalisation; or sometimes, as is attempted here, with all these things in mind as they relate to the practice of economic development itself. This book falls into the category of applied economics and is concerned essentially with the issues that arise in attempting to devise development strategies for developing countries and to implement them. We have sought to present the material and our analysis so that it will reflect the realities of development planning in a manner that will be familiar to economists concerned with preparing economic plans in the developing countries themselves, and to administrators who seek to guide the process of development and devise policies that are at the same time soundly based and politically acceptable.

The reason for the introduction of the term political economy into the title of the book is obvious. The practice of economics cannot be conducted in isolation and has always to be related to the political and social setting of the countries with which it is concerned. In such circumstances many issues are matters for debate and political consideration which extend far beyond economic argument.

The book is mainly about the poorest countries in the world and we describe the process of development with illustrations from many of them. We have provided a thumbnail sketch of two of them, Bangladesh and Mozambique, to give some idea of the very real problems facing these economies and also of the opportunities that are open to them.

In the final chapter of the book we broaden the discussion and analysis to consider various international aspects of development and some of the interrelations between developed and developing countries.

The book is intended to be easily accessible to the general

reader. The text, however, is also intended to serve as part of the material that a university student, in the second or third year, might wish to read as a supplement to the formal theoretical structures that increasingly dominate courses on economic development, sometimes with a total loss of realism

The emphasis of the book lies on policies for development. With this in mind we have tried to identify the central issues for which policies must be devised and to concentrate attention on them.

Since it is quite impossible to cover all aspects of economic development in depth in a short book, a list of further reading has been added at the end of each chapter.

We gratefully acknowledge the secretarial skills of Mrs I. Dewick and Mrs V. Garton of the University of Nottingham, and Mrs I. A. Andersen, Mrs T. Heiberg-Andersen and Mrs M. Serck-Hanssen of the Chr. Michelsen Institute. We also extend our thanks to the Librarian at the Institute, Mrs K. Hagen Andersen, who removed many blemishes from the notes and references and to Mr G. V. Reed and Dr Armindo Miranda.

Our thanks are due to the World Bank for permission to use material from *World Development Reports* and other sources; also to Frank Cass & Co., to use material from the *Journal of Development Studies*, Vol. I, 1964.

September 1985   *Just Faaland, Bergen*
                                                                                         Jack Parkinson, Nottingham

1 The development path

It is common knowledge that there are rich and poor countries. Ethiopia, the poorest country listed by the World Bank,[1] had an income of $120 per capita in 1983. At the other extreme, the inhabitants of the United Arab Emirates, with vast oil resources for their population of a little over 1 million, averaged nearly $23,000 and Switzerland, the richest industrialised country, $16,000 per head. Altogether, the World Bank identified thirty-five low-income countries, that is countries with less than $400 per head in 1983. Many of these are small and although only sixteen have a population over 10 million, two of these, China and India, with 1,020 million and 733 million people respectively, are, in terms of population, the largest in the world. Their total income, however, is far below that of the United States or Japan and less than other major industrialised countries.

With such great disparities in income and accompanying material wealth in the form of capital, it is to be expected that the poorest countries will show up badly in other ways. In general, we would expect longevity to be low, health poor, malnutrition prevalent, disease common and untreated, and educational opportunities to be severely limited. Yet, as we shall see, even with limited resources, many of these evils can be prevented. Determined policies can overcome disabilities and at the same time provide the resources needed for the development of the country. After meeting basic consumption needs, many low-income developing countries have little left over to spend on development, but China appears both to provide for necessities and to save and invest 30 per cent of the gross domestic product. Amongst the poorest developing countries, as elsewhere, generalisations may not fit specific cases.

It is curious that such differences in the performance of countries should be evident at the present time. Some countries innovate and others do not, it is true; but why do the laggards not learn from those that lead the way? Although no certain answers can be given to such a question because many factors combine to favour development, or frustrate it, it is helpful to reflect on a selection of answers advanced by some historians.

HISTORICAL EXPLANATIONS OF BACKWARDNESS

In his book, *Economic Backwardness in Historical Perspective*, Alexander Gerschenkron explains what the economic historian might be able to contribute to the understanding of the reasons for backwardness.[2]

For the quality of our understanding of current problems depends largely on our frame of reference. All decisions in the field of economic policies are essentially decisions with regard to combinations of a number of relevant factors. And the historian's contribution consists in pointing at *potentially* relevant factors and at *potentially* significant combinations amongst them which could not be easily perceived within a more limited sphere of reference. No past experience, however rich, and no historical research, however thorough, can save the living generation the creative task of finding their own answers and shaping their own future.

In a monumental study covering 5,000 years of human life, Professor Arnold Toynbee attempted to explain the rise and fall of civilisations.[3] In Toynbee's view, achievement was essentially a response to challenge presented by situations of unusual difficulty or opportunity. Thus, to take but one example, the rise of the Egyptian civilisation is attributed to the effects of a change in climate which turned well-watered grassland into the Sahara and Arabian deserts and forced some of the populations living there to move and settle in Egypt.

Such challenge had to be neither too great nor too small for new civilisations to be created. The challenge facing the Eskimos was too great to provoke a positive response whilst small changes were unlikely to be sufficiently stimulating. The process of decline was different. Toynbee considered it to be 'a failure of creative power in the minority, an answering withdrawal of mimesis on the part of the majority and a consequent loss of social unity in the society as a whole'.[4]

Modern historians would be exceedingly critical of such views, regarding them as offering little in explanation and verging on tautology. Nevertheless, the challenge of the environment is something that has to be overcome today. The threat of drought in the countries of the Sahel is unlikely on its own to stimulate the inhabitants to found a new civilisation, but it might do so if other countries were to respond to their needs. It is also very evident that many countries apparently favourably placed for development have seemed unable to develop over long spans of time, perhaps because of lack of suitable stimulation. In such conditions again, some kind of intervention may be necessary to start the process of development and in principle this can come from within or without a country. One of the countries which seems to have plucked development out of the shattering experience of war is the Republic of Korea. Nevertheless, the Toynbee thesis is too all-embracing, as well as of uncertain relevance in many instances to offer much in the way of insights as to how development may be prompted.

The approach of Professor E. L. Jones to understanding why some countries develop and others do not is very different from that of Toynbee.[5] He addresses himself to the examination of very long-term economic change as evident in comparisons of Europe and Asia, taking the period AD1400-1800 for special attention. What were the distinguishing features that set European evolution apart and which gave rise indirectly to European offshoots in what we now know as the United States, Canada, Latin America, Australia, New Zealand and South Africa? It was not so much natural advantages. 'Europe was not, by Asian standards, a lush habitat'[6] although it may have provided an environment less subject to the transmission of debilitating disease. It was much more an apparent readiness to restrict the birth rate. Marriage in Europe was not the child-bride affair of Asia, and many did not marry, so that the growth of population was restrained. This enabled land to be used for livestock husbandry and woodland, thereby providing adequate draught power and supplies of timber. Water power also provided an important source of energy. Thus by the standards of the time there was an accumulation of productive capital.

The different experience of Europe and Asia in regard to population growth is reflected in the densities of their populations in 1500, shown in Table 1.1. Of even greater moment was that by 1800 access to overseas territories through trade effectively increased the availability of land. The speculative estimates of population density for that year make an allowance for the equivalent amount of land harnessed through trade. Even without this allowance, however, the population density would have been only about half that of India of that epoch and one-quarter that of China.

Table 1.1 Density of population per km² in the main Eurasian systems, 1500 and 1800

Year	India	China	Ottoman Empire (Anatolia only)	Europe and overseas annexes
1500	23	25	8	8
1800	42	80	12	3

Source: E. L. Jones, *The European Miracle*, Cambridge, Cambridge University Press, 1981, p. 232.

Europe's forms of social organisation were more conducive to advancement than those of Asia. There was less wasteful conspicuous expenditure than the revenue-raising Asian despots were able to realise. Income was much more equally distributed and in relation to the population it was higher. The distortions of political centralisation were avoided, partly because settlement was more scattered. Sheer distance provided protection from the horse nomads of the Central Asian steppes. Nevertheless, trade flourished and new techniques and ideas were transferred from other countries, thus enhancing the activities of an inventive society.

Europe was fortunate also in being able to escape crippling exploitation by its rulers. The rise of the market offered opportunities for taxation and so was encouraged.[7] There was a general loosening of society which encouraged innovation, investment and commercial activity. Without this, technological innovation could not have taken hold; it might have done so much earlier had conditions been propitious. The adoption of new techniques is not an automatic process. The technologies developed in the eighteenth and nineteenth centuries spread rapidly amongst the European countries and their offshoots; they were slow to take hold in other places as is still evident at the present time.[8]

STAGES OF ECONOMIC GROWTH

The discussion above, brief as it has had to be, may serve to make the point that economic development is not an ineluctable outcome of human endeavour. There has to be a grouping of favourable conditions covering most aspects of social organisation before development can be assured. It can also be dangerously misleading to assume that development once started will follow some predetermined path as countries progress through various stages, as might be supposed from Professor Rostow's formulations of this theme.[9] His views have been hotly disputed but they have received too much attention to be put on one side; and in certain respects, as we shall see, they have gained some reinforcement from quantitative formulation of stylised growth paths or trajectories of key economic magnitudes.

Rostow's contention was that there were five stages of growth. The first of these is the *traditional society*. This is pre-science, not entirely static, although a ceiling exists on the level of attainable output per head. Other aspects of its nature can readily be imagined.

Emergence from this primitive stage depends on attaining the *preconditions for take-off*–the second of the stages. For this the insights of science are necessary to expand agricultural and industrial output, as happened in Western Europe in the late seventeenth and eighteenth centuries. The manner of the transition has something in common with Toynbee's views: external intrusions from more advanced societies shock the traditional society and hasten its undoing. Gradually, ideas spread and modern forms of organisation begin to emerge.

Then comes the third stage, the *take-off*. Resistance to steady growth is now largely overcome; compound interest enters, habits and institutions alter rapidly and activity surges forward. Investment rises from 5 per cent of the GDP to 10 per cent or more and change is greatly intensified.

The fourth stage is called the *drive to technological maturity*. Investment rises to some 20 per cent of GDP. Output continues to expand, but more discriminatingly. The country begins to compete effectively in export markets with new products.

What follows is an age of *high mass-consumption* with production shifting to durable consumer goods and services. We have arrived at the type of industrialised economy of the rich Western World.

It says something for Rostow's fascination with his system that he continues to classify countries according to it. The two largest of the low-income countries, China and India, are both driving to technological maturity after a take-off starting in the 1950s.[10] It took Great Britain eighty years to complete this stage before entering the era of high mass consumption in about 1920, a little after the United States. As time has gone on the whole process has been compressed and for a country like Korea twenty or thirty years may be all that is required to make the transition, although it may seem doubtful whether this will be long enough for India or China to ensure high mass consumption.[11]

When the large Asian countries make their way to maturity, as we must expect they will, there will be a vast shift in the centre of gravity of economic life. Output will reflect much more nearly the population of countries than it does at present when the low-income countries account for about half the world's population and, as a rough estimate, perhaps one-tenth of world output.[12]

Table 1.2 Economic and social characteristics of low- and medium-income countries

| | Percentage of GNP at income levels of | |
	under $100*	around $1,000
Savings	10	23
Foreign inflow of capital	3	1
Investment	14	24
Government revenue	13	29
Expenditure on education	2.6	4.3
Food consumption	41	18
Non-food private consumption	37	44
Primary output	52	14
Manufacturing and construction	13	35
Public utilities	5	10
Output of other services	30	41

* Mean value of GNP per capita $70 at 1964 prices.
Source: *Patterns of Development 1950–1970*, Hollis Chenery and Moises Syrquin, Oxford, Oxford University Press, 1975.

STRUCTURAL CHANGE

Econometricians have gone one better than Rostow in depicting the process of economic change. They have attempted to measure structural change in economies as development proceeds. Much of the pioneering work was done by Professor Simon Kuznets on the basis of historical data,[13] and the analysis has been extended and refined using current data, notably under the leadership of Hollis Chenery.[14] Such studies seek to reveal how key economic parameters change as countries develop, as may be seen from the examples given in Table 1.2 in which orders of magnitude of a series of macro variables are indicated for economies with per capita GNP of less than $100 in 1964 prices and about $1,000 respectively.

The results shown in the table have been calculated by taking figures from a cross-section of countries with various levels of per capita income and establishing the relationship between the value of the characteristics specified and income levels using econometric methods. The results can be regarded as applying to some synthetic country built up out of the averages of the performance of the countries forming the cross-section.

The nature of the changes in some constituents of the GDP can be observed by looking at the table. It may be noted *inter alia* that, in terms of percentage shares, saving rates increase as income grows; government revenues (and expenditure) increase; food consumption drops and non-food consumption increases; output of services–and, of course, also industry–increase, while agriculture falls.

Employment changes reflect the shift in output and changes in productivity. Labour in the primary sector of the economy does not fall as rapidly as its share in output; the reverse is true for employment in industry where increases in labour productivity are more easily secured.

Countries are engaged in trade; characteristically, exporting mainly primary products at low-income levels, and little in the way of manufactures and services. When per capita income has risen to $1,000, exports will account for a larger proportion of incomes and there will have been a marked shift in the composition of exports, so that the value of export of manufactures rises relative to that of primary products. Imports will

Table 1.3 Some characteristics of low-income economies

Country	Population millions mid-1983	GNP per capita		Life expectancy at birth 1983	Population annual growth rate 1973-83 (%)	Urban population as percentage of total in 1983
		In 1983 dollars	Average annual growth rate 1965-83 (%)			
1 Ethiopia	40.9	120	0.5	43	2.7	15
2 Bangladesh	95.5	130	0.5	50	2.4	17
3 Mali	7.2	160	1.2	45	2.5	19
4 Nepal	15.7	160	0.1	46	2.6	7
5 Zaïre	29.7	170	−1.3	51	2.5	38
6 Burkina	6.5	180	1.4	44	1.9	11
7 Burma	35.5	180	2.2	55	2.0	29
8 Malawi	6.6	210	2.2	44	3.0	11
9 Uganda	13.9	220	−4.4	49	2.8	7
10 Burundi	4.5	240	2.1	47	2.2	2
11 Niger	6.1	240	−1.2	45	3.0	14
12 Tanzania	20.8	240	0.9	51	3.3	14
13 Somalia	5.1	250	−0.8	45	2.8	33
14 India	733.2	260	1.5	55	2.3	24
15 Rwanda	5.7	270	2.3	47	3.4	5
16 Centr. Afr. Republic	2.5	280	0.1	48	2.3	44
17 Togo	2.8	280	1.1	49	2.6	22
18 Benin	3.8	290	1.0	48	2.8	16
19 China	1019.1	300	4.4	67	1.5	21
20 Guinea	5.8	300	1.1	37	2.0	26
21 Haiti	5.3	300	1.1	54	1.8	27
22 Ghana	12.8	310	−2.1	59	3.1	38
23 Madagascar	9.5	310	−1.2	50	2.6	20
24 Sierra Leone	3.6	330	1.1	38	2.1	23
25 Sri Lanka	15.4	330	2.9	69	1.7	26
26 Kenya	18.9	340	2.3	57	4.0	17
27 Pakistan	89.7	390	2.5	50	3.0	29
28 Sudan	20.8	400	1.3	48	3.2	20
29 Afghanistan*	17.2	–	0.5	36	2.6	17
30 Bhutan*	1.2	–		43	1.9	4
31 Chad*	4.8	–	–	43	2.1	20
32 Kampuchea*	–	–	–	–	–	–
33 Laos PDR*	3.7	–	–	44	2.2	15
34 Mozambique*	13.1	–	–	46	2.6	17
35 Vietnam*	58.5	–	–	64	2.7	20

* Very little statistical information is available about these countries and they cannot be put in order of per capita incomes on the limited information available.

Education:† numbers enrolled in primary school as percentage of age group 1982	Distribution of Gross Domestic Product: Percentages for 1983					
	Agriculture	Industry	Services	Gross domestic investment	Gross domestic saving	Exports of goods and non-factor services
46	48	16	36	11	2	12
60	47	13	40	17	2	8
27	46	11	43	17	−2	23
73	59	14	27	20	9	10
90	36	20	44	24	26	33
28	41	19	40	12	−15	17
84	48	13	39	22	17	8
62	–	–	–	23	14	19
60	–	–	–	8	5	5
33	58	16	26	21	7	9
23	33	31	37	25	11	22
98	52	15	33	20	8	11
30	50	11	39	20	−2	10
79	36	26	38	25	22	6
70	–	–	–	–	–	–
70	37	21	42	11	−1	23
106	22	28	50	23	4	31
65	40	14	47	12	−3	20
110	37	45	18	31	31	9
33	38	23	39	14	16	29
69	–	–	–	16	3	27
76	53	7	40	8	5	5
100	41	15	44	14	4	13
40	32	20	48	9	2	12
103	27	26	47	29	14	26
104	33	20	46	21	19	25
44	27	27	46	17	7	13
52	34	15	51	15	−1	11
35	–	–	–	–	–	–
23	–	–	–	–	–	–
–	–	–	–	–	–	–
–	–	–	–	–	–	–
97	–	–	–	–	–	–
104	–	–	–	–	–	–
113	–	–	–	–	–	–

† Enrolments of over 100 per cent indicate the inclusion of children outside the standard age group.
Source: Compiled from *World Development Report 1985*.

also have risen and earnings and payments will be roughly balanced.

As incomes increase, the rate of increase in population may be expected to fall in our synthesised country; the birth rate declines from 4.6 per cent per annum to 2.3 per cent. (It may be expected that a reappraisal of this statistic in the light of modern contraceptive methods would show an even greater decline.) The death rate also falls–from 2.1 per cent to 0.9 per cent. The population in this scenario, it may be noted, would still be increasing at the rate of nearly 1.5 per cent per annum, even when a per capita income level of $1,000 was attained.

Income would at first become more unequally distributed and then this movement would be reversed, so that the share of the poorest 40 per cent would at first fall from about 15 per cent to about 11 per cent of total incomes, rising later to about the initial proportion.

All the above happens in our synthesised country; however, no real country will be typical and there will be great variation from country to country. At a level of about $200 per capita (in 1964 prices) one-third of the population may be living in urban areas, according to the econometric relationships, but for some countries the proportion will be approaching two-fifths, while for others only a small percentage of the population will have left the countryside. At the same level of income there will also be a great divergence in birth rates.

Something of the degree of variation in the economic structure and social characteristics of low-income countries can be seen from a detailed examination of Table 1.3. It is helpful to look at this table to get some idea of the characteristics of developing countries and we shall refer to it from time to time later on. The information presented has to be regarded with a great deal of caution because much of it is unreliable and, in the case of some countries, it will be seen that even approximate figures cannot be provided. Great variations in characteristics are evident and this suggests that we should not set too much store on the ideas that countries follow a standard path to development, and we certainly should not expect them to increase per capita output at the same rate, although it may be possible to obtain greater conformity if countries are grouped according to certain characteristics and individual growth paths established for the groups.[15]

Growth in Britain in the nineteenth century was slow; income per capita increased by about 1.5 per cent per annum. In the United States 2 per cent was the norm but this is much less than has been achieved by some developing countries in the postwar period. Others, however, have not done so well, as is evident from Table 1.3 and from the summary Table 1.4. It will be noted that rates of growth are not on average very different between low- and middle-income countries. Industrial countries, however, have slowed down.

Table 1.4 Number of countries at different levels of growth of GDP per capita 1973-83

Average annual percentage	Low-income countries	Middle-income countries	Industrialised countries
−2-−3*	2		
−1-−2	2	2	
−1-0	0	1	
0-1	1	3	2
1-2	2	5	6
2-3	4	6	8
3-4	6	5	2
4-5	5	8	1
5-6	5	6	
6-7	3	4	
7-8	0	4	
8-9		5	
9-10		1	
10-11		1	
Total number of countries	30	51	19

* Includes Chad −5.8.
Note: Low-income countries had a per capita GDP of less than $400 in 1983, while middle countries have incomes in excess of this. Industrialised countries comprise the members of the OECD. High-income oil exporters are not included. Few figures are available for Eastern European non-market economies, which are also excluded.
Source: Compiled from *World Development Report 1985*, pp. 176-7.

It is not only in economic performance that developing countries differ. They may lean towards private enterprise and the market, or to socialism and rigorous planning; most compromise with some form of mixed economy. Often their political systems will be unstable but not always so. Economic policies will reflect the outlook and interests of the groups in power and condition the nature of development. Social attitudes will exercise major and differing influences. Opportunities will differ but there will also be common features: output will increase, as will savings and investment; modern systems of agriculture and industry will gradually percolate through the economy and much of the traditional sector will disappear. Education will exert a major influence; knowledge will spread and there will be growing signs of an international culture.

Such generalisations are not of a great deal of assistance in deciding how a country should be developed and the actions and policies that it would be appropriate to pursue. For this, the particular features of the country, its potentials and constraints have to be understood. In an effort to convey something of the realities, as opposed to the generalities of development, it has seemed worthwhile to sketch the situation of two countries, Bangladesh and Mozambique. They have been chosen, amongst other things, for their differences. The first of them is a mixed economy, the other a socialist state; Bangladesh is poor in natural resources while Mozambique is rich; they inherit different forms of civilisation, those of the Indian sub-continent on the one hand, with its British connection, and of Africa on the other, with, in this case, the influence of Portuguese colonialism. Together, and with some interpolations from some other countries also in the low-income category, they provide a means to examine various propositions related to economic development in an existing, real, rather than abstract, setting.

We also refer extensively to Pakistan, the Sudan and Botswana (in relation to planning models) by way of illustration. Further reading for those interested in these countries is suggested at the end of the chapter.

BANGLADESH

Recent history

There is no time to go into the long and variegated history of the Indian sub-continent, fascinating though it is. Suffice it to say that India achieved its independence from Britain in 1947, when it was divided into India, as we know it today, with its predominantly Hindu population (although with strong representation of other religious groups, including many Muslims), and Pakistan, at that time consisting of West Pakistan (now called Pakistan) and East Pakistan, mainly the East of the Bengal of the British Raj, which in 1971 became the Bangladesh of today.

The two Pakistans of the 1947-71 period were separated by 2,000 kilometres of uncertain communications, different languages and ethnic origins. East Pakistan, the dominant partner in population, but little else, felt itself exploited politically and economically by West Pakistan. Relations became greatly strained; civil war ensued with the West Pakistani army trying to hold East Pakistan down. In this it failed. There was armed Indian intervention; the West Pakistan army surrendered and the independent state of Bangladesh was established in December 1971. The country claimed that it had cast off two colonial yokes in less than a quarter of a century.

Political background

Sheikh Mujibur Rahman, who had long campaigned for the greater independence of East Pakistan, had the support and charisma to become the uncontested first prime minister of Bangladesh. The situation he inherited was desperate. In the war many had died; many had fled, but were returning; food production was totally inadequate to feed the population; transport, never good at the best of times, was chaotic, caused by blocked ports, damage to bridges, rolling stock, lorries and other vehicles. India, its army, and the United Nations, helped to overcome the immediate difficulties, providing food and technical assistance. After two years some vestige of normality was in sight. The country, however, remained disturbed; resistance fighters were hard to absorb into civilian life. The new government, with a civil service enlarging its responsibilities from the tasks of provincial to national administration, failed to establish a tight grip on the country and was faced with economic problems that would have taxed any governing body. Opposition developed, centred on the army. On the 15 August 1975, Sheikh Mujibur Rahman, who had recently assumed the presidency of Bangladesh, was assassinated by a group of officers and a section of the army. After a period of uncertainty and further coups, a degree of uneasy stability was imposed when Major-General Ziaur Rahman became President.

As before in East Pakistan, military rule was imposed and democratic government thrown out. General Zia's regime lasted until May 1981, when he too was assassinated by a military faction and succeeded after a time by General Ershad.

Assassination and instability of government are often a fact of life in developing countries and their effects are not very predictable. In Bangladesh the machinery of government tends to maintain some stability as officials in the public service continue to administer the country. It is natural to ask in such circumstances where power lies and how this affects the development of the country. The answer is not a simple one. The army, whether in power or in the background, is in a position to exercise considerable influence which is at its height when it constitutes the government. So too are the civil servants, as are other groups of influential people. In the context of Bangladesh, the ruling class seems to be composed of elements that stand to gain from the activities of government and from foreign aid. If this interpretation of political power in Bangladesh is correct, it has strong implications for development. The role of government and the public sector will be given emphasis and even where there may be moves towards private enterprise under the influence of capitalist ideas, or for other reasons, it is likely to take place in the context of state support.

With such a concentration of power, the influence on government of the workers and peasant agriculturalists at the margin of subsistence, or even more the landless labourers, will be slight. This will also be true locally in rural communities where the wealthier landowners (though few of them are rich by comparison with developed countries) will be able to manipulate power to their own advantage. It is against this kind of back-cloth that the strategy of development has to be devised, recognising that only some types of policies are likely to get political support.

The geographical setting and natural resources

Bangladesh has an area very slightly larger than England. It is located at the head of the Bay of Bengal. To the far south-east lies Burma; the other land boundaries are all with India. With the exception of the Chittagong Hill Tracts and parts of the north, the country is almost universally flat, a great flood plain of the Ganges, the Meghna and the Brahmaputra. Rainfall in the monsoon is high and there is heavy flooding, with a third or more of the ground under water. Amongst other things this affects communications. At the height of the floods, water may be the only means of getting from one place to another. Although there is a good main road system and rail communication, at all times water transport is a major means of moving people and goods. Partly because of the silt carried down by the rivers, the soil of Bangladesh is very fertile. This is indeed its major natural advantage.

There is little in Bangladesh in the way of raw materials: some limestone, some coal (which might be best left unmined), some clay. It is fortunate that development is not dependent on supplies of industrial materials for if it were Bangladesh would have little to support its endeavours. Even stone suitable for making re-inforced concrete is hard to come by, with the consequence that buildings and engineering structures may deteriorate all too rapidly because their aggregate takes the form of broken porous brick, with the result that water can attack the reinforcement.

The dearth of raw materials is lightened by supplies of natural gas. In relation to foreseeable consumption to the end of the century, proven reserves are adequate and offer possibilities for sale to export markets in one form or another. It had been hoped that oil would be found in the Bay of Bengal, but drilling has so far not been successful.

Agriculture and industry

The importance of agriculture to Bangladesh is evident from Table 1.3, where it may be seen to constitute about half of output. Agricultural development is crucial for the country, for population continues to grow and most of the 22 million acres (1 acre = 2.5 hectares) of available agricultural land is under cultivation. The major crop is that of rice; with three main growing seasons. The Aman rice (yielding about 7 to 8 million tons) is sown in mid-March to the end of April, or transplanted between July to mid-September. It is harvested from mid-November to mid-January. Since it is cultivated when flooding occurs, it has often to be a floating variety of rice, growing sufficiently rapidly to rise with the flood waters. The second largest rice crop, the Aus rice (yielding some 3 million tons), is sown from mid-March to mid-May and may also be transplanted. It is harvested between mid-July and mid-September. Finally, the Boro rice crop (yielding about 2.5 million tons) is transplanted from November to February and harvested from March to June. This is a winter crop depending on irrigation systems and offering opportunities for double cropping. Output of rice has risen slowly over the years, but not so fast as population. On the basis of consumption of one pound of food grains per head per day, imports of up to 2 million tons and more may be needed annually.

A number of other crops are cultivated: wheat (of growing importance), potatoes, fruits, other vegetables, oilseed, pulses and tobacco. Fish is a source of protein although not sufficient in quantity.

Output of jute provides a valuable input for the local manufacturing industry and is the major export both in raw and manufactured form. Apart from jute manufacturing, industry tends to produce for local needs. For the most part, activities are on a small scale; much of it takes the form of craftsmen serving a local market, including a great deal of handloom weaving of a domestic nature. There have been attempts to establish modern industries—steel production, shipbuilding, fertiliser, particularly urea manufacture, and oil refining—but these have not been very successful and have made only a limited contribution.

The condition of the people

It is obvious from the figures in Table 1.3 that the people of Bangladesh are very poor. They were little better off in 1982 than in 1960. For very many of them the standard of living must have deteriorated significantly if in fact, as is contended, the share of income of the bottom 20 per cent declined from about 10 per cent of the total in 1968-69 to perhaps only 6 per cent in 1976-77.[16]

Most inhabitants live in the countryside (see Table 1.3) and about three-quarters of them are employed in agriculture. Land is scarce and unevenly distributed whether measured in terms of ownership or the opportunity to cultivate it as a tenant or share cropper. Many own very little or no land; those who support themselves by farming typically have a holding of 1-2 acres.

Some, however, may have relatively large holdings. A survey of Ramapur, a village in the south of Bangladesh, brought out the not atypical fact that the two largest owners held 52 and 20 acres respectively, either in their own right or through relatives (in order to avoid the landholding ceiling imposed by law).[17]

Housing in the countryside generally takes the form of bamboo structures with only well-off people living in brick or concrete constructions. Drinking water may sometimes be drawn from a tube-well, but it is much more likely to come from a tank or pond. Sanitation is fairly rudimentary. Partly as a result of these environmental factors, health is poor. The infant mortality rate (deaths per thousand aged under one) is about 133 (compared with 7 in Japan); life expectancy at birth is about 49 years (compared with almost 80 years in Switzerland). Health care is severely limited although there is an average of one physician per 11,000 people.

About one-quarter of the population is estimated to be literate. This may rise in the future because about three-quarters of the boys and half the girls were attending school in 1981; but with high dropout rates and only limited opportunities to practise literacy in later life, attending school is no guarantee of ultimate performance. Nevertheless, it appears that 15 per cent of primary scholars will go on to secondary school with a preponderance of boys securing this opportunity.

The more limited educational opportunities for girls reflect the restricted role of women in Muslim societies. It is unusual for women to leave the shelter of their *bari* or cluster of homesteads occupied by their kin. This seclusion affects many aspects of life. It is also related to the low age at marriage and its consequences.

The poverty and general backwardness of Bangladesh is very much a function of the birth rate. Population rises inexorably and the pressure on land and other resources grows as a consequence. A population that was no more than 20 million in 1901 became 90 million in 1981 and may rise to as much as 150 million by the end of the century. Bangladesh is in danger of being caught in the poverty trap as increases in output keep pace with population but never exceed it for long, with eventually the opportunities for further progress being practically exhausted. The historical failure of Asia to produce a surplus still plagues the Bangladesh economy.

Trade and aid

Bangladesh is highly dependent on the outside world. Exports of jute, tea, hides and skins, and fish are being supplemented to some degree by other goods, but the extent of diversification has been small. Private transfers from workers overseas, particularly those working in the Middle East, amount to over half the receipts from exports of goods, but even so the deficit in the balance of payments is of the order of $1,500 million per year or about 12 per cent of the GNP. The balance is made good by aid disbursements and borrowing. One consequence is that the country is highly dependent on aid in every way: it supplements the government's budget, provides resources for investment and current use, and of course pays for imports, including food, that otherwise could not be afforded.

Such a high degree of dependence on aid may be the best way to ensure the development of the country, although this is debatable, but it is certainly dangerous both in relation to the exercise of foreign influence and the possibility that it may have the effect of reducing domestic endeavours, as some maintain. Yet the effect of rapidly withdrawing aid would be too harmful to contemplate.

Conclusion

It is not difficult to state what Bangladesh might seek to achieve within the discernible opportunities for development. Somehow population has to be controlled; agricultural output has to be greatly increased to provide the resources needed to feed the population; jobs have to be found for the expanding population and those presently without work or unproductively employed; a shift has to be made to increase industrial output, since agricultural development alone cannot provide for the needs of the people; the social system has to react to make all this possible. Whether, when and how this can be done are open questions. It will not be done without determined leadership strong enough to effect the necessary transformation. In Bangladesh this may require some form of participatory political system acceptable to the population and with the long-term stability that is necessary for development to take root and grow.

MOZAMBIQUE

History

Before independence, Mozambique was an overseas province of Portugal. This conditioned the development of its economy and led to the establishment of a plantation sector for the export of raw materials to Portugal (sugar, cotton, copra and tea), to the reservation of markets in the country for Portuguese exporters, to the construction of infrastructure, roads, railways and ports to meet the needs of South Africa and Southern Rhodesia (rather than the country itself) and to the exploitation of the labour supply in mining and other areas.[18] Through a number of agreements with Portugal, South Africa made remittances in gold to Portugal for the hire of miners from Mozambique; the miners, however, were compensated in Mozambique in local currency calculated at unfavourable exchange rates.

The colonial influence led to a lopsided development of the country. Plantations were owned by foreign capital, and large estates and medium and small commercial farms were established by Portuguese colonialists. Merchants and middlemen in the countryside organised the marketing of the surplus production of the indigenous population and provided it with basic goods. The economic activities of the Africans themselves were concentrated on subsistence production with some provision of cashew nuts and cotton for export. In other respects their function was to provide labour in an essentially dualistic economy.

The extent of the exploitation provided the seeds of rebellion. The liberation struggle, organised by FRELIMO (Frente de Libertação de Moçambique), began in earnest in 1964. One of the reactions of the Portuguese to the struggle was to group the rural populations into *aldeamentos*, or fortified hamlets, to prevent them from participating in guerrilla raids. In providing more economical units for the provision of services, this subsequently proved to have significance for development. As time went on, the population increasingly identified itself with the liberation forces. The pressures on Portugal from both within and without Mozambique and the resulting economic drain finally persuaded it, in the aftermath of a leftist military coup in Lisbon, to confer independence which was fully accomplished by June 1975.

After independence many of the Portuguese left the country. In some cases productive equipment was destroyed. The country remained unsettled and became involved in the struggle for the independence of Zimbabwe. It was not easy to keep modern installations, for which the Portuguese had been responsible, in operation. Output fell, as did exports and the ability to import, with further repercussions on production as spares and materials could not be purchased. Progress was further impeded by serious drought. The country has yet to recover from the consequences.

Political background

The years since independence have been marked by continued political instability involving South Africa and other countries. The government of President Samora Machel is opposed by the Renamo guerrillas who, by 1985, were active in much of the country. South Africa has given support to the guerrillas as a device to destabilise Mozambique, but in March 1984 it undertook to change its policy as part of an agreement with Mozambique on a non-aggression pact. In fact, this has not reduced the opposition of Renamo to President Machel's rule. The present political instability renders the task of governing and developing the country extremely difficult. It could also have the effect in the long run of modifying the economic and political philosophy currently dominating the development strategy described below.

Colonial exploitation left an indelible mark on the present rulers of Mozambique and convinced them that the country must be organised on Marxist-Leninist principles. Political education of the masses had started during the latter part of the liberation war with the formation of cadres, emphasis on collective decision-making, the establishment of targets, and responsibility and emancipation of women. Under the Constitution of the People's Republic of Mozambique, the country is declared to be 'a people's democracy in which all patriotic groups are engaged in the building of a new society, free from exploitation of man by man'. The political ideology of the country as defined by FRELIMO is designed to integrate social, political and economic objectives. The ultimate objective is full socialism. Nevertheless, the approach in the circumstances of the country has to be pragmatic. Considerable reliance on private activity in agriculture, industry and trade is accepted, because large and sweeping changes would give rise to even more disruption.

Political organisation at the grass-roots level takes the form of the operation of party cells, and the same is true at the next level of operation, the locality, where there is an elected local assembly, as is also the case in the larger towns. These assemblies elect representatives to provincial assemblies, and these in turn elect to the National People's Assembly. At the national level the Party

Central Committee is the principal policy-making body. Government work is organised in ministries, commissions and autonomous agencies. There are National and Provincial Planning Commissions. Both the government and the party are centres of influence.

Although agriculture is for the most part carried out on an individual basis, there are a number of state farms generally created from those abandoned by the Portuguese settlers. State influence is also brought to bear in other ways at the rural level. Over a million people are assembled in communal villages which are conceived of as political, social and economic units with wide responsibilities for administration, justice, security, finance, production and basic services. The organisation of the villages takes the form of a general assembly and an executive committee flanked by a party cell and a party secretary.

There is strong emphasis on cooperative activity in different areas including agriculture, fishing, industry, housing and consumer needs. These communal concerns are democratically controlled and those active in them may also be active in the party and representatives elsewhere.

The geographical setting and natural resources

Mozambique is bounded by Tanzania, Malawi, Zambia, Zimbabwe, South Africa and Swaziland, and has an extended seaboard to the Indian Ocean. The area of the country is 800,000 square kilometres with a population of only 13 million. There are three basic geographical zones, a lowland or coastal belt amounting to about 44 per cent of the total area, a middle plateau with altitudes of 200-600 metres above sea level covering 29 per cent of the country, and the highlands region more than 600 metres above sea level, mostly north of the Zambezi River, covering 27 per cent of the total area. The vegetation is highly varied and includes open as well as dense forest. There is an extensive rainy season in most parts and the average rainfall is favourable for crop production. Temperatures are high.

Mozambique has great potential. Agricultural resources are greatly underexploited, much additional arable land could be brought into cultivation, and there are opportunities for irrigated agriculture that could be measured in terms of hundreds of thousands of hectares. Rice, maize, cashew nuts, sugar, copra and bananas, amongst others, could be produced in great quantity. The tsetse fly makes it impossible to raise cattle in some areas, but other animals such as goats or pigs could be greatly increased in number; the seas and inland waters, too, produce well below capacity.

The large rivers offer the means to generate hydroelectric power and provide water for irrigation and industry. Many industrial minerals are available: coal, iron ore, bauxite, titanium, gold, asbestos, copper, phosphates and gas. Iron ore and high-grade coking coal are located close to supplies of natural gas, inexpensive hydroelectricity generated by the Cabora Bassa installation, and transport from the rail-head at Moitize or by the Zambezi (a navigable river) with access to Nacala, the finest natural deep-water port in East Africa.

Mozambique is strategically well placed for the transportation of goods to and from neighbouring countries, which is potentially remunerative and may be expected to increase as those countries increase their output. In all there are unbounded opportunities limited only by the skills and the capacity of the inhabitants of the country to exploit them.

Agriculture and industry

Potentially cultivable land is of the order of 25 million hectares. However, with primitive agricultural methods making heavy demands on human labour it is not possible to cultivate more than a third of it with the present population. The major food crops are cassava, maize and sorghum, with some rice; cotton and cashew nuts are produced for export. Yields could be greatly increased with improved methods of cultivation. Improvements in diet could be made if more maize and sorghum were grown instead of cassava and if the production of animal protein and fish were increased. The introduction of better agricultural practices is impeded by lack of personnel, transportation and other resources. In the long term it may be possible to overcome this through the cooperatives and communal action, but the process is likely to be slow.

The state farms have the potential to introduce and extend modern farming methods and could become an important source of food and agricultural raw materials. More skilled managers will be necessary if their output and activities are to be expanded.

In the twenty years from 1960 to 1980, the labour force employed in industry has increased from 8 to 18 per cent according to World Bank statistics. The construction industry provides considerable employment; apart from this, much of the industrial activity is concerned with the processing of agricultural materials such as sugar, cotton, sisal, copra, and tea for export. Consumer goods are manufactured for the domestic market and there is some light engineering. Cement is produced and there is also an oil refinery. In colonial times these industries were run by Portuguese and other expatriates.

The condition of the people

No up-to-date figures of per capita income are available for Mozambique. In 1971, average per capita income was estimated at $254, but this included the high-income Portuguese. Since then the state of the economy has deteriorated, so that the average level of income must have fallen appreciably. From observation alone, there can be no doubt that most people are extremely poor. They are dependent on what can be grown on a holding thought to average about 1.5 hectares. In normal times such an area, using primitive agricultural methods, is large enough to feed a family, but even in the absence of adverse growing conditions Mozambique has found it hard to feed itself. Flooding in 1977 and 1978, a cyclone also in 1978 followed by drought in 1979, and other similar disasters in the 1980s illustrate the need for an effective food policy. The shortage of food is unevenly distributed; in Cabo Delgado, for instance, the most northerly of the Provinces, the supply of food has been particularly inadequate. Even if supplies were available in other parts of the country, there would be little opportunity to remedy this for transport capacity is severely limited and disruptions are frequent.

In other respects also the people are badly off. Shortage of foreign exchange has severely limited imports and the supply of consumer goods. The crude birth rate (the number of births in a year per thousand of the population) is estimated at 46 and the crude death rate at 19, giving a population increase of about 2.75 per cent. Life expectancy is somewhat lower than in Bangladesh, abouty 46 years, while infant mortality appears to be less high. The availability of physicians is very much worse, about one for every 40,000 people, so that health care in rural areas is dependent almost entirely on indigenous remedies. In education a great effort is being made; again, according to World Bank figures, it appears that practically all boys in the relevant age group attend primary schools and over 70 per cent of the girls. Considerable efforts are also being made to improve adult literacy.

Trade and aid

Not a great deal is known about Mozambique's balance of payments. It appears that there is a significant deficit on the balance of trade, only partially covered by net exports of services including the sale of electricity to South Africa, transit services and remittances from emigrant miners. In recent years, Mozambique has received significant amounts of foreign assistance, but the balance of payments severely constrains both development and effective operation of existing capacity.

The pattern of trade remains typically colonialist. Exports consist almost wholly of primary products; imports include substantial amounts of food in addition to manufactured and capital goods.

Conclusion

The problems faced by Mozambique are immense. Political problems remain dominant. The main drive for modernisation comes from the government and the party. What is uncertain is how quickly the administrative organisation can be built up, in order to secure both power to influence the lives of the people and the ability to mobilise the resources that will have to be invested if the potential of the country is to be realised. The government has been pragmatic in acknowledging that the private sector of the economy cannot be replaced in present circumstances; yet it may not be easy to maintain an efficient balance between private and state-controlled operations so as not to denude the private sector of resources. The position and plight of Mozambique and its determination to develop the Marxist-Leninist tradition have aroused great interest; many countries with or without a socialist persuasion have provided aid.

The government attaches importance to industrialisation and would like to establish heavy as well as light industry. This requires large amounts of capital which can be ill afforded at the present time. The incidence of famine and the unsatisfactory level of nutrition, even with normal harvests, strongly suggest that a major drive needs to be made to improve food production. Here again there may be a clash between the resources required by state farms and the need to support traditional agriculture. Moreover, it is difficult to see what can be done to improve traditional forms of cultivation without first improving the infrastructure, notably in the form of transport. The establishment of agricultural co-operatives and communal villages may help but this again takes time and resources. The solution may have to be found by concentrating efforts first of all in areas which can be easily reached and are receptive to change.

In the long run the system of government in Mozambique will be judged both by the material progress that it can bring about and by the social structure that it is attempting to create. An important aspect of this is the opportunity to involve the people in development by mobilising their interest and activities through the party. Mozambique provides a good setting in which to try out the development strategies of socialism and to see how they can be made to work in a land of almost unlimited opportunity.

FURTHER READING

Hollis Chenery and Moises Syrquin, *Patterns of Development 1950–1970*, Oxford, Oxford University Press, 1975, reprinted 1977.

Just Faaland and J. R. Parkinson, *Bangladesh: the Test Case for Development*, London, Hurst, 1976.

J. Fitzpatrick, 'The Economy of Mozambique: Problems and Prospects', *Third World Quarterly*, Vol. 3 (1981), No. 1, pp. 77-87.

Hassan Gardezi and Jamil Rashid (eds), *Pakistan the Unstable State*, Lahore, Vanguard Books, 1983.

International Bank for Reconstruction and Development, *World Development Report*, published annually by the Oxford University Press for the World Bank (for analysis of the current situation and a convenient source of statistics).

Allen Isaacman and Barbara Isaacman, *Mozambique: From Colonialism to Revolution, 1900–1982*, Boulder, Colo., Westview Press, 1983.

B. J. Jahangir, *Rural Society, Power Structure and Class Practice*, Dhaka, Centre for Social Studies, 1982.

E. L. Jones, *The European Miracle*, Cambridge, Cambridge University Press, 1981.

Harald D. Nelson (ed.), *Sudan: A Country Study*, Washington DC, American University, Foreign Area Studies, 1982.

Lloyd G. Reynolds, 'The Spread of Economic Growth to the Third World: 1850-1980', *Journal of Economic Literature*, Vol. 21 (1983), No. 3, pp. 941-80.

NOTES

1. *World Development Report 1985*, Table 1, Basic Indicators, pp. 174-5, Oxford, Oxford University Press, 1985. The Bank excludes countries with a population of less than 1 million and figures are not available for some poor countries with, possibly, even lower per capita incomes.
2. Cambridge, Mass., Harvard University Press, Fourth Printing, 1979, p. 6.
3. It is best to refer the reader to the Abridgement of Toynbee's *A Study of History*, prepared by D. C. Somerwell, Oxford, Oxford University Press, 1947 and 1957, 2 vols.
4. See the first volume of the Abridgement, 1947, p. 246.
5. E. L. Jones, *The European Miracle*, Cambridge, Cambridge University Press, 1981.
6. E. L. Jones, ibid., p. 6.
7. E. L. Jones, ibid., p. 234.
8. In *How it All Began*, London, Methuen, 1975, p. 31, W. W. Rostow puts great weight on the use of technology: 'We conclude, then, that the critical failure of the traditional societies was conceptual: Science–lively and impressible as it was–did not teach those with access to power over resources that the physical world could be understood in ways that permitted it systematically to be transformed to their advantage'.
9. W. W. Rostow, *The Stages of Economic Growth*, Cambridge, Cambridge University Press, 1963.
10. W. W. Rostow, *The World Economy, History and Prospect*, London, Macmillan, 1978, p. 51.
11. Rostow's classification of stages of growth is not without challengers. Lloyd Reynolds prefers to distinguish between extensive growth with no increase in per capita income and intensive growth with a sustained rise. Historically, the change from one to the other comes much earlier than Rostow's take-off (see Lloyd Reynolds, *The Spread of Economic Growth to the Third World, 1850–1980*, Center Paper No. 344, Yale University, Economic Growth Center, 1983).
12. It is often misleading to compare the incomes of countries on the basis of ruling exchange rates because the real income of developing countries are often understated by this method. It is better to try to make the comparison by working out the purchasing power of the respective currencies. For some illustrations of the effect of doing this, see *World Development Report 1982*, Oxford, Oxford University Press, 1982, p. 23.
13. Published in *Economic Development and Cultural Change*, Vol. 5, 1957, and subsequent years, and in *Modern Economic Growth, Rate Structure and Spread*, New Haven, Conn., Yale University Press, 1966, as well as elsewhere.
14. Hollis Chenery, *et al.*, *Structural Change and Development Policy*, Oxford, Oxford University Press, 1979.
15. This has been tried by Chenery *et al.*, in *Structural Change and Development Policy*, ibid.
16. Bangladesh Planning Commission, *Rural Development Strategy*, Dhaka, March 1983, pp. 11-13.

17. Ann-Lisbet Arn and M. A. Mannan, *Lakshmipur Thana: A Socio-Economic Study of Two Villages*, Copenhagen, Centre for Development Studies/Dhaka, Bangladesh Institute of Development Studies, 1982. It may be noted that the detailed distribution of land in these villages does not correspond at all closely with the results shown for the 1977 Agricultural Census. A major reason for the difference is probably the exclusion of the landless and near-landless from the census.
18. For an account of labour exploitation, see Gunnar Haaland, 'Dualistic Development: Issues for Aid Policy', in J. R. Parkinson (ed.), *Poverty and Aid*, Oxford, Basil Blackwell, 1983, pp. 63-78.

2 Objectives and strategy formulation

SOCIAL AND POLITICAL OBJECTIVES

In a perfect world the objectives of development would be chosen
as a part of some moral philosophy in response to the teachings of
Christianity, Islam, or some other moral percepts related to
experience. In a world of abstraction the principles of Rawls's
Theory of Social Justice might hold sway;[1] Rawls's conception of
justice 'carries to a higher level of abstraction the familiar theory
of the social contract as found, say, in Locke, Rousseau and
Kant'.[2] It is suggested that at the beginning of the world all
mortals meet to agree on the principles of justice that they will
observe collectively in their social relationships. In Rawls's
conception it is central that the principles are chosen behind a
veil of ignorance as to what is in store for each individual. No one
knows his own qualities or the state to which he will ultimately be
called, and so all are freed from the stigma of personal preoccupation. The principles of justice once established regulate all other
acts such as the establishment of the form of government and the
choice of ends.

The real world is not established on such principles. No contract of social justice exists and had one been established it would
have been violated long ago. But the concept of justice remains
among the social, political and economic forces governing
development. Powerful and influential, it provides a frame of
reference against which alternatives may be measured and prescriptive economic judgements assessed.

Principles of justice are modifying influences on the choice of
objectives both because of their direct influence on those taking
decisions, and because too great a violation of such principles
runs the risk of provoking resistance by those whose interests may
be adversely affected and even by those prone to moral indigna-
tion.

It is right at this point to introduce a note of caution and warning. No branch of economics is more prescriptive than that concerned with economic development. The very subject matter selected for discussion is often redolent with value judgement: the virtues of free enterprise; the superiority of the state; the importance of economic growth; the damage to the environment; the needs of the poor; the desirability of reducing immigration; the failure of this or that strategy. Preconceived ideas of what ought to be done do not provide the best basis for understanding. Moreover, they demand the most careful investigation to see whether they can be justified and how applicable they are in different circumstances. Except at the highest level of generality it is not to be expected that there will be any uniformity of objectives between countries as diverse in their political systems as Mozambique and Bangladesh, Hong Kong and the Sudan, or Saudi Arabia and Botswana. In most developing countries political forces will be uppermost, and a small ruling elite, perhaps a changing one, will take the key decisions that determine the objectives of the society.

The choice of objectives in an ideological and political setting can be abundantly illustrated from Bangladesh's first years of independence, described with discerning insight by Professor Nurul Islam.[3] The objectives inscribed in the First Five Year Plan of Bangladesh (FFYP) were those assumed to represent the political stance of the ruling political party, the Awami League. Primarily a nationalist party, it represented the revolt of the middle class against the economic and political domination of Pakistan. It was basically a middle-class party in which surplus farmers (sufficiently wealthy to produce more than enough for their basic needs), traders, small industrialists and the lower echelons of the civil service all combined. The political roots were well developed. The surplus farmers were established as local leaders in government and parliament and were linked with trading and business interests. Increasingly, the party was supported by the urban elite and by the intellectuals and the professionals. During the fight for freedom it also gained the backing of the labour unions operating in large-scale industry. Although the Awami League had a large following and considerable support from all sections of the population, those who were better-off in wealth, education and in the possession of influential positions, constituted a ruling class within it, comprising greater identity of view and interest than the party itself with its diverse elements. Here lay the seeds of dissension.

Amongst students and workers there were radical elements. There were pressures for the establishment of a socialist society, for land reform and changes in the tax and revenue system. This was reflected in the constitution of the country which had been drawn up with socialist principles in mind. The constitution stressed the abolition of exploitation, the right to work and equality of opportunity, the discouragement of unearned income and the responsibility of the state to provide for the basic needs of the population. Thus the emphasis was on socialism although, as time was to show, many of the high ideals enshrined in the doctrines subscribed to by the party and written into the First Five Year Plan were to be frustrated by the forces of reaction and the resistance of those with influence.

Economists tend to describe objectives briefly and generally in statistical form. Political objectives are usually more diffuse and imprecise. The objectives for the FFYP of Bangladesh were seen in a social and political perspective based on the principles of democracy, nationalism, secularism and socialism. These pre-conceptions were to have profound effects on the approach to development adopted in the plan, but were to prove abortive in the practicalities of the emerging political situation. The concept of social justice was writ large in the statement that in a socialist society the government would take steps to ensure that the various classes of society would enjoy their due share of the national output. In the FFYP the means for change were seen in the establishment of cadres motivated by the new ideology, willing to live and work among the people and mobilise them to transform the pattern of their behaviour. Few of these aspirations were to be translated into action.

In many respects (but in reality ineffectively), the political and social objectives written into the plan paralleled those of Mozambique with its very different political organisation. This was scarcely surprising, for what was written came from a common source of socialist economics. There the similarity ended. The essential difference was not in the views of the planners as to what should be accomplished, but in the political ability, and even more desire to put socialist teaching into practice. The Bangladesh government under its founding father Sheikh Mujibur Rahman was not on balance, and in the weight of its political decisions, of socialist persuasion. On the contrary, it represented the aims of the Awami League which in its wide range of support was in fact a party directed to the political accomplishment of the aspirations of those of means, education, personal position and in many respects Western outlook.

The aims of Mozambique, in contrast, appear to be wholly consistent with the direction of government, even though, as we have seen, there is an element of pragmatism evident in the readiness to accept, subject to certain regulations, the need to rely on the private sector in agriculture, industry and trade. Nevertheless, private enterprise is certainly not regarded as an engine of primary growth or a base for political influence.

Political objectives are always multi-faceted. Although the political and economic philosophy of Mozambique professes to be founded on moral principles and has much to say about acceptable social conduct, it would be wrong to think its development objectives are concerned wholly with providing for the basic needs of all the inhabitants of the country. There is a strong element of this, of course: policies directed to the development of communal villages where basic services can be provided economically, efforts to promote basic literacy for adults as well as children, attempts to give rudimentary health care to all—all these show concern with basic needs. But these are only some of the objectives of this communist state. It wants above all to modernise, and this is an aim in itself. Modernisation requires rural development and the production of adequate food. It also implies many other things: development of heavy industry, wielding political influence in southern Africa, adopting modern technology and capital-intensive production techniques.

There can be no unanimity about what development objectives should be. Moralists, politicians, social anthropologists and economists all look at the process of development from different points of view and, consequently, wide differences emerge as to what should be attempted and how quickly. Nevertheless, most countries establish some set of development objectives consistent with their political situation; some view emerges about the role of private enterprise, the extent to which basic needs are to be met, the degree of inequality in the distribution of income and wealth that can be tolerated, and other key issues.

FROM OBJECTIVES TO STRATEGIES

Political economists also seek to influence the course of economic development. On the one hand, they are inclined to lay down objectives; on the other, they make it their business to advocate ways and means of attaining their ends. This is done on a grand scale with the intention of securing the widest application throughout the developing world. Fashions do, however, change. Any casual reader of the literature on the objectives of development might be excused the thought that there had been a radical change in the approach of economists to development round about 1970. Up till then it might appear that the emphasis had been on the growth of output to the exclusion of its distribution among people, and that subsequently the emphasis had shifted to distribution of income and away from growth.

The first approach has become known as the trickle-down strategy because it was believed that the effects of rising incomes and output would ultimately trickle down to the poor so that they would benefit as well as the rich. The second approach rejects this view and stresses the need for strategies designed to meet the needs of the poor directly. This is summed up with such all-embracing and optimistic phrases as growth with equity or re-distribution with growth, culminating in advocating concentration on providing for the basic needs (food, housing, education, etc.) of all. In many respects such labels are misleading and seem to point to a change in economic thought and under-standing of greater dimension than actually takes place.[4] The relationships between equity and growth are not very well under-stood, but that they might not move in the same direction was realised quite early, for example in Sir Arthur Lewis's seminal work, *The Theory of Economic Development*, published in 1955. Since Lewis's work was widely read it would be quite wrong to think that the question of distribution was lost sight of or that other authors did not take it up well before 1970.[5] Why, then, was there a switch in emphasis?

In the first place there was probably some disappointment with the progress of development. By historical standards the rate of increase in output in the developing world was high, averaging 5-6 per cent. The increase in population, however, was rapid and this reduced the increase in income per head to about 2.5 per cent per annum. With the rapid increase in output in industrial Europe in the postwar period and a much smaller increase in population, it was begining to look as if the developing countries, far from catching up the developed ones, would fall even further behind. The conclusion was that something must be wrong with a strategy that failed in this respect.

Secondly, it was supposed that the distribution of income was getting worse.[6] The reasons behind this rested on historical studies and cross-sectional econometric analyses. Kuznets had seemed to suggest from his penetrating examination of the evolution of the industrialised countries that this might be expected to occur, although he was careful to bring out the uncertainties inherent in generalising from his observations.[7] Other pioneering studies based on cross-sectional data appeared to point the same way. Thus Irma Adelman and Cynthia Taft Morris concluded: 'The position of the poorest sixty per cent typically worsens, both relatively and absolutely, when an initial spurt of narrowly based dualistic growth is imposed on an agrarian subsistence economy'.[8]

This was supported by the work of Montek S. Ahluwalia.[9] As mentioned in Chapter 1, it appeared that the share of the poorest 40 per cent in the national income fell from about 15 per cent, when development commenced, to about 11 per cent by the time income per capita had quadrupled. Ahluwalia's results seemed to imply that it would take fifty or more years before the original distribution was restored. His analyses were based on cross-section studies, which can be notoriously misleading and require the most careful interpretation. In a critique of Ahluwalia's work, Ashwani Saith demonstrates, using the same data, that the results are seriously in doubt because of the poor quality and variable composition of the data.[10] He goes on to show that the subtraction of one to four countries from a sample of forty-one, on the grounds that they are outliers, destroys the relationships established by Ahluwalia, or weakens them to the point that they are not convincing. It might appear that we really do not know what happens to the distribution of income as countries develop and that we should be careful not to decide policies on the basis of such uncertain conclusions and doubtful generalisations.

A third factor that led to the shift in conventional wisdom was the intervention in the debate and policy of the World Bank in the person of Robert McNamara. When he addressed the Board of

Governors of the World Bank Group in 1972,[11] he argued that even a 6 per cent per annum increase in the incomes of the developing countries during the second development decade would do little for the poorest 40 per cent of the population in countries with per capita incomes averaging no more than $275 at that time. A complete change in outlook was advocated so that the benefits of development could be diverted to the very poor. The cry that development was about the poor caught on and was pressed from many quarters, including the International Labour Office which had already launched a series of comprehensive Employment Strategy Missions, starting with Colombia (1970).

Although a strategy aimed at helping the poor was accepted by many economists, it was not universally accepted or applied. There were also doubts and opposition. It was contended that it might be inimical to growth and that immediate improvement would be purchased at the expense of the welfare of future generations. So far very little evidence to support this view has been unearthed. Professor Papanek has shown from episodic events in a few countries, and more generally by regression analysis, that there is very little systematic connection between the two. 'In a world-wide analysis, pooling cross section and time series data, we found no relationship between the rate of growth and the distribution of income, or changes in the distribution of income'.[12] Some relationship might have been expected if a distribution of income favoured the rich had the effect of increasing savings and investment, as is sometime supposed. This may not be the case, however, and other consequences of a more equitable distribution of income, such as encouraging the purchase of locally produced goods and reducing import requirements, have also to be taken into account.[13]

A strategy aimed at improving the lot of the poor has implications for rural development since most of the poor tend to be agriculturists. It is here that the limitations of the strategy may become apparent. Increasing agricultural output is not an easy task and to some large extent it may be conditional on doing other things as well; in any case, development cannot be concentrated on agriculture to the exclusion of other things. Nevertheless, the experience of a number of countries seems to show that in suitable circumstances growth and equity can be combined. Sri Lanka and China, at least until recently, as well as Korea, for example, seem to have found ways of reconciling what might seem to be conflicting objectives and getting the best from several worlds.

These things, however, come about not so much as a result of economists' recommendations, but rather because the ruling elites are ready and able to apply effective policies. Other countries may neither wish, nor be able, to follow this lead, or if they do they may find that the better-off manage to turn any programme, whether or not directed at the poor, to their advantage. Finally, what matters in the long run is not so much reducing inequalities as improving the lot of the poor.

A decision to concentrate on growth or equity or some mix of the two is not a strategy, but rather a declaration of aims. Once certain aims are decided, it is possible to consider alternative strategies, or broad directions of policies, that may enable the ends to be achieved. A list of possible strategies would be almost endless, but some alternative strategies of a general nature have been debated at length. We shall therefore review only two pairs of apparently contrasting strategies: the alternative strategies of the so-called 'big push' and 'unbalanced growth', and the issue of import substitution or export growth.

THE 'BIG PUSH' OR 'UNBALANCED GROWTH'

Should a 'big push' to industrialise be attempted with the intention of generating economies of scale and external economies and mutual support? Or, alternatively, would it be better to construct an unbalanced programme with the intention of creating leading sectors which in turn will create pressures for others to expand their activities?

The concept of linkages is central to many theories of development, although the term is often used with different meanings. In its clearest and most understandable form it relates to the connections between the various elements of an input-output table. Within such tables industries are linked to one another by their sales and purchases. Backward linkages are represented by the purchases of one industry from others, forward linkages by sales of an industry to other industries.[14] Such linkages are familiar in relation to industry but they are also relevant to the provision of services. The concept of linkages can be extended to the dynamic effects of any sectoral increase in activity on an economy's performance. The macro aspects of such relationships may work rather like Keynesian multipliers; one thing triggers off another, new demands stimulate linked sectors of the economy and encourage new activities. In some cases international trade may also be an important stimulus. Exports increase domestic activity, particularly if highly manufactured products are included. An increase in importing capacity can have similar effects, if the importation of raw materials or key components enables a domestic industry to be operated. Nevertheless, as in Keynesian economics, an increase in imports may exert a downward push by diverting demand from home products, and it should not be assumed that all linkages act as stimuli.

The effects of one sector of an economy on another are not confined to inter-industry purchases. Increases in income arising from production in one sector are used to buy the products of other sectors, as well as those of the sector in which the increase originated. Thus, if industries expand together, they stand a better chance of being able to market their outputs. If, as well, higher levels of output bring economies of scale, there may be much to be said for engineering a concerted big push.

The strategy of the big push is outlined in an early article by Paul Rosenstein-Rodan:[15]

Relatively few investments are made in the small market of an under-developed country. If all investment projects were independent (which they are not) and if their number grew, the risk of each investment project would decline by simple actuarial rules . . . Investment projects have high risks because of the uncertainty as to whether their products will find a market.

Thus the strategy of the big push was based on mutually reinforcing industrial developments which would generate sufficient incomes for their output to be sold and for economies of scale to be obtained.

The concept of the big push in its original formulation was related primarily to industrial development and as a means to create employment. It needs to be put in a wider context. Industry represents only a small part of the operations of a developing country where agriculture is of primary concern. While it is sometimes possible to concentrate a high proportion of investment on industrial activity at the expense of other sectors of the economy, a big push can seldom be applied to the whole of an economy for there are simply not enough resources to go round. If more investment is poured into industry, there will be gains from economies of scale and complementarity, but these will be at the expense of a slower rate of growth of other sectors of the economy. Naturally, such a strategy would run counter to the policies of those wishing to deflect the development effort increasingly to the poor in rural areas. Some balance might seem to have to be struck between these different approaches. Much depends on whether an autarkic policy is being pursued or whether the country is participating actively in international trade. If autarky is the rule, demand will have to be met from internal resources and production will have to be organised to meet it. In practice this may mean that the opportunity to accelerate economic development by a big push is severely limited.

The whole picture changes if we consider an open economy operating in freely moving, world trade conditions. Internal requirements can now be met with the aid of an additional degree of freedom represented by the opportunity to draw on the possibilities of world specialisation in different types of productive activities. Those manufacturing activities which depend on technology and large-scale operations for economical production might be left to the developed world where capital and markets are to be found in more ample abundance; while industries which can work efficiently on a small scale and require labour might be established locally. (Note also, however, that multinationals may also establish themselves in modern industrial operations in developing countries in order to avail themselves of cheap labour. We return to this issue in Chapter 8.)

It is possible that the strategy of the 'big push' would have fitted the needs of Eastern European countries for which it was advocated. For less developed countries elsewhere it seems to have a rather limited application, mainly because it may be difficult to reconcile a big push concentrated on industry with the need to achieve 'balanced growth' in a wider context and in strongly agricultural countries.[16] By this we mean trying to keep most activities of a country in step so that, at whatever income level can be sustained, the goods and services produced and consumed (and exported and imported) would represent an optimal mix of activity with the emphasis on balance in growth rather than on a big push. It seems to us that balanced growth is a result that would appeal to most planners, though not, however, to A. O. Hirschman, as we shall now see.

A. O. Hirschman believed that a community needed some mechanism to induce decisions and actions to promote growth and that a strategy of unbalanced growth might be conducive to getting things done. The linkages here are not of the technical-economic character discussed above, but spring from the opportunity to make high profits by increased investment and activity in individual sectors or product lines, when conditions there are particularly favourable, and from the readiness to exert political pressures on the state to create such favourable situations. In Hirschman's view, the promotion of investment was the key to progress:

The investments of one period are often the principle motivating forces behind some additional investments of subsequent periods ... Thus investment in the production of A sets up strong pressures for an increase in the production of B and strong incentives for the start of the production of C.[17]

Thus once the initial start is made, momentum is gained by linkages operating between the commodities involved in a time sequence.

Such a start might be expected to be hesitant and uncertain but, if it should take hold, to have some prospect of being self-perpetuating. Development will neither start nor be maintained unless sufficient incentives are there to make it worthwhile. In Hirschman's model the impetus comes from a process of unbalanced growth; one sector of the economy over-extends and so improves the prospect for other sectors which are encouraged to move forward in turn, sometimes themselves over-extending and providing further incentives for movement elsewhere. Behind this process lies the assumption that technical complementarity is sufficiently powerful to be a factor activating investment.[18]

Hirschman's view of how one thing sparks off another can be illustrated in terms of investment in different types of capital, that is, those that are made with the intention of providing for directly productive activities, such as manufacturing something, referred to by the acronym DPA, and those that are made in social overhead capital (SOC) or infrastructure. There is no reason why the proportions of the two may not be varied. A factory can construct its own roads, but it will have lower costs if it can use public ones, particularly if they are of good enough quality to reduce wear of its vehicles; it could educate its own labour force, but it would save money by leaving this to the public system if suitable education were provided, and so on. If there is insufficient SOC, a manufacturer (or his manufacturers' association) will pressurise the government to provide more. Suppose that the government responds and that the manufacturers' costs are reduced. This may stimulate him to increase output and the process might be repeated. Of course, the sequence might go the other way. The important thing is that imbalance between SOC and DPA, however it occurs, produces pressures to do something about it.

Hirschman's views about how things get done and how people are motivated can be extended further. It may be a mistake to build roads so well that they will require little in the way of repair for several years; it may be better to construct roads of lesser quality that last long enough to demonstrate their usefulness and then become full of holes. Those using them will then, it may be hoped, be motivated to repair them, and new activities will be set in train, so helping to fan the wind of change. In practice, of course, this may not happen, as many field workers have observed.

If the arguments developed by Hirschman seem a little strained at times, they become more convincing when applied to planned industrial linkages. In Bangladesh the establishment of the government-owned Sugar Corporation for the refinement of sugar demonstrated that supplies of sugar cane were inadequate to work the plant at full capacity. This led the Corporation to consider ways and means of increasing the output of cane and getting growers to deliver it to the factory.

It is easy to find illustrations of linkages between agriculture and industry and between industries where one provides the other with raw materials or other inputs. But are such linkages of substantial benefit or only a minor factor in development? For the most part they do not appear to be very strong influences. An inspection of input-output tables prepared for less developed countries reveals many nearly empty economic boxes. Moreover, the expectation that linkages should be important rests on the assumption that it is possible and economical to conduct different stages of production in the same country. This is often not the case.

Propositions of the kind put foward by Hirschman are impossible to prove, and are only uncertainly disproved, because they may be valid in some countries or circumstances and not in others. The attempts of Yotopoulos and Nugent to correlate growth and linkages gave no support to the Hirschman thesis.[19] While any study of this type is full of pitfalls, it suggests that unbalanced growth may not be a productive strategy to pursue. We also are inclined to reject the Hirschman thesis as an acceptable general strategy for development, while conceding that some projects may be successfully designed to stimulate the activities of others.

IMPORT SUBSTITUTION OR EXPORT GROWTH

Most developing countries are prone to balance of payments difficulties. Many of the goods they need are not produced domestically and there may be little opportunity to increase exports quickly. It might be thought that given time, market forces would take care of balance of payments difficulties, but Raul Prebisch has argued that this may well not be the case.[20] 'It is a well-established fact that the income elasticity of demand for imports of Latin American primary commodities by the centers is generally lower than the income elasticity of demand for Latin American imports of industrial products from these centers.'[21] Prebisch goes on to argue that the consequence of this will be that the rate of growth of the Latin American countries will be tied to the rate of growth of the 'centers' (industrial countries) by the balance of payments constraint and in such a way, given the orders of magnitude of the elasticities, that the rate of growth of the developing countries will probably be less than that of the centres.

The remedy is to employ import substitution. It may be that, on the face of it, this appears uneconomic; comparative costs would dictate otherwise. But this is not the real issue. The important thing is that restricting imports breaks the tie to the 'centers' and so allows growth rates in the Latin American countries to be unrestricted by it. It might be added, in the context of the debt burdens of the Latin American countries in the 1980s, that these countries were forced to accept rates of growth that were tied to their ability to service the debt that they owed to the 'centers'. Import restrictions to improve the balance of payments also have the effect of reducing rates of growth.

Prebisch's thesis is clearly liable to fierce attack. Countries can and do adjust the structure of their production; they do not need to be rigidly tied to the demands of industrial countries for their exports, and they do not need to impose restrictions in order to be able to do this. As development proceeds, industrialisation, even without special measures of protection, might reduce import dependence automatically. Prebisch contends, however, that even this is unlikely, for the developing countries may find themselves moving into an area of activity where they do not have comparative advantage, and the effect of this will be to make their terms of trade deteriorate.

These arguments are often seen against a back-cloth in which the export-orientated economies of Japan, Taiwan, South Korea, Hong Kong and Singapore may be seen to be progressing more rapidly than other countries with an inward-looking strategy. Protectionist measures, it is argued, distort prices, raise costs, enable protected companies, whether domestic or foreign, to make excessive profits and give rise to excess capacity.[22] Moreover, such policies may be associated with the inefficient use of administrative controls,[23] while export can take place only if efficiency in production, marketing and economic activity is attained, and is considered to be a powerful generator of growth.[24] It is sometimes ignored that policies directed at export promotion by the use of subsidies or other means may also be inefficient and suffer from much the same defects as those engendered by import substitution. It may also be that if all developing countries were to concentrate hard on the export of manufactures to the industrialised countries, import barriers would be raised against them, so curtailing development by this route. Furthermore, export markets are not without other risks. International competition, as well as promoting efficiency, may make it difficult for newcomers to get established, and shifts in competitive power, even after establishment, may drive them out of the market.[25]

This chapter has outlined a number of strategies or general approaches to development. While all of them are worth considering, few of them in isolation can be regarded as providing some unfailing key to development. There are strong subjective elements in all of them. To the extent that any of them may be adopted, they are likely to require the most careful tailoring to the needs of particular countries. Strategies have to be reconciled with the aspirations as well as the social, political and economic structures of the countries for which they are designed. No general rule of thumb can replace a careful study of all these aspects individually.

FURTHER READING

Montek S. Ahluwalia, 'Inequality, Poverty and Development', *Journal of Development Economics*, Vol. 3 (1976), No. 4, pp. 307-42.
Gary S. Fields, *Poverty Inequality and Development*, Cambridge, Cambridge University Press, 1980.
Nurul Islam, *Development Planning in Bangladesh: A Study in Political Economy*, London, Hurst, 1977.
Raul Prebisch, 'Commercial Policy in the Underdeveloped Countries', *American Economic Review*, Vol. 49 (1959), No. 2, pp. 251-73. (Papers and Proceedings of the 71st Annual Meeting of the American Economic Association, 1958.)
Ashwani Saith, 'Development and Distribution', *Journal of Development Economics*, Vol. 13 (1983), No. 3, pp. 367-82.

NOTES

1. John Rawls, *A Theory of Justice*, Cambridge, Mass., Harvard University Press, 1981.
2. Ibid., p. 11.
3. Nurul Islam, *Development Planning in Bangladesh: A Study in Political Economy*, London, Hurst, 1977.
4. See A. W. Arndt, 'The "Trickle-Down" Myth', *Economic Development and Cultural Change*, Vol. 32 (1983), No. 1, pp. 1-10.
5. See, for example, Jagdish Bhagwati, *The Economics of Underdeveloped Countries*, New York, McGraw-Hill, 1966, Chapter 1, and his address to the Asian Development Bank, Manila, on 6 October 1983; and A. W. Arndt, op. cit.
6. There are several ways of attempting to measure inequality of income distribution. The share of selected percentages of the bottom or top households, or individuals, in total income is often used to give such an indication, as is done in this chapter. From such data it is possible to derive the Gini coefficient. This measures the extent of deviation from an equal distribution of income on a scale 0-1 with 0 representing perfect equality. A coefficient less than 0.5 is often regarded as acceptable, though values of 0.3 are found in countries with outstanding equality. Another measure is the T coefficient which measures deviations from average income. It represents in effect the proportion of income that has to be transferred from the rich to the poor if perfect equality is to be attained. A figure for the Sudan in the mid-1970s is 28 per cent, which may be placed against a Gini coefficient of about 0.4 to 0.5. There are many other possible measures and the fact that they may give different results must be borne in mind.
7. Simon Kuznets, 'Economic Growth and Income Inequality', *American Economic Review*, Vol. 55 (1955), No. 1, p. 24: 'Is the pattern of the older

developed countries likely to be repeated in the sense that in the early phases of industrialization in the underdeveloped countries income inequalities will tend to widen before the leveling forces become strong enough first to stabilize and then reduce income inequalities?'

8. Irma Adelman and Cynthia Taft Morris, *Economic Growth and Social Equity in Developing Countries*, Stanford, Calif., Stanford University Press, 1973, p. 179.
9. 'Inequality, Poverty and Development', *Journal of Development Economics*, Vol. 3 (1976), No. 4, pp. 307-42.
10. 'Development and Distribution', *Journal of Development Economics*, Vol. 13 (1983), No. 3, pp. 367-82.
11. Address to the Board of Governors, Washington DC, 25 September 1972. Others had, of course, been saying similar things but the Bank carries weight.
12. 'Aid, Growth and Equity in Southern Asia', in J. R. Parkinson (ed.), *Poverty and Aid*, London, Blackwell, 1983, pp. 169-82.
13. See the study carried out by Dr Mehmet Kaytaz, *Potential Effects of Income Redistribution on Economic Growth: A Simulation Based on the Turkish Economy, 1968-1972* (Ph.D. Thesis, Nottingham University, 1978). He demonstrated that attempting to achieve a more equal distribution of income would have both positive and negative effects on growth of the Turkish economy. On the one hand, savings might be reduced and, on the other, import requirements (one of the scarce inputs in development) might also be reduced. Depending on how income was transferred, it could be shown that greater equality in the distribution of income might increase the rate of growth of national output. Even if it did not have this effect, redistribution might be considered to be beneficial because the poor would benefit. The study demonstrated that the consequences of adopting particular strategies require detailed investigation if they are to be fully understood. Unfortunately it is seldom possible to do this with the thoroughness that the issue deserves.
14. Note that to get a measure of the full effect of linkages the input-output matrix needs to be fully inverted. The purchases of industry A affect the output of industry B which in turn affects the output of C, D and perhaps also A through purchases from that industry.
15. 'Problems of Industrialisation in Eastern and South-Eastern Europe', *Economic Journal*, 1943, pp. 204-7.
16. For a discussion of balanced growth see, for example, Ragnar Nurkse, 'The Conflict between "Balanced Growth" and International Specialization', in Gottfried Haberler (ed.), *Equilibrium and Growth in the World Economy: Economic Essays by Ragnar Nurkse*, Oxford, Oxford University Press, 1961, pp. 241-58; and S. K. Nath, 'The Theory of Balanced Growth', *Oxford Economic Papers*, Vol. 14 (1962), No. 2, pp. 138-53.
17. A. O. Hirschman, *The Strategy of Economic Development*, New Haven, Conn., Yale University Press, 1958, p. 42.
18. Hirschman, ibid., p. 67. Technical complementarity occurs whenever an increase in output of A lowers the marginal cost of producing output of B. This may happen when (i) A is an output of B and is produced under conditions of decreasing costs; (ii) B is an input of A and is itself produced under conditions of decreasing costs; or (iii) A and B are joint products (or because B is a by-product of A) and are produced under decreasing costs.

19. Pan A. Yotopoulus and Jeffrey B. Nugent, 'A Balanced Growth Version of the Linkage Hypothesis: A Test', *The Quarterly Journal of Economics*, Vol. 87 (1973), No. 21, pp. 157-71. See also by the same authors, 'Morphology of Growth, the Effects of Country Size, Structural Characteristics and Linkages', *Journal of Development Economics*, Vol. 10 (1982), No. 3, pp. 279-95, in which they conclude that balanced growth is favourable for the long-term growth of less developed countries.
20. 'Commercial Policy in the Underdeveloped Countries', *American Economic Review*, Vol. 49 (1959), No. 2, pp. 251-73. (Papers and Proceedings of the 71st Annual Meeting of the American Economic Association, 1958.)
21. Ibid., p. 252.
22. Anne O. Krueger, 'Import Substitution Versus Export Promotion', *Finance and Development*, Vol. 22 (1985), No. 2, pp. 20-3.
23. For a discussion of various aspects of this, see Ian Little, Tibor Scitovsky and Maurice Scott, *Industry and Trade in some Developing Countries*, Oxford, Oxford University Press, 1970; also, Bela Balassa and Associates, *The Structure of Protection in Developing Countries*, Baltimore, Md., Johns Hopkins Press, 1971, particularly Table 4.1, p. 82 and *World Development Report 1983*, Oxford, Oxford University Press, 1983, pp. 60-3.
24. Lloyd G. Reynolds, in 'The Spread of Economic Growth to the Third World', Center Paper No. 344, Yale University Growth Center, lays great stress on the historical importance of exports as generators of growth in developing countries.
25. See Paul Streeten, 'A Cool Look at "Outward Looking" Industrialisation and Trade Strategies', *PIDE Tidings*, Nov./Dec. 1982.

3 The nature and scope of planning

There are many types of planning but all have common features: they try to instil order and method and to integrate activities in a coordinated way. The range of planning activities can be illustrated from the experience of the United Kingdom. In the Second World War every aspect of the British economy, civil as well as military, was planned and, by the end of the war, quite effectively. It was a command economy and market processes had scarcely any role. This is as near as a capitalist country can be expected to get to planning in the Russian mould, but only in wartime; in peacetime it does not find favour. In 1965, under a Labour government, an effort was made to introduce an indicative plan (indicative of objectives) prepared along French lines, but this was a dismal failure and was soon abandoned. Nevertheless, it would be wrong to regard the United Kingdom of the present day as being unplanned in every respect. Governments have objectives and they plan how to attain these objectives through the exercise of policies, including fiscal and monetary measures, and a good deal of direct intervention (when they can get away with it). This kind of planning may be regarded as setting a framework within which the economic activities of individuals, households and enterprises are conducted.

Although many aspects of planning are not concerned with economic issues, the economist has a special role to play, for he is trained to consider alternative courses of action and to weigh their net advantages. He is also trained to adopt a systematic approach to the organisation of economic activities and the optimal use of resources, taking full account of interactions between the many sectors of an economy.

The role of the economist is not confined to the technical preparation of a plan; he, in the company of others in an operational context, has to relate to political masters. The involvement of the politicians in the planning process is crucial. The essentials of a plan must be approved by those who hold real power: the president, the cabinet, the junta, the civil servants, whoever it may be. This means that the ruling faction, or some of those concerned at least, must accept responsibility for the planning process and adopt it as an apparatus for deciding what to do. Politicians frequently shy away from committing themselves and have to be convinced that decisions must be taken and cannot be postponed indefinitely. This in turn involves reconciliation of the aspirations of ministers and their departments, and political as well as economic coordination; in this a plan can help.

Although the aims of planning may seem unexceptional, it does not follow that planning is the one and only, or even the best way of attaining them. The industrial revolution in the United Kingdom took place without any conscious effort to plan it. It was promoted by the actions of a great many individuals taking their decisions in an environment in which government direct action played a minor part. Ultimately, it spread to almost every kind of economic activity. There was no plan, but the activities taking place were coordinated through the market, by buying and selling and in response to market signals in the form of prices and costs. This might seem to be a successful way of organising things and, in default of better alternatives, one to be adopted, but it also has its defects, as has been abundantly demonstrated.

In the first place, leaving things to private enterprise does not necessarily result in growth. Private enterprise has not emerged as a driving force in many countries in the way that it did in Western industrial nations and, when this is the case, other stimuli to growth may be necessary.

When India was partitioned, the Hindus living in West Pakistan, who predominated in trade and commerce, were driven out. Who could take their place? Few of the members of the leaders of the old civil service of India remained and in any case they were not primarily development-orientated in their training. How could business or government be coordinated and the development of the country promoted? It was felt that one necessary condition was to ensure that national plans were prepared and put into action. While the circumstances of Pakistan were peculiar to it, it is quite usual to find that adequately educated people, used to dealing with national rather than personal affairs and to getting things done, are all too few in an emerging developing country. Coordinated direction of the economy may help to use them efficiently and for this a plan can be useful in identifying what needs to be done and giving impetus to development. Another reason advanced for planning is that it is technically efficient. It is thought in some places and by some enthusiasts that with the aid of computers planning can give better answers to economic questions than the market. In some respects planning and planning techniques do give superior answers to economic questions, but it does not seem to us that this is so often the case as to be a compelling argument for having a national plan. In fact it is extremely hard to plan well, a great deal of judgement is involved and things often go wrong. Sometimes, as might be expected, planning and the associated policies may have quite harmful effects, as we shall illustrate later.

In the eyes of many people political considerations give powerful justification for planning. This is most obvious in the traditional Soviet model where it is axiomatic that the economy should be directed by the state, the means of production owned by it, and economic freedom limited, so giving only small scope for decision-taking by individuals.

In market economies, planning may be advocated as a means to correct deficiencies. How well do such economies function? Does the market really establish the right prices on which to base economic decisions? It is in the nature of externalities that they are not taken into account by private decision-makers, so that public welfare may be adversely affected by economic decisions in the private sector. It is often argued that market-based systems of economic organisation may give rise to high unemployment and to a markedly skewed distribution of income and wealth, and may fail to provide opportunities for all sections of the community. The corollary is assumed to be that planning could correct these defects.

Most present-day developing countries prepare economic plans to guide their economies, but the nature and extent of the contribution of these activities to economic development is contestable. The future, except in the roundest terms, may be virtually unforeseeable; the facts and information on which planning has to be based are often inaccurate and always incomplete. This itself points to the potential advantages of decentralisation of decision-taking to operational units where information may be more readily available and better understood. It also points to the advantages of relying on markets to guide and promote economic activity where the man on the spot can make the best possible decision in detail.[1] In spite of these misgivings about planning we think that the process is likely to be beneficial for developing countries. It helps to identify the options open to a country, coordinate economic activities, trace the consequences of economic decisions, force decisions, and coordinate the machinery of government. The final point is more important than may appear to the uninitiated.

In developing as in developed countries, planning can also take a variety of forms. It may be directed mainly to planning the government's own activities or setting particular programmes for development. Or it may attempt to embrace some or all of the activities of the private sector. The market may be relied upon to some degree, or every effort may be made to dispense with it as an instrument for deciding what economic activities should be pursued. Whatever system is adopted, it is likely to change and evolve over time.

While planning does not necessarily require the preparation of a comprehensive single document covering all aspects of the economy in a consistent and coherent fashion, there are advantages in doing so. The plan represents guidelines for government policies that would not otherwise become easily available to civil servants and others, and it enables arguments to be structured in relation to explicit aims. Without agreement on aims the plan may become no more than an instrument of dissension. Generally, the plan is also intended to be a document available to the public. It is sometimes the practice to submit draft plans to wide public scrutiny with the object of eliciting criticism, securing support and disarming critics.

In Mozambique, contrary to what might be expected, there appears to be no detailed plan available for public discussion. The main objectives, including the increase in outputs that it is hoped to achieve, have been disclosed but with little indication of the measures that will be taken to bring this about. It is possible that the absence of a published plan may be explained by the fact that there is insufficient information available and insufficient time to construct a thoroughgoing plan, but confidentiality may also be a factor; in this respect as in some others, Mozambique has adopted the practice of other socialist states.

Another reason for having a plan is that aid agencies frequently demand a coherent (though not always well-reasoned or organised) picture of economic policies and performance in the form of a plan before they are prepared to consider giving assistance. Private bankers seem to get on without this; aid agencies, with governments to answer to, consider it to be essential.

All in all, there seem to be some good reasons for preparing plans for less-developed countries, most of which make considerable efforts in this direction. This does not always ensure that the preparation of a plan improves the performance of government or that those engaged in preparing plan documents might not be better engaged elsewhere. There is bad planning as well as good.

THE ORGANISATION OF PLANNING

The preparation of a well-considered plan requires a massive flow of information in the form of statistics and reports on operations. It also requires the services of hundreds of people. In a very low-income developing country only a few of the planning staff will be experienced planners and they are likely to share the responsibility of determining the structure of the plan and making the decisions incorporated within it.

We shall refer to the agency responsible for planning as the planning commission, the term used in Bangladesh and many other countries. It may be a separate government agency with or without a minister in charge of it and sometimes under the nominal charge of the prime minister or the president, in an attempt to build up its reputation and influence in the affairs of government. Frequently planning is a responsibility of the ministry of finance, and the planning commission will be one of the arms of that department. The location of the commission within the government is a debatable matter. The arguments in favour of one or another location generally fluctuate between the amount of influence the planning commission is expected to command and, alternatively, the ways in which such influence can be limited. There are also arguments about how its location is likely to affect its technical efficiency. Will it be better able to contribute usefully to day-to-day policy decisions if it is in the ministry of finance rather than on its own? And, often vital, how will the relations with top civil servants work if the planning commission is isolated from the normal structure of government? It will have to have well-developed contacts with other ministries if it is going to be a real force. Its basic function is to give a lead to policy and combine and coordinate economic activities; it is not in itself an executive agency. It will draw heavily on information provided from other ministries and will need to be involved with them.[2]

Interrelations with government are also reflected in the way in which the planning commission is organised. Often it has two, and sometimes three, basic divisions. One of these would typically be concerned with micro or sector aspects of planning and the other with macro aspects. Within the micro division there will be sections concerned with specific sectors of the economy, often corresponding to ministerial responsibilities. Thus there will be sections dealing with agriculture, industry, transport, power, education and so on. It will be their responsibility to understand the needs of those sectors, how they expect to develop, what development projects are in hand or under preparation and what contribution they are expected to make. Most of such information will come from the executive ministry, but the staff in the planning commission will have to examine it critically, both in relation to the sectors concerned and the totality of the plan. They cannot do this without becoming expert in their field.

The macro section of the planning commission, as the description implies, is concerned primarily with the operation of the country as a whole. It will consider the general economic strategy and the relations between the various sectors of the country. Amongst other things, it will have to consider, and sometimes determine, how much money can be found for development, how much aid is likely to be available, how domestic and international prices may move, and how big the private sector of the economy should be. It will also be asked to outline the economic policies that government should follow in order to realise the plan. It has a broad span of responsibility, but it will not generally need to be staffed on the scale of the micro section as economic analysis makes less demands on administrative coordination than work in the micro field. A third division, which in some cases may form part of the macro division, may be concerned with all aspects of external resources: the receipt and use of aid (including some aspects of the administration of it) and the balance of payments. For most developing countries this is vital and so is singled out for special attention.

A major part of the time and effort of a planning commission will be concentrated on the preparation of medium-term plans, typically of about five years' duration. However, planning work with a longer-term perspective, say, a twenty-year period, as well as short-term planning, typically for a budget year, are also important responsibilities. Thus, when several years may elapse between the preparation and execution of projects it is essential to plan ahead, both for investment and subsequent operation, to ensure a coherent framework. Yet the further ahead planning is attempted, the more difficult and speculative it becomes.

As a general rule, the planning effort might best be limited to the period over which current actions are likely to exert significant influence. In the case of a factory it may not be necessary to look much further ahead than ten years, since that may be the economic life-span of its operations. Other planning decisions may have consequences far into the future. Planning a town is of this nature; twenty-five years is seldom long enough for a town to be completed and what is done in those twenty-five years will produce effects for decades or even centuries thereafter. In economic matters the same may also be true. Extending primary education in the next five years is not likely to have much immediate effect on the quality of the work-force, but it may be a very desirable thing to do in relation to the more distant development of the country. Geological surveys may have very little effect in the short term, but they may make all the difference to the ultimate prospects for the country.

In a wider context, it is helpful to assess what the cumulative effects of development might be expected to be. If development proceeds at some preconceived rate, will material standards improve sufficiently in the next twenty-five years to satisfy the people, or must more be done if there is to be confidence that development can be sustained? Where will the country be in twenty-five years' time? Will there be enough jobs, adequate institutional infrastructure, good educational standards and so on? These are some of the reasons for attempting to look at the evolution of the economy over one or two decades or more and for preparing perspective plans. These are necessarily of a broader character than medium-term plans and more general in content.

Perspective plans can be quite instructive in pointing to future dangers. The revolt of East Pakistan against West Pakistan in 1971 reflected, amongst other things, discontent as economic progress in East Pakistan fell progressively behind that of West Pakistan. A perspective, if not a plan, prepared many years before the revolt of East Pakistan by the Pakistan Planning Commission,[3] had drawn attention to the need to support development in East Pakistan which lagged behind West Pakistan. It was not acted on sufficiently, in part because planners and politicians were not able to find effective means of accelerating development in East Pakistan. More recently, the need for thinking about the future of Bangladesh in terms of longer-term perspectives is just as evident. How to feed the population in 2000 and find work for it are just some of the issues that need consideration now.

Most countries, developed as well as underdeveloped, take the opportunity to review government policy and objectives before presenting their annual budgets. For a developing country operating a medium-range plan, a systematic review of the plan will also take place to see if changes need to be made in the light of evolving economic circumstances and to some extent with the intention of rolling it forward. It is also possible, as the implementation of the plan moves forward, to spell it out in the sort of detail that cannot be encompassed in a document intended to serve as a broad guide for a fairly long period. Out of this arises a plan of action for the coming year.

An important aspect of the preparation of annual plans is to relate them to the government's annual budget. It is only when the latter is drawn up that a reasonably reliable estimate can be made of the resources that are expected to be available for current or development purposes. This covers not only the use of domestic resources, but foreign currency requirements as well, for in most developing countries the two cannot be regarded as interchangeable. The availability of foreign currency will depend on how far it has been possible to reach agreement with foreign donors about the level of aid to be made available in the coming year.

At the time of the preparation of the annual plan, spending authorisations can be issued to government departments giving substance to the proposals made in the medium-term plan. With these as a basis, financial control can come into operation and with it machinery for monitoring progress in implementing the plan.

At the same time as the annual plan is prepared for development expenditure, other forms of government activity will also be decided. If the economy uses controls to allocate foreign exchange, for example, decisions relating to this will have to be taken so that government finance in its entirety may be co-ordinated. As part of this exercise, instructions will be issued to the banks detailing the form and extent of restrictions to be imposed.

It might be thought at first sight that the annual plan would give the opportunity for a radical review of existing policies and that drastic changes to the development programmes could be introduced at this stage. Some changes can of course be made and they can be quite drastic if the economic pressures are really severe. More generally, however, changes are not so easy to introduce. Government agencies always have built-in interests; they are reluctant to stand down in the interests of other departments, and activity is very hard to cut back as a result. One of the arguments that departments use to protect their interests is that the activities and the development projects that they are supporting are 'on-going' and to reduce them, let alone terminate them, would be wasteful if not impossible. Often this may also be used as a device for the introduction of new schemes under the cover of the completion of old ones previously approved. Even within an expanding programme only a small percentage of budgetary expenditure is made up of new schemes distinctly separate from previous programmes. This is a further argument for a strong planning commission or ministry of finance which has the knowledge and power to ensure that the right pattern of government expenditure is established.

We complete this section by emphasising that if planning is to be of value it must be operational. This applies particularly to the annual plan. It must emerge from an interchange between central planners and the ministries that will enable the latter to see the economic situation as a whole and how operations fit into it. In many cases this will demonstrate the need to economise, to be less ambitious, or to abandon favoured plans. The process, however, is two-way: the ministries begin to understand the effect on them of the constraints exposed by the central planners, who in turn learn about the consequences of the ministerial programme for other sectors of the economy and indeed for its (the economy's) total functioning. Without this interchange, policies and performance would be much weaker, resources would be wasted and the development of the country retarded.

MACRO PLANNING

The aim of a plan is to provide guidelines for the evolution of an economy, typically in the case of a medium-term plan over a period of five years. It is a mistake to think that because plans are seldom precisely fulfilled planning is doomed to failure. The aim of planners is not to forecast what will happen; nevertheless, the plan will include quantitative values for key economic variables describing how the economy is expected to evolve over the time-period chosen for the plan. It is also desirable to establish how the plan is to be phased over the five years. This will be necessary not only to indicate the rate at which projects, programmes and policies are intended to be executed, but also to provide a picture of dynamic interrelation. Efforts have to be made to ensure that the elements of the plan will be consistent and, ultimately, all ends have to meet and tie. Gaps and inconsistencies revealed in the planning process have to be resolved, perhaps after confrontation and long discussion between ministries, and after acceptance of fundamental changes that are needed. Sometimes prophets and mountains may both be immovable, and the economy may shudder on from one crisis to another.

It is possible to start the preparation of a plan by specifying any of its major elements and proceed from there to work out the implications for other elements. Initially, discussions about the plan will be in political terms as much as economic or technical terms, as we described in Chapter 2. A good starting-point for plan preparation is to specify objectives.

Rather broad objectives need to be specified to begin with in order to get the main lines of the plan established, uncluttered by too much detail. Although the GDP has considerable drawbacks as an indicator of welfare and says nothing about income distribution, the rate at which it increases is often regarded as the key indicator epitomising plan performance. It is necessary to consider how large an increase should be proposed. Whatever figure is proposed, it will be subjected to prolonged discussion with the following considerations in mind.

1. Investment is expected to enable consumption to be increased in the future but in all probability at the expense of present consumption. How far is it justifiable to contain or even reduce

the consumption of the present poor in order to increase that of the future rich?[4]

2. A low investment effort reduces the rate at which poverty can be eliminated. With a 3-1 capital-output ratio, a population increase of 3 per cent, and investment of 15 per cent of the GDP, output per capita would increase by only 2 per cent per year. This might be too low to be politically acceptable.
3. The rate of increase attained in the past and the strains imposed by it are of significance.
4. Does the country have the absorptive capacity to carry out the proposed programme? In other words, does it have the skilled manpower, know-how, organisational capacity, infrastructure, etc., to do what it wants to do?
5. Will it be possible to use the increased capacity provided by investment profitably, or will a shortage of inputs mean that it cannot be operated at capacity?
6. An ambitious programme might qualify for more aid than one that is more limited.

Politicians are likely to be involved in setting targets for increases in output and will consider whether the planners' judgement about the rate of increase that can be achieved is politically acceptable. In these respects the predictions of planners and the aspirations of politicians are likely to coincide; both will be inclined to set their sights high. Thus in the second five-year plan for Bangladesh it was ultimately decided to aim for an increase of 7 per cent per annum in GDP, partly because of presidential pressure to increase food output. As a guide it may be said that it is most unusual to attain an increase of as much as 6-8 per cent in GDP over a period of years (see Table 1.4 for an indication of past increases in income per capita for low-income countries); a plan aiming at more than this would be suspect, unless there were unusual circumstances to justify it.[5] In most cases a much more modest growth rate would have to be accepted for the plan to have credibility.

In the end, planners and politicians will reach some compromise view on the rate of increase in output to be used for the planning exercise. This is not the end of the matter; it will have to be reconsidered later in the light of what the rest of the planning exercise shows. Nevertheless, the preparation of other aspects of the plan can now go ahead. Although it might seem convenient to determine the size of the plan first and to proceed to work out its details later, the preparation of other elements of the plan will proceed in parallel with the macro analysis. Finalisation of plan objectives will not take.place until a great deal of preliminary work has been completed. Much of this takes place in the micro division.

The function of the micro planners is to consider how their sectors can be made to function efficiently and be further developed. They may seek to increase output and productivity, expand health care, reduce the birth rate, build roads and many other things.

The preparation of programmes for the individual sectors of the economy is a painstaking and difficult task. Often there will be very little experience within the country of preparing development projects. Although domestic technical experts can in many instances be reinforced by consultants from outside the country, the novelty of what may be attempted, the fact that it often represents a quantum change not closely related to what has gone before and, above all, the pitfalls of trying to do things in developing countries with little of the general facilities so widely available in industrialised countries, all throw a heavy responsibility on those called on to recommend projects for adoption.

Just as the micro sections have to spell out the details of what they are to put in their programmes, so will the macro planners seek to investigate in more detail how the economy is likely to fit together in terms of aggregates. A key aspect of this is international trade. Estimates of the balance of payments will have to be prepared in order to see if the implications of the import requirements of the (as yet, very tentative) plan can be met. There is no ready-made way of doing this. Estimating the value of exports for five years ahead, depending as it does on assessing price movements, production possibilities and market prospects, is extremely hazardous. Forecasting economic variables with confidence over such long periods is a virtually impossible task. How is it possible to judge the rate at which new products for export will become available? What are the prospects for exports of timber, fish or manufactures in the face of protectionism? What prices will they fetch? What is the chance of discovering oil? Import requirements may be more readily assessed in relation to the programmes being evolved by the micro division using import coefficients. Here again, however, there are great uncertainties.

What will happen to the prices of imported oil and food? The assumptions and calculations of the first five-year plan of Bangladesh in 1973 were made irrelevant by price increases which doubled the cost of imports within a year. Unforeseeable disturbances of this magnitude have to be dealt with as they arise.

Just as the balance of payments must be consistent with the plan as a whole, so must many other aspects of the operation of the economy. One good question to ask is whether domestic savings will be adequate to finance that part of investment expenditures which is not to be met by aid or other capital inflows. Will the increase planned in the supply of money be consistent with the assumed increase in output and prices?

On the micro side of the planning exercise, consistency will also be necessary. Will the requirements of industry for electricity be met by the capacity that is expected to be in operation? Will port capacity be sufficient to accommodate the flows of imports and exports? Is land prepared for the number of houses that are to be built and can the public services needed for them be provided in time? Not all such questions can be answered in the form of a plan document but the most important of them need to be considered. The plan is a guide as to what can be done and must pass a number of broad checks on the feasibility of what is proposed. Even so, it will require interpretation and almost certainly modification from a very early stage in its implementation.

The need for flexible planning must not be allowed to obscure the fact that it is also necessary to observe the discipline of the plan. Officials, ministries and ministers like to get their own way, achieve their own objectives and make life easy for themselves. The plan can be uncomfortable and attempts will be made to escape from its compulsions. This has to be resisted. To argue that changes will destroy the plan can sometimes have salutary effects, particularly when combined with the employment of the familiar challenge: 'If you get more who gets less?'

No plan is complete without a list of policies to go with it. Some parts of the plan lend themselves to direct implementation because they concern action to be taken in the public sector of the economy for which instructions can be given. Even here administrative policies may have to be devised if departments or government agencies are to be kept under control. Depending on the system of government, it may also be decided to operate the private sector within a strait-jacket of controls and commands.

While the expansion of the private sector can be constrained by government instructions, it is much harder to make it respond positively, when that is needed, by instruction alone. Indeed, to have a private sector of an economy subject entirely to direction by government is a contradiction in terms. The point of having such a sector is to give scope for individual action because it is thought that it can make a contribution to development which government agencies could not themselves provide. It is also arguable that public sector agencies should be allowed freedom to do their job without too much interference. Nevertheless, freedom to act cannot be totally unrestrained. There has to be some regulating framework even if it amounts to no more than fiscal and monetary control.

The major elements of policies to be applied in respect of both public and private sectors need to be spelt out in the plan in some explicit detail. The planners may not wish to leave this to the ministry of finance and other government agencies and may wish to make recommendations about the determination of prices, the size of sectoral investment programmes, and many other matters such as regional issues related to the distribution of activity within the country, physical planning, administrative reform and the mobilisation of cadres.

THE USE OF COMPUTING AIDS AND MODELS

Many of the consistency checks indicated above can be carried out with the use of an inverted input-output table, as is increasingly done. The same matrix can also provide the base for consideration of the implications of different sizes of plan expenditure for the economy. With a suitable input-output table and computer facilities the import content of alternative strategies, involving different amounts of development expenditure and alternative compositions, can be worked out electronically for consideration, so relieving planners of the tedium of carrying out many detailed calculations in a sometimes uncoordinated way.

The limitations of such methods need to be understood. Even if the model is well constructed, it can only be a partial approximation of how the economy really works and the available data may be very poor. Still another difficulty is that developing countries change rapidly. Imagine what happens within five years to a country growing at the rate of 10 per cent per annum. A matrix appropriate at the beginning of the planning period might seem very inappropriate at the end of it. To some extent changes can be accommodated by modifying the model; nevertheless, this imposes considerable elements of judgement as to what the shape of the economy is really going to be when it is destined for profound and far-reaching change. This is not in any way to belittle the contribution that suitable computing techniques can make to plan formulation, but they will aid and not replace the contribution that the planners themselves have to make, which, as we have seen, depends very much on understanding the programmes devised for the various sectors.

To illustrate the use of a model in policy determination we take one constructed for Botswana in connection with the preparation of that country's National Development Plan, 1979-85.[6] What follows describes the Botswana economy as it was perceived at the time the model was constructed. As the operation of the Botswana economy is dominated by only a few main features, the model could be a fairly simple one. The crucial aspect of the economy was the support given to government revenues and export earnings by diamond mining and the export of meat. Partly because of this, the government was so well endowed with revenue that the development effort could be said to be limited mainly by the absorptive capacity of the economy.

The model starts with making assumptions about production levels in leading sectors of the economy. These comprise the cattle sector, other forms of agriculture, diamond mining and selling, other mining and prospecting, the Botswana Meat Commission, manufacturing, water and electricity, and central and local government.

There are, of course, other production sectors in the economy, but they could be considered to follow the movements of the leading sectors. Having established production levels for the various sectors, it was possible to calculate the investment needed to attain them and the manpower that could be employed. In a similar way, the implications for household incomes and expenditures could be traced, by dividing recipients according to whether they are high- or low-income classes and in the rural or urban areas of the country. A further step was to establish relationships between production and consumption and exports and imports.

So far we have been describing the real side of the model's

construction. This may all be translated into current prices either by assuming that prices are exogenously determined, as in the case of export prices, or as a function of the costs incurred by producers, assuming that cost changes are reflected in prices. From this it is only a step to calculating the components of government revenue. These cover mining revenues, customs revenue and revenue from other sources as well as grants. Expenditure figures for the government can also be assessed.

What can a model of this type tell us? In the 1979-85 plan for Botswana it was used to test a number of alternative scenarios and to trace their effects on the economy. It was decided to work out what would happen to the main forecasts included in the plan if the country were to face either drought, or foot-and-mouth disease, or slower development of the mineral sector than had been assumed, or a combination of these factors. Some of the findings are described below.

Drought in Botswana does not take its toll immediately; it may take up to three years of water shortage before the cattle population is drastically reduced as a result of inadequate grazing. The first effect of drought is that cattle owners would find it in their interest to reduce their herds and therefore they increase their cattle sales to the abattoirs of the Botswana Meat Corporation; this may take place progressively during the drought years. As a result, when the rains return, the volume of sales to the Botswana Meat Corporation would be reduced for several years, say up to five years and by as much as 40 per cent. These effects of drought were calculated to amount to a reduction in the overall rate of growth over the plan period from 10 per cent to 8.9 per cent. The effect of lower rates of output on government revenue was very small, no more than 0.3 per cent over the plan period, and it was found that foreign exchange reserves would actually be somewhat higher at the end of the plan period both because of the higher beef exports during the drought years and a relative decline in imports in later years, reflecting reduced incomes. In summary, a severe drought could hit the incomes of rural people directly and hard, but foreign exchange reserves and government revenues would hardly be affected.

The effect of an outbreak of foot-and-mouth disease occurring at about the middle of the plan period, very serious as it may be for individual cattle owners and particular rural areas, was shown by the model to cause very little aggregate reduction of GDP and disposable income. Foreign exchange earnings would be 3 per cent lower by the end of the plan but government revenue again would hardly be affected.

Diamond production bulks large in Botswana. There were great uncertainties in trying to estimate its contribution during the plan period. Capital and operating costs might vary greatly from predictions, the time at which a new mine at Jwaneng would come into production was not known with confidence, and the volume of output, the quality of stones that would be found, and the prices that might be got for them were all the subject of the utmost uncertainty. The plan based its calculations on a set of assumptions roughly corresponding to the median of the range of those that might reasonably occur. In order to test the effects of deviations from this possibility, a more pessimistic set of assumptions was fed into the model, both for the diamond sector and for the rest of the mining sector. It was found that the effect of doing this was substantial, as may be seen from the Table 3.1. The effects fell on government revenues and on foreign exchange reserves. Botswana was fortunate in having a strong balance of payments and so could absorb an adverse movement in the

Table 3.1 Impact of deviations from assumptions in Botswana's 1979-85 plan[7]

Consequences	Nature of disruption		
	Foot-and-mouth disease	Drought	Slower mineral development
Percentage GDP growth rate falls from 10.1% p.a. to:	10.1	8.9	7.4
Percentage change in GDP over plan period	−0.2	−4.0	−12.0
Percentage change in foreign exchange reserves at end of plan period	−3.0	4.0	−55.0
Percentage change in government revenue over plan period	–	−0.3	−13.0
Percentage change in personal disposable income over plan period	−0.4	−7.0	−0.6

reserves for some time without being forced to change policies or curtail government expenditures dramatically. Since, however, the mineral industry affects mainly government revenues and the foreign exchange position, because other activity is little connected with it and the development effort is restricted by absorptive capacity, the effect on other sectors of the economy was shown to be small. Personal disposable income, it was calculated, would fall by only 0.6 per cent across all income groups and even this would be caused mainly by a slight reduction in the government recurrent and development expenditures assumed in the plan. The effect of these deviations from the plan assumptions is summarised in Table 3.1.

SECTOR AND PROJECT PLANNING

There are several stages in preparing a development programme. The overall shape of it should be determined by the objectives set by the country and reflect the development strategy that has been adopted. A development strategy based on industrialisation imposes a composition of investment of one kind, while a strategy directly orientated to meet the basic needs of the population requires quite a different pattern of investment. Whatever broad objectives are set there are likely to be a number of alternative ways of achieving them and various sets of projects from which to choose. How should this choice be made?[8]

It is the task of the economic administrator to bring order and method into the process by which investment decisions are taken. Some rules have to be elaborated which, if they are to carry conviction, must have intellectual respectability as well as practical applicability. They will be severely tested when they lead to the conclusion that projects that are being pressed hard should be rejected. The process of choice is complicated by reason of the fact that priorities have to be established amongst vaguely phrased objectives which may often seem to be incapable of direct comparison. How is it possible to decide on investment programmes which will lift the economy from the conditions of take-off to the stage of self-sustained growth; achieve a regionally balanced, self-reliant and accelerated economic development; double real per capita income by the turn of the century; carry out a major expansion and improvement in the fields of education and health, as well as in the production of essential consumer goods; effect a gradual improvement in the balance of payments; ensure intensive training and fuller participation of women within an open and outward-looking economic policy? These questions (not in context and run together) are taken from the six-year plan for the Sudan 1977/78-1982/83 to give some idea of the problems that face the planners in determining priorities.

How does the value to be obtained from an extensive training programme compare with money spent on achieving the fuller participation of women or on investments directed at improving the balance of payments? What species of arithmetic can suffice to resolve such dilemmas without appeal to the predilections of politicians? But, it would be wrong to take such decisions without some quantitative assessment of their implication when this is possible or, when the alternatives being considered involve similar types of investment, to fail to compare their yields with rigour, however tenuous the outcome may be.

Since the Second World War in particular, economists have elaborated systems for analysing the costs and benefits involved in investment in the public sector of the economy. They differ in many respects from those appropriate for use by the private sector. They specifically seek criteria to calculate the return on investments in terms of social values, which may be quite different from those that would be used by firms or individuals in the private sector attempting to maximise their own economic return. Any system, whether designed for use in the private or public sector of the economy, must establish criteria for making choices and decide what it is intended to maximise. There may be differing views about what such criteria should be and no settled political or economic consensus may emerge. In the private sector it is fairly easy to appeal to the market-place as the criteria for success; in the public sector criteria are likely to be hotly debated and to depend on what faction is in power or commands the intellectual fashion.

Cost benefit analysis involves determining the costs and benefits implied in following some course of action and comparing them with alternatives and, when a choice has to be made, accepting those projects offering the best returns in relation to costs. The first step is to try to establish the physical facts relating to inputs and outputs–how much is needed, how much will be produced–so that an economic analysis can be made.

It may be of some interest to give a brief description of the way in which projects emerge for consideration and testing against economic criteria when an international aid-giving organisation is deciding whether it can offer support. In most cases an economic appraisal of the potentialities of a country will precede any attempt to develop and select suitable projects. The purpose of this is to find out what areas of the country and which types of activity seem likely to have promise. The International Fund for Agricultural Development, for instance, might send a mission to a country to try to ascertain whether there are suitable opportunities to expand agricultural production. It would not be desirable to do this in isolation without regard to the nature of the country's economy, its needs and aspirations; large agricultural projects have to be seen in relation to the economy as a whole and not just some narrow segment of it. In reaching its recommendations the mission is likely to consider a portfolio of projects already prepared for the government of the country. As a result of the mission's assessment of them it may select some activity with potential for examination such as, for example, opening up new areas of land, providing irrigation facilities or improving marketing arrangements. These possibilities would then be examined with greater thoroughness by experts capable of assessing the technical feasibility of agricultural operations and their potential benefits. A favourable report would lead to the engagement of another team of experts, local or international, to prepare a detailed project. As a result of their activities, information would emerge about where the project would be located, how much land would be needed and what it would cost, what products would be produced and where they would be sold, what inputs would be needed and what they would cost, and how the project would be owned and managed. This work would not, of course, be done without regard to costs and benefits but final judgements about these matters would be left to still another team of experts who would appraise the project in order to determine whether, according to the criteria laid down by the organisation concerned, it was soundly based. On the basis of this review a firm recommendation might be made to proceed with the project, and if this were accepted by the IFAD board and government concerned and other interested parties, the operational details of the project would be finalised and a starting date fixed. It is a very time-consuming and complicated business which may result in ultimate rejection of the project or a lengthy period of preparation as well as implementation.

Once the physical nature of a project has been determined and the amounts of its inputs and outputs become clear, it is possible to proceed with an economic appraisal of it. What rules should be adopted for this and, above all, what prices should be assigned to the various inputs and outputs that are involved? A private entre- preneur would use market prices and would be concerned only with purchases and sales that affected his financial position. The decision-maker in the public sector might feel that the rules followed by the private sector were incomplete or inappropriate for the public sector for a number of reasons. Fundamentally, he might feel that the prices established in the market-place failed to reflect social priorities. No system of prices established is sacro- sanct. If one or a number of things were modified—if there were to be a redistribution of wealth, if investments were to be put into agriculture rather than into industry, if rural workers were forced to seek work in the city—prices would change. A change in the aspirations of individuals or in the objectives pursued by society produces a different set of prices, reflecting the scarcities asso- ciated with those different aims.

Irrespective of ultimate objectives, a socially orientated planner would look at things from the point of view of society as a whole, including the effects on people and sectors not directly involved. The effects of investment could be harmful, for example, when private investment decisions lead to the elimination of gainful employment opportunities for others, for instance, when power looms replace hand looms, tractors replace farm workers, etc. Other effects may be beneficial: creating markets, increasing the demand for products which are subject to increasing returns of production scale, training manpower and so on. Decisions taken by a collective rather than by a collection of individuals might be expected to take these externalities into the reckoning and in some cases this might give a very different picture of the costs and benefits involved in a particular operation. Nevertheless, it may be suspected that the major difference in decision-making between private individuals and collective entities lies as much in disparity of objectives as in externalities.

Many of the differences that arise can be regarded as finding their expression in the choice of prices to use in making economic calculations. Once it is felt that one price is out of line, it follows that nearly every other price must be so too, for prices are inter-related. Nevertheless, when planners talk about differences between prices viewed from a private or public point of view, they are generally concerned with only a limited number of those they consider to be of special importance, often including, but not limited to, the following six:

(i) Some planners take the view that money is worth more in public than in private hands. It is sometimes argued that the level of investment in a less developed country is too low and that income frittered away on needless consumption by those in the private sector is worth less than it would be if it could be transferred to the government to invest. We are not convinced that investment programmes in less developed countries are universally too low in practice.[9] From a theoretical point of view concerning growth paths, very high levels of investment can often be justified. Frequently, however, absorptive capacity and administrative factors affecting the operation of an economy lead to excessive investment and unused capacity. This was certainly the case in Pakistan in the 1960s. 'Less and better executed' may sometimes be a good motto to follow. Channelling money to the state may also be advocated in the belief that the state is intrinsically superior to the individual, representing some form of collective goodness. Others, and even planners, may not agree with this, believing that governments are extravagant, self-seeking and in-efficient.

(ii) Another area for discussion is the high market price of labour. Wage earners, it is contended, are paid more in industry than they could earn in agriculture. The real cost of employing them from the social point of view is not what they are paid in industry, but rather the opportunity cost represented by the loss of output in agriculture when they take up some new employment. Since this loss is light in many cases, the argument continues, the real cost of employing labour is low and much lower than the rates of wages in industry. This situation could be corrected if the use of labour were subsidised in industry, thus reducing its costs. But is this really the right way to look at things if it entails the use of public money; should it instead be used to increase investments, rather than to pay wage earners who spend it on consumer goods? On this finding, the employment of labour is far from costless. Looked at another way, the cost to the state of employing labour is greater than the benefit (judged by the state) received by labour. On balance, therefore, the use of labour involves a cost to society. (iii) It is sometimes argued that the price of capital is too low. This may be the case, for instance, if the cost of credit made available by the banks to the modern sector is subsidised by one means or another. By contrast, the cost of credit in the traditional rural sector is often considered to be too high, equating high demand of arguably high social and economic value to a supply of credit which is too limited.

(iv) Frequently the price of foreign exchange may bear very little relationship to its real scarcity, as would be revealed if world markets were allowed, or able, to work free of government interference in conditions of perfect competition. Many less-developed countries have exchange rates that are overvalued, so that goods bought and sold in international trade have unrepresentative price tags attached to them. Imports in such circumstances are too cheap and exports too dear to give a rational direction to economic activity, rational, that is, in terms of free market economics. Sometimes an overvalued exchange rate may be justified, for instance, when a country is the main producer of some goods and wishes to exploit its monopoly position.

(v) Still another anomaly may be provided by geographical differences. Some regions are very poor and the benefits they receive may therefore be valued at a level in excess of that denominated solely in terms of units of currency. A *taka* in Sylhet (the tea-growing area of Bangladesh) may be worth more in real terms because of the poverty of the people there than a *taka* paid to industrial workers in Dhaka. For the very poor individuals, increasing consumption may be much more important than increasing investment programmes, in effect, the value of a given sum to a poor man is greater than that of the same sum to a rich man.

(vi) It may also be necessary to deal with artificial distortions of prices resulting from the imposition of taxes which may make the price of goods appear artificially high. Of course, such distortions are not necessarily socially bad or economically unjustified, for example, when they increase the price of scarce energy, but in other cases the distortions tend to exaggerate the costs to society of beneficial activities.

If distortions of the kind described above could be eliminated or substantially reduced by some means, there would be no need to dream up an alternative system of 'shadow' or 'accounting' prices to use as a guide when assessing the desirability of various investment projects. In fact, some but not all distortions could be removed by this means. Distortions introduced by fiscal measures are the result of actions taken to achieve government's objectives and so cannot readily be eliminated without misrepresenting that government's priorities. Control of the exchange rate may also fall into the same category. It may be held at an artificial level as a device to control the working of the economy. Excessively high wages in the modern sector, where they exist, can also be the product of government action (such as minimum wage legislation) and so in principle are remedial. Nevertheless, once such distortions are established, they are hard to remove.

It seems that it would not be easy to correct many of the distortions between market and (what may be judged to be) social prices. In some cases this may not matter very much but in other cases the differences may be sufficient to warrant corrective action. One device to correct for price distortions is to use a set of shadow prices when working out the cost benefit implications of investment projects, particularly those in the public sector.

TECHNIQUES OF PROJECT PRICING

Many systems of project pricing have been devised. They include that of Little and Mirrlees, and of UNIDO, as well as others.[10] Dealing as they do in the main with the same problems of quantification of observed or presumed distortion, they have much in common in respect of both methodology and applicability. The presentation in the following pages refers particularly to the Little-Mirrlees system, but much of it would be equally relevant to alternative techniques for project pricing to allow ranking and choice between prospects.

The essence of the Little-Mirrlees system is that costs and benefits are measured in terms of international currency and that particular importance attaches to social income.[11] First, why social income? Largely because we are concerned with the welfare of society as a whole and so need to work out all the effects of economic actions on society, and not just on the individuals or institutions that perpetrate them. Thus, replacing a taxed industrial import by home production may be industrially beneficial, but it results in a loss of income to the state which is a cost in terms of social income in the Little-Mirrlees calculus. This is just one example of externalities that need to be taken into consideration; there may be many repercussions less easy to account for and add into the calculation. Yet another consideration in the Little-Mirrlees system is that not all income is equally regarded from a social point of view. They seem to take the point of view that income in the hands of a government is superior and, rupee for rupee, worth more than income in private hands. They would also ascribe different values to income of the poor from income of the rich, again on a rupee-for-rupee basis. While in some cases it may seem valid to make distinctions of this kind it would be impossibly complicated to do it in all cases. We shall return to this when we discuss how to value labour in relation to project evaluation.

The reasons for measuring in terms of foreign currency may be understood in terms of Pareto optimality, which in an uncontrolled, tax-free and competitive economy would imply that internal prices of commodities would be in the same ratios, one to another, as prices in international trade. If this were not so, arbitrage would be possible and there would be opportunities to increase welfare by shifting production and consumption patterns by altering the trading pattern until arbitrage was no longer possible. It is important to emphasise that it is relative prices that we are concerned with here.

How can we measure items of cost and benefit in terms of convertible foreign exchange? For some items this is easy. When commodities are directly imported or exported, the value of trade in them can be recorded in terms of the international currency that was paid or received. More often, however, there will be some elements of cost or benefit that are incurred domestically and cannot readily be translated into terms of international currency. It is useful to distinguish between labour and other forms of costs that are domestically incurred. In some cases, domestic goods or services could be exported if they were not used at home and consequently a price can readily be ascribed to them; in other cases, the alternative to supplying them domestically would be to import them and again they can be appropriately priced. For other goods, it may be possible to build up implied foreign exchange values. In a freely adjustable economy, factor inputs of goods and services can be regarded as transformable at the margin. Inputs used for domestically produced and consumed goods could be transferred to producing goods for export or replacing imports. Thus, such inputs can be priced implicitly in terms of foreign exchange. Once this is done, the implicit cost in terms of foreign exchange of domestically produced and consumed goods becomes apparent. As a short cut, and after appropriate study, it may sometimes be possible to adopt an approximate conversion factor that will enable expenditure on domestic goods to be equated roughly to its international equivalent.

The cost of labour remains to be evaluated and this brings us back to the concept of social income. It might appear at first sight that labour should be treated like any other economic commodity so far as the determination of its price is concerned. Consultant services paid for out of foreign exchange might be treated in this way. For unskilled labour things are not so straightforward. Suppose a man transfers from agriculture to a new project in the public sector and there is a loss of agricultural output in consequence. This features as a social cost to be set against the project. There is also the further cost to the project of the man's wage which is assumed to be paid out of uncommitted social income. Against this we have the benefit of the wage to the man himself which it is assumed is spent on consumption. Consumption, however, in the Little-Mirrlees calculus is regarded as of less value than investment and so has to be written down in some proportion representing the judgement of planners as to the difference.

All these effects can be rolled into one by combining costs and benefits to give a net cost of employment called the shadow wage rate (SWR), as shown in the formula:

$$SWR = C - \tfrac{1}{s}(C-m)$$

C represents the payment to the workers; $\tfrac{1}{s}$ is a coefficient giving the social value of consumption; $C-m$ represents the increase in consumption that comes from the employment; m is the loss of output assumed to take place in agriculture because the worker moves to the town.

Such coefficients are not constant for all time. The difference in the valuation of consumption against investment may be high today, but as the country gets less impoverished the difference will decline until the social judgement deems it to be no more important to increase investment than consumption. When this will happen is uncertain and decisions about it are likely to be rather arbitrary.

We now have an outline of the mechanism for valuing inputs and outputs in terms of accounting prices and acknowledging both international and social valuations. Rates of return can be calculated and projects can be ordered by these. The cut-off between acceptable and unacceptable projects will be determined by accepting those projects with the highest returns up to the point where available investment funds are exhausted.

The above account is no more than an outline of how the Little-Mirrlees method is to be applied. It is capable of much elaboration and refinement but in practice many approximations and judgements have to be made. So many, in fact, that planners have to ask themselves whether it is worthwhile given that there are both practical and theoretical reasons for questioning whether cost-benefit analysis of the above kinds will improve the quality of economic decisions in a less-developed country, as even their proponents are aware.

(i) In the Little-Mirrlees system, it is assumed implicitly that the economy is an open one or at least that it can relevantly be analysed by analogy with an open economy. The reason that the system makes comparisons in terms of international prices is that international trade represents an opportunity for the country to exchange its products at the ruling world prices. These determine the transformation rates and opportunity costs facing the less-developed country. If there are impediments to trade either because of import duties, domestic restrictions, or foreign actions limiting export markets, or if world prices are excessively volatile and comparative advantage and relative prices are often changing, the optimal structure of the economy could be very different from that in conditions of free trade. While an economy like those of the centrally planned countries might be better off if it traded with the world on a greater scale, so long as it does not it is better to have regard to the transformation ratios between commodities within the country itself rather than those obtaining outside.

(ii) The Little-Mirrlees system seems to assume that a central office of project evaluation could be omnipotent and able to apply the system of accounting prices throughout the economy. In every country of the real world this is manifestly impossible; control is too difficult to achieve for this to be the case. In many countries there will be a private sector of considerable importance and this is most unlikely to follow guidelines laid down centrally for project selection. It should be remembered that the system is concerned with social costs and benefits and that these may be different from their private equivalents. A project in the public sector of the economy, which would lead to a net reduction in unemployment, would be assessed by putting a lower cost figure on labour inputs than the payment actually made to an employee, because the benefit obtained from increased consumption by those initially unemployed would be regarded as a significant part of the benefits to be derived from the project. Such benefits do not accrue to a business in the private sector and so would not be taken account of. It follows that a project with high labour cost might show a profit after allowing for increased consumption by those employed in the project, and might show a loss on a private system of bookkeeping. If such projects were to be made financially attractive to a private businessman, it would be necessary to pay a subsidy to him. Moreover, this action could in itself render the project unprofitable because it would require government mobilisation of the resources to cover the subsidies.

(iii) Generally, the system is extremely complicated. Even much simpler systems have proved hard for administrators and project designers to follow. This is not an insuperable objection to the adoption of the system but it requires suitable training courses to be instituted and procedures enforced. The cost of doing this and operating the system has to be weighed against the improvement in project selection that it is hoped to bring about. Even the estimation of prices of traded goods can present difficulties, when alternative sources of supply or markets have to be considered and when the price of goods may fluctuate considerably and unpredictably. It will frequently be tiresome to attempt to establish the international prices appropriate for domestically traded goods or even for international goods when these do not enter into trade to any extent because of transport costs or other forms of market insulation.

(iv) An administrator may not easily find acceptable the shadow prices that are laid down by an office of project evaluation. Its officials may not wish to disclose some of the shadow prices that they are using. To prescribe an exchange rate much lower than that being operated might be to invite criticism of the rate adopted and speculative activity against the currency. The arbitrary use of shadow prices may lead to their being challenged when it is inconvenient to accept them, and in consequence they may become even more arbitrary.

(v) Will administratively established shadow prices readily respond to changing economic circumstances, as do market prices, or will they stick at some level laid down in the handbook and be altered only at long intervals? To operate on out-of-date prices could greatly impair the benefits of using the system.

(vi) Can public authorities be relied upon to follow the guidelines laid down? Will they genuinely act as though interest rates were as high as those laid down in the manual, if in fact they are able to borrow much more cheaply on the market? Only, it may be suspected, if they are obliged to pay the higher rate.

(vii) If shadow prices are to be applied by administrators they will have to be of a fairly uniform nature, which may tend to disguise differences in local conditions. Market rates respond to changes in market forces, but administrative rules tend to be inflexible for fear of introducing complications and establishing precedents that would lead to further argument and modification to the rules.

The criticisms outlined above prompt the question as to whether the aims sought to be achieved by the adoption of shadow prices can be more easily established by other means. Often, as we have seen, market prices are at odds with social priorities and this again is often the result of government interventions in markets. Interest rates can be controlled to some extent by the adoption of suitable monetary policies; overvaluation of the exchange rate is generally also the result of government intervention in the interest of either improving the terms of trade or preventing unrestricted access to foreign exchange by a rationing or allocation system. A change in government policies in the direction of allowing market prices freer play might be preferable to attempting to work on the basis of a theoretical price structure designed by planners.

Finally, the extent of the improvement that might be expected to result from the use of shadow prices requires some consideration. The experience of those who have worked in less-developed countries is that it is the conception and execution of a project that is most likely to determine its profitability. It may also be suspected that the more grandiose the project, the more likely it is to go wrong; few things are worse in this respect than the construction of dams.[12] By comparison with the real things that can go wrong in a project, errors arising from inappropriate prices are likely to be minimal and when they occur are more likely to arise from a misjudgement about the market situation than about the precise shadow prices that should be used.

INSTITUTIONAL DEVELOPMENT

Few economists take kindly to the study of administration. Yet the study of economic systems is really concerned with a particular form of administration, that of organising an economy so that it works efficiently. Most economists with experience of planning in developing countries would agree that one of the greatest obstacles to getting things done is inefficient administration. This is one reason why plans frequently have a section on public administration suggesting how improvement can be made. The discussion is likely to be far-ranging, covering administrative organisation and procedures, budgeting, the public services, organisation and methods, and extending to public corporations and authorities.[13]

There is also likely to be some discussion of institutions and how they may be changed and developed. This covers both social customs, laws and relationships within the society or community as well as establishments (institutions) founded for a particular purpose. The very poorest countries with which we are concerned have a strongly traditional sector as well as a modern sector of society and economy. They are the dual economies as described by J. H. Boeke, the Netherlands civil servant who was one of the first to comment on the existence of two or more economies within the same country.[14] In Boeke's experience the modern sector did not have the effect of transforming the traditional sector in its image; the two existed side by side with a minimum of contact and a century or two between them. Since it is frequently desired to change and modernise the traditional sector, this may have to be engineered.[15]

Generally government takes on the responsibility of building and managing interrelated processes of nation-building, economic growth and social change. This is not without its dangers for governments; proposed changes may prove unpopular to the point of rejection and overthrow of the government itself. Social change may be attempted by prodding, coaxing, bribing, inspiring, or coercing those who have it in them to transform the country, its society, economy and outlook. But, above all, it is a matter of creating suitable institutions and working through them.

All these processes can be illustrated from actual experience. Changing the outlook of people is central to the strategy of the Mozambique government, and the party is directed to it. This is backed by the policy of establishing communal villages, and bringing influence to bear on inhabitants to change traditional ways of life by establishing new institutions such as cooperatives and assemblies. In Bangladesh, many aspects of rural life have changed little in a century or more. Here the cooperatives have been enlisted as instruments of social change as well as a means to improve agricultural performance. The importance of institutional change in China is too well known to require further comment. War in China and in Korea has been the progenitor for social change.

A great deal of institutional promotion is not concerned with nation-building so much as creating organisations that can serve particular purposes. The need for organisational change very often starts with government itself. It is generally necessary to expand, train and redirect the activities of those in the administrative services. A civil service diminished in numbers of experienced personnel after independence and used to looking at the functions of government through colonial eyes must expect to see its shape and function change in relation to new needs. Reforms will shift the focus of power, affect rewards, promotion prospects and status so that it is to be expected that they will be resisted. The nature of required changes may be discussed in the plan, but the sensitivity of the subject is such that it will need to be handled with political acumen and probably after detailed study by some committee or commission that can command political support.

Disruption of existing administrative functions must be avoided while reforms are put into effect. If this is not possible, a choice will have to be made between holding up the development effort until the reform can be consolidated, proceeding very slowly, or maintaining the status quo. The danger of disruption is considerable, for it will generally be necessary to exert pressure at a number of points simultaneously, since changes in one part of the structure will almost certainly require changes in other parts. Reform of the structure will be closely linked to the expansion of activities. Training programmes will be necessary to produce the kind of officials that are needed.

Some major aspects of economic organisation are concerned with the extent, composition and method of control of the public sector. The Pakistan involvement in public enterprise started from a framework and outlook inherited from colonial times and the provision by the state of infrastructure, communications, power, irrigation and related development works, and some social facilities in the form of education, health and housing associated with public activities. After independence, the involvement of the state in economic activity was greatly extended not only through the establishment of public corporations and other agencies but also by pump-priming activities including the establishment of financial institutions. How much should be left to private enterprise and how much retained for the state and parastatal organisation to perform is a matter that will have to be considered when preparing plans.

However large or small the public sector may be, it has to be controlled and coordinated. Even within the state or parastatal sector, market mechanisms may play a role in determining activities, and this is certainly the way in which private sector operations are generally designed to operate, although they too may be subject to other forms of direction.

The public sector will be expected to operate within a frame of reference laid down for it by the government. The nature of this requires detailed consideration. Devolution of responsibility for operations is an essential element of efficiency but some ultimate control has to be exercised to ensure that public institutions perform as they should. What sort of checks need to be imposed? At the very least, top appointments are likely to be made by government, and in a planned economy public institutions may be expected to organise their operations so as to conform to the plan. Other controls may also be exercised on wages, finance and performance. Again, the nature of these relationships requires consideration and forms an essential part in planning the operations of the economy.

The question of devolution of responsibility to public institutions arises also in relation to local government. Often there is great reluctance to devolve in this way. The few highly experienced administrators operate from the centre and distrust local initiatives. Often there is no adequately functioning system of rural administration to form a basis for development and the scattered nature of the population may make it hard to establish local services that can function economically.

In Bangladesh, the density of population is such that local government can play a useful role but centralisation of administration is against it. Programmes for rural development have until recently been operated very much from the centre and although there is a move towards devolution this may not go very far, for many of the programmes for rural development are organised by the 'line' ministries: agriculture, industry, irrigation, etc. Moreover, financial provisions for local operations are very inadequate and the money to be spent there tends to be kept in the hands of the central administration. The transfer of political power that an increase in the responsibility of local government would bring about is another reason for reluctance to encourage local activity. These are all matters that have to be considered in framing policies for development.

CONCLUDING REMARKS

We started this chapter by discussing the nature of planning and the alternative forms that might be adopted. Some doubts were registered about the contribution that planning could be expected to make to development. Inherent in these doubts were questions about the form that planning and government direction of an economy might usefully take. In the postwar period, planning in developing countries was widely adopted in the belief that national resources should be centrally managed to meet national objectives. As time has gone on, there has been some disillusionment with this approach from both ideological and practical considerations and with the acceptance of *dirigisme*. According to Ramgopal Agarwala, plans in Latin America appear to have had very little effect on economic decision-taking, and Mexico with a strong economic performance had no plan at all.[16] In Bangladesh disappointments with the First Five Year Plan led to concentration on planning in key sectors, such as food, and accepting greater reliance on prices and markets in other areas. In China there has been a movement away from the concept of all-embracing central planning. In Mozambique compromises have also been made. It appears that the retreat from central administration has occurred not just because of dissatisfaction with technical insufficiencies in the preparation of plans, or even with their execution, but because of doubts as to whether total planning is the most efficient method.

Agarwala also suggests that the countries that performed best in the 1970s were not those that adopted *dirigiste* planning but those like Korea, Malawi, Malaysia, Colombia, Ivory Coast and Kenya that 'by and large relied on streamlining incentives for guiding the private sector, but also provided a macroplanning framework for their public investment programmes'.[17] Planning, it is suggested, should be focused on key themes appropriate to the country in question, perhaps linking up with the idea of strategic planning discussed earlier. Key themes suggested are: for Bangladesh, food; for Malaysia, improvements in income and wealth and their distribution between Malays and non-Malays; for Botswana, trying to convert mineral wealth into human and physical capital.

If the approach to planning outlined above is accepted, it has, of course, implications for government policy. It means, for example, that ways have to be found to provide an economic framework in which the public and private sectors of the economy can coordinate their activities. A particular aspect of this is the need to ensure that prices and incentives are geared to enable the private sector of the economy to function efficiently as is discussed in the following chapter.

FURTHER READING

A. K. Cairncross, 'Programmes as Instruments of Co-ordination', in *Factors in Economic Development*, London, Allen & Unwin, 1962, pp. 320-38.
International Bank for Reconstruction and Development, *World Development Report 1983*, New York, Oxford Economic Press, 1983, pp. 66-73.
Nurul Islam, *Development Planning in Bangladesh: A Study in Political Economy*, London, Hurst, 1977.
Tony Killick, 'The Possibilities of Development Planning', *Oxford Economic Papers*, Vol. 28 (1976), No. 2, pp. 161-84.
I. M. D. Little and J. A. Mirrlees, *Project Appraisal and Planning for Developing Countries*, London, Heineman Educational Books, 1974.
Irving Swerdlow, 'The Usefulness of the Institution Building Approach', in *The Public Administration of Economic Development*, New York, Praeger, 1975, Chapter 7, pp. 210-40.

NOTES

1. See, for example, Ramgopal Agarwala, 'Planning in Developing Countries', *Finance and Development*, Vol. 22 (1985), No. 1, pp. 13-16.
2. For a further discussion of these and other issues, see Albert Waterston, *Planning in Pakistan: Organization and Implementation*, Baltimore, Md., Johns Hopkins Press, 1963; Nurul Islam, *Development Planning in Bangladesh*, London, Hurst, 1977; and Mahbub ul Haq, *The Strategy of Economic Planning: A Case Study of Pakistan*, Oxford, Oxford University Press, 1963.
3. The perspective was further elaborated in a book by the (then) Chief Economist of the Pakistan Planning Commission, Mahbub ul Haq, *The Strategy of Economic Planning: A Case Study of Pakistan*, ibid.
4. One issue here is whether the increase in output will more than compensate for the fact that the marginal utility of consumption is assumed to fall as incomes increase. For a difficult but illuminating discussion of these considerations, see J. Black, 'Optimum Savings Reconsidered, or Ramsey without Tears', *Economic Journal*, Vol. 72 (1962), June, pp. 360-6; and R. M. Goodwin, 'The Optimal Growth Path for an Underdeveloped Economy', *Economic Journal*, Vol. 7 (1961), December, pp. 765-74. See also J. R. Parkinson, 'Determining the Size of the Development Effort in Bangladesh's First Five Year Plan', in Peter Maunder (ed.), *Case Studies in Development Economies*, London, Heinemann, 1982.
5. Japan, however, averaged 10 per cent for 1960-70, as well as Hong Kong. A number of oil exporters, Libya amongst them, increased GDP by nearly 25 per cent. Botswana also increased output at about 10 per cent per annum at this time on the strength of diamond output.
6. The model was constructed in the Ministry of Finance and Development Planning by P. Granberg of the Chr. Michelsen Institute.
7. Based on Table 2.16 of the *National Development Plan 1979-85*, Botswana, Ministry of Finance and Development Planning, 1980, p. 52.
8. It is sometimes possible to arrive at an answer by using linear programming techniques. This was done for Bangladesh, for example, by the World Bank economists to establish the sequence in which steps to increase the net output of agriculture should be undertaken. See the *Bangladesh Land and Water Resources Sector Study*, Volume III, Technical Report, No. 4, *The Land Water Sector Sequencing Model*. In practice, even when such exercises can be carried out they are unlikely to carry the day. They are best regarded as a technical input into a decision process in which social and political considerations rank uppermost.
9. As may be seen from Table 1.3, investment as a percentage of GDP is quite high in many of the countries shown.
10. For a general discussion, see Deepak Lal, *Methods of Project Analysis: A Review*, Baltimore, Md., Johns Hopkins Press, 1974 (also World Bank Staff Occasional Paper 16). Details of the UNIDO system are to be found in *Guidelines for Project Evaluation*, United Nations, 1972.
11. The numeraire, the unit in which measurement is made, is defined as 'uncommitted social income measured in terms of foreign exchange'. This

definition is less precise than it looks. Its meaning, amongst other things, depends on how the social income is or might be spent, which Little and Mirrlees dismiss as an unavoidable nuisance representing a genuine difficulty in project evaluation; *Project Appraisal and Planning for Developing Countries*, London, Heinemann Educational Books, 1974, p. 146. We shall in fact use it as though it referred to government investment expenditure, while appreciating that social income is used for many purposes and not just for investment alone.

12. See J. Faaland and J. R. Parkinson, 'The Economic Price of Natural Gas in Pakistan', *Pakistan Development Review*, Vol. 13 (1974), No. 4, pp. 481-4.
13. See, for example, Chapter 5 in *The Second Five Year Plan 1960–65*, Pakistan Planning Commission, June 1960.
14. *Economics and Economic Policy of Dual Economies*, International Secretariat Institute of Pacific Relations, New York, 1953.
15. Not everybody would agree with the objective of modernisation but most might be persuaded that an improvement in welfare is something to be attempted. Should we leave the bushmen of Botswana as they are—survivors of the original population of the African Continent?
16. Op. cit., note 1, p. 14.
17. Ibid.

4 Instruments of policy

This chapter considers how various policy instruments may be used to assist in the implementation of the plan. In a mixed economy, it is necessary to consider the public and private sectors of the economy individually, as well as in their interaction. In principle, the government is capable of controlling the public sector directly. Each ministry or agency may be required to provide its own plan of action, consistent with what has been decided in the general plan, and to execute it on agreed lines and within a defined time schedule. Appropriate monitoring can be introduced to check on progress and remedial action can be taken in response to this. In short, those responsible for action can be told what to do and how to do it.

In a command economy of the Russian type where the public sector is extensive, much economic activity can be promoted, organised and controlled by issuing instructions, without reliance on market responses to price signals. Such a system, however, presupposes public ownership of most productive enterprises; where this is not the case and there is a large private sector, alternative methods of control, stopping short of complete management, have to be devised. These may include the use of selective controls operating in key areas. It is common for governments in developing countries to control the flow of imports through licensing systems which may go as far as to fix import entitlements for individual firms, so in some cases effectively controlling their level of activity. Permission may also have to be obtained to set up a business or to extend it; price controls may be imposed, affecting profitability; so, too, may many other means be used to regulate private sector activity. Even in the absence of controls, efforts may be made to persuade firms to modify their activities to suit the government's needs.

Command economies are difficult to operate and they may function very inefficiently. Partial controls may also operate inefficiently, and an extensive system of (probably inconsistent) bureaucratic controls can be a considerable drag on private economic operations. Most developing countries are likely to develop a package of controlling measures. The public sector is likely to be given its instructions; the private sector is likely to be subject to some controls but will also be guided and affected by fiscal, monetary and trade policies in a general, but extensive, way.

An alternative to direct controls can be found in the use of fiscal, monetary and international trade policies, although their effects will generally be less specific. Thus, fiscal policy may be used to restrict consumer spending, regulate profitability and free resources for government use. Monetary policy may be an acceptable alternative to price control and can be used to regulate investment. Trade policy may be used to protect the balance of payments in conjunction with exchange rate policy, and it may be used to vary the profitability of different kinds of production and to stimulate or constrain consumption of particular items or groups of goods and services and other use of resources.

Reliance on fiscal, monetary and trade policies to regulate the activities of the private sector is likely to confer greater freedom on that sector to govern its own affairs than if it were under a regime of direct controls. This may not, of course, be desired either by bureaucrats or governments wishing to maintain power and control over the economy in their own hands. Establishing an economic framework that determines the operation of fiscal, monetary and trade policies does, however, have the advantage of allowing market responses to govern economic activity and can be a very efficient way of allowing an economy to operate. With such an armoury of means of control, care has to be taken in the choice of the instruments selected to attain particular ends. Consideration also has to be given as to how the measures selected interact together. This can require detailed and complicated analysis. The effects of tariffs and taxes on incentives to produce can be large and can seriously distort prices, so that they do not reveal real needs or promote the best use of scarce resources.

The rest of this chapter is concerned with instruments of policy aimed mainly at the operations of the private sector of the economy, although indirectly and sometimes directly they may affect the operations of public institutions. The public sector is assumed to be controlled mainly by government instructions, although these are often framed so as to leave some room for discretionary action within a general framework of requirements.

FISCAL POLICY

The objectives of fiscal policy

The purpose of all fiscal policy, in developing as in developed countries, is to intervene in the economy so as to influence the amount, composition or distribution of the gross national product. This requires financial resources which may be raised and spent in a variety of ways.

The scope for fiscal policy is wide. It may be concerned with channelling resources into the provision of such basic needs as health care or education. It may also try to suppress or reduce certain activities, such as the production of luxury goods, to free resources for other uses judged to be of greater social value. Fiscal policy may be directed towards the pursuit of autarky or to the protection of domestic producers from the competition of imports from other countries. Special assistance may be given to small industry, to deserving regions of the country, or to deprived ethnic groups. Not all such objectives will be wholly consistent with one another or build up to a completely integrated or coherent policy. In fact inconsistencies can have serious consequences, as we shall see.

Efforts to influence the distribution of income may also take the form of encouraging certain types of activities rather than others. Attempts to reduce inequalities in income and wealth by progressive taxation have limited scope and are difficult to put into operation in low-income countries. Another approach is to promote such activities that directly benefit the poor rather than the rich, and government expenditure may be an instrument to achieve this. Supplementary policies include differential taxation of luxury goods, fixing the price of essentials or subsidising them, and more direct actions such as land reform to reapportion wealth.

The control of government expenditure and the design of systems of taxation is complicated because a number of conflicting objectives have to be reconciled. In reviewing the government budget it is useful to keep some guidelines in mind. First, it is very easy to spend too much on capital development without making provision for essential and desirable current expenditure. Second, so far as possible, the proportion of GDP raised in revenue should rise as output grows and it is helpful if the taxation structure has some built-in elasticity of this nature, although part of the progression can come from the addition of new taxes. Third, taxation systems are inclined to change in a higgledy-piggledy manner as governments introduce changes to achieve varying political ends. The resultant pattern of taxes can be very harmful to the economy if prices and costs become seriously distorted.

Policy issues relating to taxation and public expenditure are no less important for revenue mobilisation in socialist states, such as Mozambique, than in Bangladesh or other market or mixed economies. The instruments for doing so are much the same. Indirect taxes are levied on items of consumption, taxes imposed on industrial profits, and some attempts made to effect progressive income tax on wages and salaries in the face of the usual difficulties in taxing small incomes. As the country's economic activities expand, opportunities to increase government revenues will occur. It may also be possible for state-owned public utilities and other similar bodies to create a surplus above their operational costs.

Government expenditure

Governments in poor countries are under the same kind of pressure as governments anywhere else. They are expected to provide for law and order, for basic services, such as education and health care, for infrastructure that would not otherwise be built and for the promotion of development, either through their own activities, or by giving assistance to other sectors, sometimes simply by channelling finance to would-be users who would otherwise be unable to raise it.

The demands on government resources practically always exceed what government can raise by taxation or borrowing. One perennial difficulty is to provide for normal non-development expenditure on running the country, such as paying for the armed forces, teachers' salaries, road maintenance and so on. The pressures are all too often in the direction of financing development expenditure and, not infrequently, too little regard is given to whether the resources needed to operate new facilities can be made available. This is not peculiar to developing countries, however. There are new hospital facilities in Britain and Norway, for example, that nobody can afford to operate. It takes firm budgeting to avoid such imbalances and a strong treasury is an essential part of the operation of government finance.

Table 4.1 Current government expenditure, in
Bangladesh, 1981-82 budget

	Percentages
General administration	16
Justice and police	12
Defence	18
Education	14
Health	6
Agriculture, manufacturing and transport	7
Debt service	8
Food subsidy	6
Other	13
	100

The 1981-82 budget for Bangladesh is used to illustrate the composition of current government expenditure in that country (see Table 4.1). Administration, justice, police and defence account for 46 per cent of the total and education and health for 20 per cent. Very little is spent on the productive sectors of the economy. The provision of aid to Bangladesh for development made it possible to plan for investment expenditure in 1981-82 at a level of about twice the government's current expenditure, and about 40 per cent of this was in the private sector. Two-thirds of the total was financed from aid and other foreign sources with the government surplus properly defined making no contribution.

Other aspects of the control of government expenditure include the need to do more than just ascertain that money is used for the purposes for which it is issued. Regular audits are made to ensure that no irregularities occur, but they are also needed to make sure that the money spent achieves the aims intended. The appropriate amount of money may have been genuinely spent on building a school, but did it result in the amount of physical construction that it was supposed to? If it did not, the funds allocated will prove to be inadequate and the provision for the construction of the school will have to be made good out of later budgets. To guard against this, further checks need to be carried out to detect over-optimistic budgeting or inefficient spending, and more rigorous control may be needed. This comes under the heading of performance budgeting, designed to relate the expenditure of money to physical performance. All this may seem to be very elementary, indeed it is; but, the need to emphasise it arises because it is so very often neglected. Administration is a skill that needs to be cultivated in developing countries as elsewhere and it plays an important role.

Level and composition of taxes

Taxation placed on income or expenditure may reduce consumption or savings, or both; it may also reduce taxation yields and in extreme cases it may have serious political repercussions. Whether increases in taxation result in higher savings will depend on where they fall. If taxes are placed on necessities purchased by people who save little or nothing, then savings rates may be increased perforce. If, on the contrary, taxes fall on the rich, there is a strong possibility that part, if not all, of the increase in taxation will be absorbed by a reduction in savings. Even here, however, there may be advantages. In Bangladesh, for example, the savings of the rich arc not always invested productively. They may be salted away abroad, they may be used to buy up land, so enhancing its price and aggravating its distribution; they may be invested unproductively in jewellery or in the creation of luxury housing. Thus a reduction in private savings offset by an increase in government investment could represent a gain to the economy. This might be enhanced if a fall in the construction of luxury housing released, say, scarce cement for activities of greater value to society. On the other hand, if the effect of enhanced taxation rates is to increase tax evasion by more than the increase in tax imposed, the government may be much worse off. Figuratively speaking–and sometimes in fact–three sets of books may be kept by a business: one for the tax authorities, one for the shareholders, and one for the manager. Paying tax can often be avoided when transactions in cash can cover a multitude of sins. It is difficult to predict how taxation yields will be affected by changes in taxation rates when so much is unknown about people's attitudes to taxes and when so many opportunities exist for concealment.

So far we have considered the effects of increasing taxation in a static context, when income levels can be taken as momentarily given. As per capita incomes grow over time, there is greater scope for raising the proportion of the GDP collected in tax. In very poor countries there is very little surplus over minimum consumption levels to be diverted to investments, public or private; as incomes increase so does the surplus and more can be raised in taxes. As a matter of observation, it is true that wealthier countries tend to raise more revenue relative to income than those on the poverty level. As income levels rise, most developing countries increase the share of government expenditure in the national income, perhaps because they consider this to be a superior use of resources relative to private expenditure or perhaps because the goods and services they wish to consume are most efficiently and economically provided by the public sector.

It cannot, however, be said with conviction that higher rates of taxation will be conducive to higher rates of growth. Indeed, the evidence seems to be the other way round. An analysis by Keith Marsden suggests that for a limited sample of twenty countries of varying income levels an increase of one percentage point in the ratio of tax to GDP would decrease the rate of growth by 0.36 per cent and that the response was even greater in low-income countries.[1]

No simple rules can be devised to indicate what the progression of the incidence of taxation should be or, even more difficult, at what rate it is likely to be practicable to increase it. Surveys of developing countries' performance in raising revenue indicate great variations even within particular bands of income. Table 4.2 shows central government revenue as a proportion of GDP (in 1981-82) for a selection of countries with per capita incomes of up to around $1,600 in 1982. The differences in the performance of the countries are striking. Amongst countries with less than $400 (low-income countries) per capita income, the amount of revenue raised varied from 3 per cent in troubled Uganda to nearly 30 per cent in Togo. At somewhat higher levels of per capita income it is also evident that there is great variation. The very different performance evident between countries is not readily explained by generalisation but it seems that a number of factors contribute. These include administrative capacity, the importance of trade,

Table 4.2 Relationship between levels of taxation and per capita
income

	Income per capita in US$ 1982	Total current revenue as per cent of GNP 1981-82
Low income countries		
Nepal	170	8.7
Mali	180	15.5
Zaïre	190	21.6
Burma	190	16.2
Burundi	190	13.4
Burkina	210	14.0
Malawi	210	17.4
Uganda	230	3.1
India	260	13.6
Tanzania	280	19.6
Haiti	300	13.9
Central Afr. Rep.	310	16.4
Madagaskar	320	13.6
Sri Lanka	320	17.2
Togo	340	29.1
Ghana	360	5.4
Pakistan	380	14.6
Sierra Leone	390	11.6
Kenya	390	22.8
Middle income countries		
Sudan	440	11.8
Senegal	490	20.1
Liberia	490	25.2
Yemen Arab Rep.	500	20.4
Bolivia	570	5.6
Indonesia	580	22.2
Zambia	640	24.9
Honduras	660	14.8
Egypt	690	37.9
El Salvador	700	12.0
Thailand	790	13.9
Papua New Guinea	820	21.5
Philippines	820	11.2
Zimbabwe	850	31.3
Morocco	870	26.5

	Income per capita in US$ 1982	Total current revenue as per cent of GNP 1981-82
Cameroon	890	18.5
Nicaragua	920	27.6
Guatemala	1,130	10.2
Peru	1,310	16.8
Dominican Republic	1,330	10.7
Ecuador	1,350	11.9
Turkey	1,370	22.0
Tunisia	1,390	33.9
Costa Rica	1,430	20.4
Colombia	1,460	11.7
Paraguay	1,610	11.7

Source: Figures given in *World Development Report 1985*.

the extent of modern industry, plantation and extractive activities, the degree of inequality, the resistance of the ruling elite to higher taxation and their political ability to escape it.

In order to understand the significance of these factors it is helpful to look at the structure of taxation in Bangladesh and Botswana (see Table 4.3), which may illustrate the great differences in revenue-raising opportunities. As is shown, Bangladesh is heavily dependent on indirect taxation for revenue. Further analysis shows that almost the whole of the revenue raised depends on trade. Customs and excise receipts account for nearly half of the revenue and much of the sales tax collected is placed on manufactures dependent on imports, or in the form of a supplement to duties on imported goods. Taxes on income account for less than 10 per cent of the total and land revenue is so small as to be almost negligible. The low level of land revenues reflects political as well as economic forces. The Awami League, which was the governing party when Bangladesh came into being, set its face against such taxation and virtually abolished the imposition of land revenue. The small amounts raised are gathered mainly from the commercial tea garden sector. Before independence land revenue contributed about 8 per cent of revenue raised in the

Table 4.3 Composition of government revenue, 1980-81

	Bangladesh		Botswana
Customs and excise	47	Customs and excise and	
Sales tax	14	other direct taxes	35
Income tax	9	Direct taxes	29
Land revenue	1	Property and	
Non-tax revenues	29	entrepreneurial incomes	20
		Other	16
	100		100

Source: National budgets and *United Nations Statistical Yearbook 1981*, p. 209.

province of East Pakistan, but it would be extremely difficult now to restore land revenue as a major revenue contributor.

The composition of revenue in Botswana is of an entirely different nature. Customs and excise duties are considerable but direct taxes, mining royalties and dividends paid to the government come to nearly half the total revenue. Single Tax George, the Californian who in the last century advocated the transfer of rents from landlords to government as a major source of taxation, might find his wishes coming true with the rents obtainable from the rich mineral deposits of Botswana.

One of the advantages of being able to raise revenue from mineral exploitation is that there is no great internal pressure group resisting the government's claim on the proceeds. The mineral rights are in the government's keeping. The revenues from exploitation do not accrue to individuals of great wealth and influence, nor for that matter do they accrue to poverty-stricken farmers. The international companies engaged in exploitation must be offered a satisfactory reward for taking the risks and meeting the costs involved, but this is something over which the government can exercise control so as to ensure that returns are reasonable; if necessary, a clause can be written into the agreement enabling the government to claim a higher percentage of the returns if they prove to be greater than expected, for whatever reason: richness of deposit, price, or the successful exercise of monopoly selling power.

The resources of Botswana are probably large enough in relation to a population of about one million for revenues from minerals to expand for a time much more rapidly than other sources of income, but eventually the composition of government revenue will approach a more usual distribution. For Bangladesh efforts to increase government revenue are likely to consist of attempting to increase the yield of existing sources. Imports are easy to tax because they come through relatively few ports; excise duties are also relatively easy to administer because it is always possible to put a revenue officer into large factories and to ensure within limits that he carries out his duties; sales tax, essentially an addition to these taxes, is similarly capable of reasonable enforcement. Other things are not so easy to tax. Few incomes come into an income tax range that promises large tax receipts; evasion is comparatively easy; and there is little prospect of taxing the myriad of small-scale manufacturing and service activities that go on. More important, the opportunities to levy taxes on agricultural activities, quite apart from political considerations, are circumscribed. The reasons for this are not far to seek; they have to do with subsistence farming and the very size of the operation needed to deal with millions of small agricultural holdings.

The traditional way of taxing agriculture is by way of land taxes. The Moguls in India are said to have appropriated 30 per cent of the output of agriculture into the coffers of government by this means. In comparison, the efforts of British administrators to raise revenues, though successful by modern standards, must have seemed insignificant. An equitable system of land revenue is neither easy to devise, impose or enforce. Yet in theory a tax of this nature has much to commend it. In essence it is to be regarded as a tax on rent and therefore unlikely to disturb incentives or distort markets. In practice, the imposition of a tax means that every plot of cultivable land has to be assessed and its natural fertility and market potential established. When this is done, taxation can be levied to remove some of the surplus when output is more than sufficient to sustain the cultivator and his family. However, the labour involved in such assessment is great and there is considerable room for dispute. Also, the original assessment cannot be left for all time. Rivers change course, salinity develops, irrigation fails, market situations alter, and with bad monsoons a succession of crops can fail.

In modern times, inflation also plays a part and the relative prices of crops shift in response to market forces. Land correctly assessed ten years ago in relation to its inherent properties and to market prices may be overvalued or, much more likely, undervalued ten years later. So the whole thing has to be done again, or rule of thumb adjustments introduced, either permanently or for the duration of some emergency such as crop failure. It is not surprising, therefore, that land revenue is a bad tax to administer. Moreover, where there is shifting cultivation, where there is no shortage of land, or where agricultural conditions are greatly variable, it may not be practicable to levy systematically on land. As a result, other ways of taxing those engaged in agriculture may have to be found. If crops are exported, export taxes may be imposed; this is not uncommon. In Bangladesh jute has frequently been subject to the imposition of export taxes. Still another possibility is to impose taxes on the sale of produce through local markets.

It is desirable to levy taxes on agricultural output in some form or another for a number of reasons. First, agriculture constitutes a large part of the GDP, and while per capita incomes in this sector are small, the need to raise revenue persists. Some sectors of agriculture even in poor countries may be capable of sustaining reasonable income levels. In other cases the introduction of new methods of cultivation can greatly enhance output and returns. In those areas of Bangladesh where irrigation may be practised, the supply of water can make it possible to grow another crop with the effect of doubling output from the same plot of land; and seeds used in the right way may again double or even treble yields. If growing incomes are to swell the yield of taxation, then agriculture may have to be made to contribute. In part, this may sometimes be done negatively by reducing subsidy payments. The conventional wisdom has been that, when agricultural improvements are first introduced, the new inputs needed for more advanced systems of cultivation, seeds, fertilisers or water, should be subsidised in order to create sufficient incentive for farmers to try out the new methods, knowing that they will involve risks and uncertainties in branching out into the unknown. Once acceptance of new methods is gained, there should be no need for subsidies, which therefore, could be withdrawn. This might seem too obvious to mention were it not for the fact that political resistance to such moves is bound to be strong and, as recently experienced in Bangladesh, it has been convincingly argued that withdrawal of subsidies may affect output unfavourably. All four alternative ways of raising revenue from agriculture–taxing land, income, input or output–present difficulties, yet taxing incomes is likely to be the hardest.

As suggested above, the amount of taxation that it is appropriate to impose can be determined only in relation to specific cases. Nevertheless, it is tempting to generalise from the experience of different countries in order to try to get a mental picture of what it is reasonable to expect in a typical case, if such can be considered to exist. An interesting piece of analysis by Raja Chelliah attempts to give some answers to questions of this kind.[2] His study considers the change in the incidence of taxation in twenty-seven developing countries over the period 1953-55 to 1966-68. It demonstrates, amongst other things, that the income elasticity of taxation receipts was approximately 1.5. In other words a 1 per cent increase in material income was associated with a 1.5 per cent increase in the yield of taxation. If this were typical, the effect would be that taxation starting at, say, 10 per cent of the GDP would in twenty years amount to about 20 per cent of the enlarged total income for an economy growing at about 7 per cent per year. The type of taxation showing the greatest income elasticity was that placed on internal production transactions. Amongst the countries studied, income taxes accounted for about one-quarter of the total, taxes on internal trade to about the same, and taxes on external trade to about one-third; a very different pattern from that of Bangladesh as might be expected, since one of the poorest countries is compared with a more representative cross-section.

If the maximum increase in taxation yields is to be achieved, considerable attention will have to be given to the structure of taxes and to enforcing taxation law. The high elasticity of taxes on industrial output revealed in another study by Raja Chelliah points to the need to bring new manufactured goods into the taxation net.[3] An increase in direct taxation becomes possible as a country gradually modernises and the scale of economic activities increases, and with it personal incomes.

The problem of tax evasion has also got to be tackled. Some simple things may help in this respect: checking lists of licensed traders against persons paying income tax, and watching for signs of ostentatious spending where tax payments do not suggest an adequate income to maintain it. The use of even simple checks will depend on having sufficient tax officials to carry them out, and, since such people are often in demand for other administrative tasks, it is unlikely to be possible to employ enough of them to prevent substantial evasion. In this respect, there is always the danger that those wishing to escape tax will try to reach some understanding with those whose job it is to enforce it.

Local government and parastatal organisations

A discussion of government revenues would be incomplete without some consideration of the role that local governments and parastatal organisations can play in raising revenue. Local governments frequently complain that they are deprived of the most productive sources of revenue. Nevertheless, they are generally left with some sources of revenue peculiar to themselves. Taxation levied on property is a frequent source of revenue. In Bangladesh this takes the form of a house tax. The *octroi* (a duty on goods brought into towns) can be a substantial source of revenue. Licence fees may be imposed on those practising professions, on traders and others. A lucrative source of revenue might be a tax on land values in urban environments. Land around developing centres increases greatly in value as urbanisation takes place. Taxation may be imposed when the land is developed or redeveloped or, as an alternative, the land may be purchased by the government before it has acquired potential value. Strong resistance to such proposals is to be expected from those that own the land and this is frequently sufficient to frustrate the imposition or collection of a tax on such land development.

The impact of local taxation tends to be heaviest in the towns and to reflect the greater provision of services that is made there. In areas of scattered settlement, migratory movements and small villages, the imposition of local taxation may appear to be virtually impossible. This need not be so, however, if the principle is observed of trying to make people pay for the whole or part of the public services that they consume, and sometimes, perhaps, in kind rather than in cash. In the Sudan it has become the practice to collect an income-graduated education fee from families with school-age children. The graduation was based on local knowledge of the circumstances of the families and, at least in one locality, those administering it seemed to be fairly confident that this could be done with objectivity based on personal observation.

Nationalised industries, public utilities and other parastatal organisations in the public sector of the economy can be a potential source of public profit. They may also, of course, be a source of loss. If the latter, the first necessary step is to try to bring them back to profitability. Losses in the public sector are not always due to the faults of those operating them. Sometimes the cause may lie in government policies; in the case of the nationalised jute-manufacturing industry in Bangladesh in the 1970s, for example, there were many contributory causes, including an over-valued exchange rate and the imposition of export duties in an effort to increase revenue directly. Moreover, inflated wages and overmanning, also a reflection of government directives, played their part. Often attention is centred on the prices charged by nationalised undertakings. It would be wrong to assume that such prices are always too high. In less-developed countries the operators of public utilities often believe in the concept of the just or fair price. They may even be found to argue that the interest of the consumer is at least as important as the interest of the state. In this case planners may intervene and press major public utilities to order their pricing policies and profitability with a view to providing resources for investment. Price increases effected with this object in mind may be regarded as akin to taxes. Where there is opposition to raising prices because costs are being covered, an alternative means of raising revenue may be to impose a tax on sales.

The question of profitability and pricing policy of the public sector is of concern to aid-givers, as well as to government. One of the conditions imposed by the World Bank on a loan for the provision of a piped water supply in Dhaka was that the water should be paid for by meter. The opposition of the Bangladesh authorities to this measure was overruled and attempts were made to base charges on consumption. It proved to be extremely difficult to enforce, and of doubtful value. To begin with, meters for monitoring the use of water had to be imported, as they were not available from domestic production; and when they arrived, they proved to be wrongly calibrated and so could not be used for imposing charges immediately. There was also strong consumer resistance. Bengalis are averse to paying for water, which falls in such over-abundance. In the streets it was sought to impose the same discipline on users of water from standpipes which, more often than not, are not turned off. Therefore, spring-loaded taps were installed which turned themselves off when not in use; but these in turn were resented and the taps were simply knocked off by enterprising souls. No doubt the taps are still running as a symbol of a natural right of all Bengalis to the water the heavens—

and now government–provide. The application of strict logic is not an end in itself and in this instance to raise the house tax in order to pay for the cost of providing piped water might have been a more reasonable thing to do.

More normally the determination of prices fixed by the parastatal sector is likely to be a matter for general discussion between the organisation and the planning authorities. There are strong arguments for letting parastatals conduct their own affairs with the minimum amount of interference from government, but in practice bureaucracy takes hold and insists on having some say where the policies adopted by parastatals have implications for the conduct of economic affairs. When aid-givers are also involved, as they often are, many conflicting points of view may have to be reconciled.

MONETARY POLICY

Money supply and deficit financing

Mainly subsistence economies have very little use for money. As time goes on and income increases, more of the economy will come into the monetised sector, more produce will be bought and sold, greater cash balances will be held, and more sophisticated means of payment will gradually come into operation. The money supply will have to be adjusted to keep pace with the increasing demands for means of payment. It will also have to accommodate rising prices, which are features of most economies in conditions of increasing output and growing prosperity (and often without this stimulation). Moreover, the monetary authorities will have to consider whether the rate of increase in output can be accelerated by the use of deficit financing, even if this means that prices may increase more rapidly. All too often it will appear that the government is incapable of meeting the financial needs of the public sector from taxation and from the increase in the money supply that may be justified by the expected real increase in marketed output. Furthermore, governments very often resort to deficit financing under the pressure of circumstances irrespective of macroeconomic considerations, sometimes without weighing the consequences of such action.

Is there some optimum level of deficit financing that will result in maximum rate of growth of output? The evidence on this is uncertain. There are circumstances in which deficit financing may facilitate higher growth rates. In wartime, governments do not hesitate to use deficit financing so as to ensure that they can lay their hands on the money they need. These actions are, however, generally backed up with measures designed to limit the consequences of their actions, such as rationing and the direct control of the operation of the economy. Without these devices the consequences of deficit financing would be of much greater import; the government would in effect be bidding against other buyers for available resources and, in this process, prices would rise.

It is possible to envisage a variety of reactions to habitual deficit financing. Consumers facing rising prices might decide to reduce their savings in order to maintain their consumption; or they might find themselves affected to varying degrees by differing types of money illusion. The rate at which prices rise could also have significant effects on behaviour. Small increases in prices might be shrugged off, but larger rises might produce a quantum change in behaviour, even to the point of loss of all confidence in the value of currency. When this happens a new standard of value has to be established and conventional money disappears from the scene in favour of some alternative which is expected to keep its value better. When this is not possible chaos may ensue—barter is no substitute for market efficiency.

Laos is an interesting example in which failure to maintain the value of the domestic currency has led to the use of the American dollar as a medium of exchange, establishing a parallel monetary regime. In such circumstances, the government may attempt to direct the economy by controls in an effort to overcome its lack of financial resources. This is much more difficult than it sounds; it is possible, as we have seen, in a wartime economy with sophisticated administrative arrangements, but it is likely to be beyond the capability of a country with rudimentary administrative resources, as Mozambique's experience illustrates.

There may be levels of inflation that an economy can accommodate and others that will prove to be so high as to be disastrous. In practice, it is perhaps surprising how well an economy can adjust itself to high levels of inflation and still continue to function without much loss of efficiency. Attempts have been made to see if savings increase in response to rising prices. Interesting evidence on this assembled by A. P. Thirlwall seems to show that for poor countries, with incomes below $200 per head (as an average of 1958 and 1968), saving as a proportion of income tended to be adversely affected by rising prices.[4] For countries with higher per capita incomes the relationship seems to go the other way with savings increasing along with prices. Operating with a more sophisticated non-linear model, Thirlwall found it was possible to argue that there was an optimum amount of inflation that would maximise savings ratios. His equations suggested that the optimum rate of inflation in poor countries might be about 20 per cent, but the curve as calculated appeared to be very flat and the optimum might, more informatively, be described as lying between 4 and 36 per cent.

Interesting though such investigations are, they provide no ready-made answers. More practically, it might be assumed that the precise state of a country's economy at any period of time would weigh more heavily in determining what policies to follow than would such research findings. Nevertheless, they do conform to the planners' intuitive feeling that although some degree of inflation can reasonably be tolerated without obviously harmful effects, it would be unwise, except in dire emergency or loss of control, to plan for high rates of price increases.

The effect of a given amount of deficit financing in a developing country is likely to be less significant than in a more advanced country because credit multipliers are much smaller in low-income economies as a result of the proportionately much greater use of cash in transactions. An initial increase in a bank's reserves is substantially reduced as cash flows out to the market-place and remains there.[5]

The standard monetary instruments include changes in the reserve ratio imposed on the banks to ease or tighten credit, moral suasion (leaning on the banks), or simply telling them what they must do. All methods have their advantages and disadvantages, but in a developing country there cannot be anything like the sophistication of money markets in advanced countries.[6] Thus interest rates are not likely to figure prominently as a means of regulating the money supply in poor countries, but some consideration needs to be given to them for other reasons. The scarcity of capital makes it desirable to keep them at rather high levels as a means of screening projects for profitability. Whether this will also have the effect of increasing saving is doubtful. Attempts to establish a firm connection do not seem to be successful.[7]

Mozambique looks at monetary management rather differently from what may be appropriate in more market-orientated economies. In that country plans are made in real terms and the finance needed is expected to be provided either out of surpluses generated by the enterprises concerned or from funds provided by the banks. Thus finance and activity are planned to be exactly matched. The two major banks are not independent agencies with freedom to lend as they might wish. They are bound by the economic plan for which finance is provided and the provision of such finance does not yield an increase in reserve assets as the basis for still further credit creation. In practice, things may not work quite according to the planners' design. Enterprises may find that they need more finance than they expected for the plan provided. If this were to be the case, more money might have to be created in the same way as in market economies, and with similar consequences. The growth in purchasing power would increase the demand for consumer goods; either prices would rise or queues would grow longer, or both. If this were greatly resented and foreign exchange were available, imports might be increased; or if things went so badly wrong that the need for increased amounts of bank finance indicated that the resources available were insufficient for the plan to be executed, expenditure might have to be reduced or spread over a longer time-period.

The banking system in Bangladesh has been remodelled in recent years as private banking has been pushed ahead. In the 1970s, when the banking system was largely nationalised, it fell between the two extremes of the classical model and the fully planned economy. The rate of credit creation was planned along with other things. The credit requirements of the nationalised corporations were worked out in much the same way as in Mozambique and some provision was made for the needs of the private sector. Even so, things did not always go according to plan in Bangladesh, as elsewhere. It is an interesting experience to hear the chairman of a public corporation telephoning the manager of a nationalised bank to explain that if he does not have more money he will be unable to pay his workers (who are entrenched in a strongly organised union), only to be told by his bank manager that he has exceeded the credit limits laid down for him. In such circumstances something has to give. In the first round it is more likely to be the bank manager than the manager of the public corporation, although in the second round the manager of the corporation may find himself replaced in the interest of maintaining financial discipline. With private banking reasserting itself, it will not be possible to plan the operations of the banks in the same direct manner and more conventional methods of control will have to be used.

Control of banking operations and the money supply needs to be conducted in the context of the increase in money supply necessary to meet the requirements of the economy. This can be worked out in an appropriate manner by adding an allowance for the percentage increase (if any) in prices that it is assumed will take place during the planned period to the percentage increase in output that is expected. This gives the percentage by which the money supply should be allowed to increase after making some adjustment, as appropriate, for further monetisation of the economy or changes in the velocity of circulation; this in turn sets a limit to the amount of credit that can be created. Part of this will be needed for the government's own requirements; the remainder can be used to sustain other borrowers.

In many developing countries, as well as in advanced economies, the place of time deposits in these calculations requires some consideration. Does an increase in time deposits count as an increase in the money supply? The conventional answer is no, because time deposits are customarily regarded as a form of saving. The justification for assuming this really lies in the assumption that the velocity of circulation of time deposits is distinctly less than that of demand deposits. In Bangladesh, in fact, this probably is so, although money will be used from time deposits periodically for making current payments. If it can be assumed that such deposits are for the most part firmly held, the increase in them can justifiably be classified as savings. Nevertheless, since financial assets of various kinds are relatively easily interchangeable, unexpected shifts in the supply of credit, as well as the demand for it, may well upset the predictions of any calculations, particularly in the short term. If the money supply is allowed to increase beyond certain limits it will be a factor contributing to increases in prices and pressures on imports in a less-developed country, just as anywhere else. If these pressures are to be contained, the growth of the money supply must be curbed.

Generally, developing countries are more prone to price fluctuations than industrialised countries, partly because unavoidable and irregular fluctuations in harvests cannot readily be compensated for by equivalent changes in the flow of food imports. Often there are few reserve stocks of food available, particularly just before a harvest, which could be used to make good a shortfall. Fluctuations in prices set in train by movements in production will often be aggravated by speculation, particularly in conditions of shortage. A small crop failure can easily lead to a much greater shortfall in the supply available on the market, particularly if the speculators over-react to the reduction in supply. Apart from the effects of speculation, when the marketable surplus from producers dries up, they naturally supply their own needs first. Since, even in good times, their surplus production is small, much of the shortage may be transferred to urban consumers and those in rural areas who depend on buying their food in the market. The impact on prices thus becomes very large.

Monetary institutions

In developed countries banks are to be found in every high street. Firms are well provided for by a vast variety of financial institutions, ranging from clearing bank facilities to the specialised skills of merchant bankers and highly developed stock exchanges. International links provide still greater flexibility in the provision of finance for large firms and multinationals. It is different in poor developing countries. To begin with, distances are often great and communications bad. Scattered village settlements are characteristic of Bangladesh; in the Sudan distances are immense and communications poorly developed; and in many areas nomadic herdsmen move across the country in a seasonal pattern.

In the towns the situation may be very much better. Ordinary banks will certainly exist and some of them may be run by, or at least owe their origins to, foreign banks through which they maintain contact with the outside world. Internally, they cater for most of the financial needs of the business community, and yet they will not always have the resources, expertise or readiness to provide all the financial facilities needed for a developing country. Capital markets will be rudimentary. Characteristically, the flow of investment capital to the private sector will be from the retained profits of those who have somehow managed to establish themselves in business successfully, supplemented, in some cases, by investment from government resources. As the flow of investment capital is so restricted, government policies may be framed to make entry to industrial activity possible for a few entrepreneurs and to provide large incentives sufficient to generate the profits required for the extension of activities.

In order to hasten and regulate the development of financial institutions, many developing countries follow a conscious promotional policy. This does not necessarily mean that banks and other financial institutions will be government-owned, but it is likely that if private financial institutions are encouraged, they will be subjected to considerable control. Foreign banks, if not taken into domestic ownership, are likely to find their operations circumscribed.

What do governments seek to achieve by setting up new types of financial institutions and extending the operations of those in existence? The first objective is likely to be the encouragement of saving. Savings are likely to be restricted if they cannot be invested productively or lent with security.[8] Without this, any savings that are made may go into the relatively unproductive accumulation of assets, including cattle, as in the case of Sudan.

The provision of more local banking facilities may go some way to deal with such difficulties but it will not eliminate them. Local banks may not be regarded as safe depositories; and they provide no protection against inflation as goods might do, or even cattle on the hoof, although ownership of these is not without risk from drought, theft or disease. Nor, very often, do bank deposits earn much in interest to compensate for the erosion of inflation. Thus the link between institutions and savings may be a tenuous one and, even if positive, the costs of providing the institutions may exceed the benefits that they generate in the way of increased savings. It may also be suspected that where money is lodged in banks it is not very likely to benefit the countryside whence the savings were generated; if some had been passed on to the money-lender, perhaps there would have been some effect, although such rural lending is often concerned with financing consumption rather than investment–providing for the purchase of food after a harvest failure or meeting the costs of a daughter's wedding. When industrialisation is the object of development and investment in the towns is required, there will be pressures to channel resources from rural to urban areas. Thus the extension of the banking system may not work to the benefit of rural areas unless special measures are taken.

This points to some of the advantages as well as the disadvantages that the concentration of savings in the hands of banking intermediaries could be expected to have. If it were not for the existence of some means for channelling savings from savers to borrowers, each act of saving would have to be carried out as an act of personal investment. This might in fact be impossible and as a result savings would serve no purpose, or it might mean that the savings were used much less productively than if they had been invested in some other project of a different kind, or in a different part of the country. One aspect of this is the need to accumulate large amounts of funds for investment projects that require more capital than could be saved by a single individual. Moreover, the use of financial intermediaries may help in assessing whether investment projects are well thought out and likely to succeed.

It follows from the above that monetary authorities should be circumspect in pushing ahead with institutional development. As the economy extends and expands so should the financial institutions that go with it, but not perhaps much in advance of evident requirements. All this points to the need to give careful attention to the types of institutions that are required: where they should be established; how they would be staffed; and the rate at which their activities should be expanded.

Although generating savings and investing them profitably may seem to be a purely economic operation, in important respects the operations of financial institutions are extensions of administrative activities. One of their functions is to decide what activities should be supported by loan capital and what activities should be rejected by refusing to lend. This view of banking becomes more apparent in relation to the functions of specialist institutions, such as those concerned with providing the long-term capital needed for fixed investment. In Pakistan, in the late 1950s for example, it was thought that industrial development would be accelerated if the state set up an institution to invest in new industrial undertakings. It was decided to establish the Pakistan Industrial Development Corporation with the aid of government money. This institution was in effect both an investment bank and an industrial holding company. It had to decide where the funds placed at its disposal should be invested, what types of industry should be established, and on what scale. In this respect it was both administrative and executive, deciding how the money should be spent according to the criteria laid down for it by government, as well as undertaking the action needed to carry out its decisions. The result of its activities was to establish industry which the private sector of the economy could not have been expected to undertake.

It is only a further step in the same direction to set up other types of institutions with the slightly different functions of lending money provided by the state (or other lenders) for the creation of private industry.[9] The function in this case was not to invest directly, but to provide the funds needed by others to invest on their own account and on their own responsibility. This was the function of PIFCO, the Pakistan Industrial Finance Corporation and PICIC, the Pakistan Industrial Credit and Investment Corporation. Note that it is not unusual to set up more than one institution with similar and overlapping functions, as was the case with these two. While competition may be stimulating, there is generally too little trained and experienced talent in developing countries to allow institutions to proliferate.

Development banks, of which PIFCO and PICIC are examples, may be so organised as to provide both domestic finance and foreign currency. The latter service may be crucial for obtaining the required permission to import–or to pay for imports–which is often the prime instrument in the operation of exchange controls. PICIC, for example, was given loans from the World Bank and from other sources. By using these funds for its own lending in support of development of local industry, it was in effect acting as an administrative agency, freeing both the foreign lenders and the government of the problem of day-to-day administration and decisions relating to the acceptance or rejection of loan applications. Again, while such banks may specialise in giving loans to particular sectors of the economy, scarcity of skilled manpower may lead them to become responsible for lending to a wide range of sectors. For the most part, the finance they extend is likely to be in the form of loan capital, but there may also be arguments for equity participation. In developing countries it may be necessary for banks to accept a higher degree of risk than they might be prepared to assume in industrial countries. When a venture succeeds, it may be possible to sell off the bank's equity holding and in this way revolve funds for other uses.

Opportunities for companies to augment their capital may be provided by arranging for their shares to be quoted on a stock exchange, where new issues of capital can be made, too. Operations of this kind are sometimes described as trying to extend share ownership on a democratic basis, but this may often be a misleading description. To those issuing the shares they are much more likely to be considered as a means to extend their affluence still further by drawing in outside funds, while not necessarily paying a great deal in dividends, if profits can be fed to some related but separate and wholly-owned company.

The problem of the small borrower

Institutions of the type described above tend to be directed to large industry and to the affluent. They do little for small entre-preneurs or for agriculture. To some extent this may be due to inherent biases in the government's perceptions, but this is not the full story. There are considerable difficulties in lending to small businesses and agriculture that require consideration. What does lending to small business really mean? In the context of less-developed countries it means providing funds for the rickshaw-wallah to buy his own rickshaw, for the small transport operator to buy his secondhand lorry, for the fisherman to buy his nets or small boat. There is very little security for such transactions: rickshaw-wallahs may disappear together with their rickshaws; lorries run off embankments and in a land without recovery vehicles they are difficult to get back on the road; nets get lost and boats sink. Bankers normally do not like this sort of transaction. Apart from the risk of total loss, repayments may be slow. A great deal of administrative time is needed for little result. A margin of as much as 5 per cent on money lent may be too little to cover the costs and work involved. The financial results at the end of the day may be disastrous. Bad as this looks from the point of view of the bank's operations, it may be even worse from the point of view of the country, because scarce resources have been used with little to show in productive results.

In rural communities the traditional sources of credit are rela-tives and friends, who provide more than 50 per cent of loans in Asia and Africa (but only an estimated 10 per cent in Latin America), and local money-lenders, shopkeepers and merchants who may provide about 30 per cent.[10] Interest may not be charged on loans from friends, but the cost of borrowing from money-lenders or traders may be very high, not necessarily in terms of interest alone, but also in forcing sales of produce or purchases of inputs through the channels of the lender. Attempts have been made to improve the flow of rural credit in many countries but satisfactory results are notoriously hard to achieve.

Lending for agricultural operations may be even less satisfactory than other rural credit. A typical form of organisation for this purpose consists of setting up a central agricultural bank with funds to be placed at the disposal of a number of regional branches or, if it is a cooperative bank, local cooperative societies. The organisational chart is a simple one: an apex bank and a series of local outlets lower in the chain, which have the responsibility of actually making loans to farmers. There are great practical difficulties: contacting the farmers, judging whether they have the know-how to use loans efficiently and, possibly most important, assessing whether they really intend to use the money for the purpose for which they say they intend to borrow it. It is not surprising that recovery rates are low and that agricultural output does not visibly increase because of an isolated injection of bank credit.

In the face of such difficulties, cooperatives can function very well; yet in fact they often function very badly. Loans to cooperatives can be diverted to large affluent landowners rather than to the small members of the cooperative and, moreover, recovery rates are often as bad as, or worse than, those applying in the case of banks giving loans on an individual basis. The issues here are not primarily economic, they are concerned more with influence, power and local political organisation. Thus cooperatives in Mozambique may well function much better than cooperatives in Bangladesh; if so, the reason is not far to seek. In Bangladesh there is little discipline, in Mozambique the party apparatus exercises a controlling influence and more rigorous supervision may be possible. In Bangladesh failure to repay a loan may result in little happening to a recalcitrant debtor. In Mozambique the reaction is likely to be much tougher: a driver in government service who crashes his car is liable to find that he will have to contribute to the cost of its repair.

The major conclusion to draw from this is that credit needs to be combined with other institutional and administrative measures to ensure that it is allocated and used efficiently. The World Bank has suggested that ten criteria may serve as a guide in lending to small farmers:[11]

(i) *Accessibility*: Small farmers have difficulty in reaching lending agencies; this can be overcome if field agents visit the farmer in his surroundings.

(ii) *Packaging*: Credit should be accompanied by information on technology and the timely supply of inputs.

(iii) *Distribution in kind*: Farmers may not use the money advanced to purchase the required inputs or they may have difficulty in doing so; therefore, distribution in kind is preferable.

(iv) *Timing*: Credit must be available in time for the inputs to be purchased and incorporated into the agricultural cycle.

(v) *Selection*: The smallholder needs to be assessed for credit worthiness in terms of his reputation and the technical feasibility of the proposed investment.

(vi) *Individual liability and group responsibility*: The repayment of the loan is the borrower's responsibility but social pressures can be brought to bear to encourage repayment.

(vii) *Control*: Payment and repayments need to be geared to the liquidity of the borrower.

(viii) *Flexibility*: It may be necessary to reschedule the repayment of loans if things go wrong.

(ix) *Continuity*: Programmes must be continued for some time if they are to succeed.

(x) *An open-ended approach*: Programmes may have to be modified in the light of needs and experience.

TRADE POLICY

Gains from trade

There are sound reasons for urging developing countries to take advantage of trading opportunities. Not all do so to the fullest extent. There may be political objections to trade with certain groups of countries, reluctance to become dependent on food imports, aversion to the risk of fluctuations in export receipts or import prices, and fears of the effects of market changes.

Analytically, the key to the advantages of trade lies in the theory of comparative advantage. The reasons for specialisation in the production of certain products are sometimes fairly obvious though not always totally conclusive. Fuels or raw materials may be easy to extract and hence natural candidates for exploitation, for example. But acquired advantages can be just as important as natural ones. A well-educated population, technical know-how, well-developed institutions, and accumulations of capital in the form of productive resources may be far more important than natural advantages. In fact, if we were to attempt to contrast the advantages of the developed with the less-developed countries, we might ascribe to the former acquired advantages and to the latter, in some cases, natural advantages. This classification is dangerous and does not get us very far; yet it directs attention to the importance of assessing the comparative strength of a country's endowments, whether natural or acquired, with a view to identifying what it might be expected to concentrate on in the medium term, at the same time using its resources to the best advantage.

This brings us to the Heckscher-Ohlin theory of international trade as applied to the less-developed countries.[12] In its simplest form the theory might lead us to conclude that the less-developed countries should concentrate on labour-intensive activities, because they appear to be plentifully endowed with labour relative to the capital they possess, while the reverse applies to developed countries, which with their relative capital abundance might be expected to produce capital-intensive goods. The Heckscher-Ohlin theory has been subjected to intensive analytical and statistical analysis to determine the conditions under which it may be valid. These are quite restrictive and there are a number of circumstances under which the very simple propositions outlined above might not be valid. In spite of this, the theory has some practical applications in suggesting where comparative advantages should be sought. For a less-developed country the issue is generally how the (often) large amounts of unskilled labour can be put to good use with the limited amounts of capital available, and what are the implications of this for international trade. In crude terms, this may suggest establishing industries such as textiles and clothing, where the labour content of production is high; in fact, in many cases this is how industrialisation in the less-developed countries has been introduced.

The Heckscher-Ohlin theory has further implications for world trade and for the distribution of income between labour and capital in the developed as well as the less-developed world. It has been shown by Samuelson, on the basis of certain restrictive assumptions, that the effect of trade between countries may be to equalise factor rewards, so that in effect labour (at given levels of skill and productivity) would be paid the same in all the trading countries, and similarly for capital.[13] The theoretical conditions in which this would be true do not, however, obtain in the real world where it is a matter of common observation that the remuneration of workers varies greatly from country to country.

Nevertheless, there is a very real sense in which the proposition can be seen to be working. In countries that have gone far with industrialisation, wage levels have risen; the level of wages in Japan has caught up with that of the United Kingdom. Moreover, the competition offered by the less-developed countries to those already industrialised will not act only in the direction of raising the wages of the former, since competition in third markets will limit the prices that can be obtained by industrialised countries and hence the remuneration that it is possible to pay their workers. These tendencies are bound to get more marked as increasing numbers of the less-developed countries industrialise on an accelerating scale.

So far we have argued that it will be in the interest of the less-developed countries to trade, because they can exploit their comparative advantages and so increase their incomes. Most of the propositions that we have been advancing rest on assumptions about freedom to trade without restrictions, that production will in fact be permitted and possible in whatever area comparative advantage might seem to dictate, that market conditions approximate to perfect competition with no government intervention in the form of taxes, import duties or quantitative regulations, and also that there is no dominance by private monopoly. In practice, of course, this will often not be the case. Market conditions may not bring about the results that theory might seem to suggest; there is great uncertainty about where comparative advantage lies and how it will change as time goes on. It will also be necessary to relate the pattern of trade to what the world trading system will accommodate.

Take, for instance, the decision whether to push industrialisation or agricultural development in relation to trading opportunities. This falls into the type of strategy decisions discussed in Chapter 2 with the possibility that there may be strong predilections for industrialisation, quite irrespective of what may be judged to be the economic merits of the case. The relative ease or difficulty of getting the desired increase in activity in the two sectors will be another consideration, which in the past has tended to give a bias to industrialisation. Suppose, however, that the decision turns on which of the two sectors would be most likely to contribute to improving the balance of payments by increasing export potential. A prime consideration would be how the world markets for industrial and agricultural products would be expected to develop over the next ten or twenty years. It might be argued, for instance, that the demand for agricultural products is not as income-elastic as that for manufactured products and that, partly as a consequence or independently, the price of agricultural products would fall relative to those of industrial goods. Therefore, the argument might go on, it would be best to concentrate on industrial products. Would this be a sound conclusion? The answer depends amongst other things on the expected terms of trade between the two.

The movement of the terms of trade for the less-developed countries, both as a group and individually, has been a matter of much discussion. A study of the terms of trade between primary products and manufactures over the period 1870-1960 has been carried out by Sir Arthur Lewis.[14] During this period, the developing countries of today were largely exporters of primary products and importers of manufactures, so that the ratios of the prices of these two categories of products gave some indication of movements in the terms of trade as they affected the developing countries. Over the whole period there seems to have been some deterioration in the terms of trade defined in this way, but it was probably not very great. What was evident from the study was the extent to which the terms of trade fluctuated. In conditions of boom the primary producers did well; in times of slump they did badly. The terms of trade were largely determined by changes in manufacturing output, with the prices of primary products falling or rising in response. A later study by Professor Thomas Wilson and others takes the story further and shows that the terms of trade deteriorated for the developing countries by about 10 per cent between 1950 and 1965;[15] roughly matching gains accrued to the developed countries, as might be expected.[16]

Studies such as these, the interpretations put upon them and the use of particular periods for comparisons, led to the view formulated by Raul Prebisch, that there might be some phenomenon that would lead to continuing decline in the terms of trade of the developing countries.[17] Changes tending to bring this about might be the increasing use of substitutes for raw materials, more economical use of them, and a switch to the consumption of products with less material content. If this were expected to be a continuing trend, it might be advisable for the developing countries to concentrate more on producing manufactures than on primary products; yet the argument may be totally inconclusive.

Writing as we do at a time when world activity is increasing only slowly, it is possible to believe that in relative terms many commodity prices will tend to fall, but it would be extremely rash to base a development strategy on an assumption that they would necessarily do so. The increase in the price of oil in the 1970s illustrates vividly how volatile prices of primary products can be if their production is restricted, or if supplies appear to be in danger of running out, or simply if activity increases. Pressure on world food supplies may also give some indication that prices of primary products may improve relative to those of manufactures. Whatever happens, in the long run it is to be expected that the production of primary commodities at some level of output and in some developing countries will be profitable. In any event, commodity or net barter terms of trade are not the only consideration. Costs of primary products may fall because they can be produced more easily using improved methods of production or new techniques. In these circumstances deteriorating terms of trade do not necessarily signify a worsening position. Again, it may sometimes be necessary to accept a deterioration in the terms of trade if the volume of exports is to be increased. What matters is whether developing countries consider it worthwhile to maintain or increase exports of primary products in order to be able to pay for more imports. In this respect it is helpful to consider the income terms of trade, which are arrived at by multiplying the index of net barter terms of trade by an index of the volume of exports. A rise in this combined index indicates that a country can get a larger amount of imports from its exports. In fact, Professor Wilson's study showed that the ability to increase imports had increased very considerably for most countries over the period investigated, because exports had outpaced changes in the terms of trade. When barter terms of trade change there are winners and losers, but with income terms of trade everybody can win, reflecting a general expansion in world trade.

The above discussion may serve as a warning about the dangers of generalisation about the terms of trade and the conclusions to be drawn from movements in them. A further word of warning is needed. It is, more often than not, unhelpful to generalise about the terms of trade of the developing or the developed countries taken as blocs. Patterns of trade vary greatly from country to country. A striking illustration of this is the experience in the 1970s of oil-exporting developing countries, who derived the benefits of increases in the price of oil to a level 15 times greater than in 1972-73, far greater than the costs imposed by some off-setting rise in the price of manufactures.

Protection

We repeat that cases have to be considered on their merits and considerations affecting the terms of trade do not seem to dictate either dependence on industry or reliance on primary products to generate exports. For some countries industrialisation will be an end in itself and where this is the case, or even where it appears justifiable on grounds of comparative advantage for industrial development to go ahead, a call to protect industry against foreign competition is part of the game. This is almost certain if the objective of industrialisation is to replace imports; it may also apply, as in Korea, if industrialisation is directed to exporting to foreign markets.

Theoretically, protection is extremely difficult to justify. In the words of Harry G. Johnson: 'Contemporary arguments for tariffs in underdeveloped countries can be classified into three broad kinds: economic arguments, non-economic arguments, and non-arguments'.[18] The non-economic arguments for the imposition of tariffs are those concerned with industrialisation as a matter of national pride, or as a basis for political and military importance, etc. The non-arguments fall into the category of logical mistakes, for example, arguments of the kind we have already considered: that because the terms of trade are getting worse or the returns from commodities fluctuate, they should not be produced, or that the solution of balance of payments difficulties dictates imposition of protection rather than other means of adjustment.

The best-known economic argument for protection is the infant industry argument. This argument maintains that some industries will start by making losses, but will ultimately become viable and, over the whole of the life of the investment, will be profitable. If so, it is asked, why should there be a need to protect the industry; the losses can be sustained, for example, by borrowing, and subsequently they will be more than recouped. However, it is possible in this case that private enterprise, faced with the certainty of initial losses, may feel that the risks of things not turning out well in the end are too great, or it may not be possible to raise the capital needed in imperfect markets. Thus private enterprise might not be prepared to undertake the investment and the state might feel justified in offering a subsidy for a venture that it considered sound on social criteria.

A less well-known argument for protection, but one that may have some merit, is that of optimal tariff. By imposing restrictions on imports through the imposition of tariffs or quantitative regulation, the effective demand for imports can be considerably reduced and, therefore, fewer export receipts will be needed to pay for imports. If the demand for the country's exports is inelastic this will mean that the reduced export quantity can be sold at higher prices and the terms of trade thereby improved. All this assumes, of course, that retaliation can be avoided. Before jute fell prey to the use of synthetics and bulk transport (which did not require the use of jute sacks), it was to Bangladesh's advantage to limit the amount of jute exported and so obtain higher prices. This provided some justification for the export duties that were imposed at times on raw jute, although there were also other reasons.

The use of tariffs for purposes other than the regulation of imports can be strongly criticised on theoretical grounds. Appendix 1 shows how the use of tariffs to correct domestic price distortions may affect welfare adversely. It must be accepted, however, that tariffs may be imposed in order to protect industrial activities. Appendix 2 discusses the implications of this for the levels of duties imposed on different commodities and shows that in principle they should be different.

The destructive effects of ill-thought-out tariff structures can be illustrated from the history of Pakistan and Bangladesh. When the Second Five Year Plan of Pakistan was drawn up in 1960 it was decided that domestic manufacturing should be encouraged. The obvious way to bring this about was to impose taxes on imports competing with goods that were or could be manufactured in Pakistan. It was also felt that protection should be arranged in such a way as to encourage full-scale manufacture of goods from basic raw materials rather than from intermediate components. In less-developed countries it is quite usual to start a manufacturing process by importing components and assembling them. Thus kits with parts for Vauxhall cars were sent to Bangladesh in the 1970s for assembly there, in the hope that the operation would gradually be enlarged until many of the components needed for the fabrication of the cars would be manufactured locally. However, in Bangladesh the domestic market is too small to justify full-scale production and therefore the capital needed for it could not be made available unless domestic production could be linked to export markets. For other kinds of manufacture this would not be the case. In textiles, for example, the market is large enough to permit efficient production. If it is desired to encourage complete manufacture rather than assembly, an obvious ploy seems to be to give greater protection to finished and semi-manufactured products than to raw materials. Cheap raw materials relative to the price of the final product give good profit margins on the processing of such materials, particularly when the prices of the finished goods are kept high by protection. This was certainly the case in the 1960s in Pakistan, when the rate of duty imposed on unprocessed raw materials was about 25-50 per cent and that on processed raw materials about 50 per cent, while duties on finished goods ranged from 50-100 per cent.[19]

Another aspect of the selection of rates of duties imposed on imported goods is the effect of trying to restrain the consumption of luxury goods by making their price very high. Since in Pakistan many such goods were imported, high tariffs were imposed as a means of taxing the rich. The duty on imports of essential goods was fixed at about 50 per cent, that on semi-luxuries at 100 per cent, while that imposed on luxury goods was about 150 per cent. Still another consideration is that investment might be encouraged by making the duty on capital goods low; in Pakistan such duties were about 17 per cent. In this case, however, the duty on materials needed for the construction of capital goods was about the same.

The combined effects of all such incentives offered to producers are difficult to assess, and the tariff structure that results may in fact be quite illogical. In the first place, the high rates of duty imposed on finished goods and the much lower rates on materials mean that profit margins are potentially much higher than those of producers abroad. Secondly, the profit margins to be earned from producing luxury goods are much greater than those obtainable from producing non-luxury goods, while these in turn are higher than those obtainable on the production of essentials. So luxury goods would be produced rather than essentials whenever a choice was available. All of this was evident in Pakistan in the 1960s. Other consequences of the structure of duties adopted in Pakistan were that the profit to be earned from the production of capital goods was small, giving little incentive to produce them. Yet in many instances there were opportunities to earn large profits in industry as a result of the protection given—an issue to which we return in Chapter 5. Pakistan's system of protection was not unique; distortions of incentives resulting from ill-thought-out taxation systems are quite usual.

In the Sudan the distortions introduced in the 1970s by disparate rates of tariffs on imports combined with taxes on exports were of a different nature.[20] The effect of taxes on exports of agricultural products was to make the remuneration obtained from them about 27 per cent less than it would have been without the imposition of the tax, whereas the combined effect of taxes on industrial imports and duties on raw materials was to raise the potential margin of profit obtainable on domestic industrial production to about 150 per cent more than that obtaining overseas. Thus, the effect of the fiscal system was to encourage would-be entrepreneurs to seek their fortunes in industry rather than in agriculture. Fortunately this is not the whole story, for investment in industry was controlled by a licensing system, while agricultural activity was not interfered with, so that the incentive provided as a result of the operations of the combined tariff and tax systems was to some extent frustrated.

The moral to be drawn from these practical illustrations is that fiscal systems should be designed in their entirety if their adverse effects are to be minimised. In practice this is seldom done; tariff structures are never developed *ab initio*. There is always an existing tariff structure which is progressively modified as time goes on without much thought given to the consequences of such modifications; there may be a scream for protection from some industry hard hit by competition; there may be negotiations in GATT that affect some commodities more than others; there are negotiations with the Common Market and other bodies; and there are the (not always well-considered) recommendations of tariff commissions. A closer inspection of the tariff rates imposed in

Bangladesh enable such changes and some of their effects to be traced. In total, the result is a hotchpotch of inconsistent and contradicting patterns.

Nevertheless, discouraging and difficult as it may be, changes in tariff rates should not be considered in isolation from the effects discussed above. A golden rule might be that only a strong case should be accepted as justifying special protection to a particular activity which others are not afforded, and it should always be remembered that, as with subsidies, protection once granted is very difficult to remove.

Further information about the effects of tariffs in giving various degrees of protection to different types of industry and the distortions that this introduces is given in Appendix 3, which defines and discusses effective protection.

Quantitative restrictions

The discussion so far has proceeded largely on the assumption that the only impediment to trade is created by the imposition of tariffs. Many countries do not rely exclusively on tariffs for protection; Bangladesh, the Sudan and Mozambique certainly do not do so. As an alternative or supplement, quantitative restrictions may be imposed. Typically, such restrictions will limit the amount of particular goods that can be imported; generally the amount allowed in will be less than the amount that users or consumers would be willing to buy if they could import freely at prices equivalent to world prices, plus custom duties when applicable. Quantitative restrictions raise a set of market imperfections of their own. As a general rule, the cost of the imports will be below the price that can be obtained in the market and the goods that are imported will command a premium over their landed cost. Amongst other things, this will add to the protection afforded to local producers, making it greater than might be assumed from looking at customs schedules only. It will also affect calculations of the degree of effective production.

Like tariffs, quantitative restrictions have the effect of distorting price relativities. They also distort market forces in another way because an importer or trader lucky enough to secure supplies of imports, which command a premium, can often make handsome profits. The government may attempt to prevent this by employing price control, but it is very hard to make this stick.

Another effect, as we shall discuss in Chapter 5, is that industrialists may spend more of their time trying to get their hands on
imports in short supply than managing their own businesses. The
administration of quantitative restrictions also takes up the time
of officials, and since it is they who issue the licences they will be
exposed to attempts of would-be importers to obtain supplies
with the aid of suitable sweeteners.

TARIFFS, TAXATION AND EXCHANGE RATES

Fiscal, monetary and trade policies, along with direct interventions and other government actions, as we have emphasised,
ought not to be discussed in isolation without regard to their
interaction. Devaluation, for example, increases internal prices of
imported goods just as a tariff does; both increase the com-
petitiveness of domestic producers. Export subsidies encourage
exports, as does devaluation. All these measures affect price relativities and they can have strong effects on the profitability of
different economic activities.

Before Bangladesh broke away from Pakistan, the taxation
systems imposed on the two countries and the rates of duty
imposed on imports were the same. The effects on the two countries, however, were very different because the composition of
their output differed markedly. Pakistan was predominantly agricultural in the 1960s, but its industry was developing rapidly in a
fairly diversified fashion. Bangladesh was very largely an agricultural producer, and its very limited industrial sector was
mainly concerned with the production of jute goods for export.
The domestic manufacture of jute was given some protection in
relation to corresponding operations in other countries using
Bangladesh's jute, since an export tax was imposed on sales of jute
abroad, thus increasing its cost to competitors.

Although Bangladesh had high export earnings from raw and
manufactured jute, the receipts of producers was less than they
would have been with freely operating markets because the
exchange rate overvalued the rupee. This was possible because
the amount of imports allowed into the country was controlled by
a licensing system which restricted them to much less than would
have obtained without such controls. The effect on Pakistan's
exporters of the overvaluation of the rupee was much reduced by
the 'export bonus' system which had the effect of subsidising

exports of manufactures from that country.[21] This served to keep the profits on manufacture high enough for export to take place, while at the same time the domestic market was remunerative because, as we have seen, industrialists were producing in a market protected both by import duties and the restrictive effects of import licences. The net effect of all these measures on Bangladesh was definitely adverse.[22] They served to turn the terms of trade between agriculture and industry against agriculture and, in the process, against Bangladesh whose jute sold for little and whose purchases of imported manufactures, whether from Pakistan or the outer world, were increased in price by the protection imposed. These effects were a contributing factor to the political unease within Pakistan in the 1960s which terminated in civil war in 1971 and the creation of Bangladesh.

The above discussion brings us to a more general point in relation to the exchange rate: how appropriate are uniform exchange rates for less-developed countries? Multiple exchange rates have some advantages in relation to exports, when the demand for some types of exports is inelastic while for others it is highly elastic.[23] The effect of multiple exchange rates can be contrived by the imposition of different rates of duties (or subsidies) on imports, by differential subsidies (or taxes), or by other means. To differentiate in this way inevitably leads to considerable complications in the structure of taxes and duties.

One of the recurrent issues, often in relation to recommendations by the IMF, is the appropriate level of the exchange rate and whether adjusting it (downwards) is likely to be beneficial to the balance of payments. Simple tests for this include looking at the relative increase in costs and prices over time, differences between official and black-market prices, and forecasts of the domestic absorption of resources and trade prospects.

If the exchange rate appears to be overvalued will devaluation be helpful? Whether this is the case depends on the elasticities of supply and demand for imports and exports and how the country reacts to a shift in prices and profitability. Will exports respond, for example, to the greater profitability induced by devaluation and to what extent and at what rate? Similarly, will imports contract, so saving foreign exchange? When the IMF urged Bangladesh to devalue in the 1970s there appeared to be little reason to think that import needs would be reduced or that the supply response would be very great, and there was some preference on the part of administrators for the adoption of alternative measures to encourage exports.[24] Bangladesh, however, is always a special case. More generally it appears that supply-and-demand elasticities are favourable to devaluation.[25] If, as is contended, exports increase, there is opportunity to increase imports and extend the international division of labour.

FURTHER READING

Bela Balassa *et al.*, *The Structure of Protection in Developing Countries*, Baltimore, Md., Johns Hopkins Press, 1971, Part I.
Graham Bird, 'Should Developing Countries use Currency Depreciation as a Tool of Balance of Payments Adjustments?', *Journal of Development Studies*, Vol. 19 (1983), No. 4, pp. 461-84.
Raja J. Chelliah, 'Trends in Taxation in Developing Countries', *IMF Staff Papers*, Vol. 18 (1971), No. 2, pp. 254-331.
Harry G. Johnson, 'Tariffs and Economic Development: Some Theoretical Issues', *Journal of Development Studies*, Vol. 1 (1964), No. 1, pp. 3-30.
Deena R. Khatkhate and Klaus-Walter Riechel, 'Multipurpose Banking: Its Nature, Scope and Relevance for Less Developed Countries', *IMF Staff Papers*, Vol. 27 (1980), No. 3, pp. 478-516.

NOTES

1. *Links between Taxes and Economic Growth: Some Empirical Evidence*, World Bank Staff Working Paper, No. 605, World Bank, 1983.
2. Raja J. Chelliah, 'Trends in Taxation in Developing Countries', *IMF Staff Papers*, Vol. 18 (1971), No. 2, pp. 254-331.
3. See Raja J. Chelliah, 'Taxation of Consumption Expenditures, with Special Reference to India', in Richard M. Bird and Oliver Oldman (eds), *Readings on Taxation in Developing Countries*, Baltimore, Md., Johns Hopkins Press, 1967, pp. 301-10.
4. A. P. Thirlwall, *Inflation, Saving and Growth in Developing Economies*, London, Macmillan, 1974.
5. In 'The Promotion of the "Banking Habit" and Economic Development', *Journal of Development Studies*, Vol. 2 (1966), No. 4, pp. 346-66, Richard C. Porter shows how the money supply is related to the monetary base on alternative assumptions relating to reserve ratios and use of currency.
6. For a discussion of some of these issues, see R. B. Stevenson, 'By What Measures Can a Central Bank Exercise Control in a Young Economy?', *Journal of Institute of Bankers*, Vol. 82 (1961), Part 5, October.
7. See Alberto Giovannini, 'The Interest Elasticity of Savings in Developing Countries: the Existing Evidence', *World Development*, Vol. 11 (1983), No. 7, pp. 601-7.

8. For a discussion of some of the issues, see V. V. Bhatt and J. Meerman, 'Resource Mobilization in Developing Countries', *World Development*, Vol. 6, (1978), No. 1, pp. 45-64; and Richard C. Porter, op. cit.

9. See, for instance, W. Diamond, *Development Banks*, Baltimore, Md., Johns Hopkins Press, 1957, and *Development Finance Companies: Aspects of Policy and Operation*, Baltimore, Md., Johns Hopkins Press, 1968, edited by the same author; and Deena R. Khatkhate and Klaus-Walter Riechel, 'Multipurpose Banking: its Nature, Scope and Relevance for Less Developed Countries', *IMF Staff Papers*, Vol. 27 (1980), No. 3, pp. 478-516.

10. International Bank for Reconstruction and Development, Agricultural Credit, Sector Policy Paper, World Bank, May 1975, p. 28.

11. Ibid., pp. 62-3.

12. For a discussion of this see, for example, Chapter 3, in Bo Södersten, *International Economics*, 2nd edn., London, Macmillan, 1980.

13. P. A. Samuelson, 'International Trade and the Equalisation of Factor Prices', *Economic Journal*, June 1948, pp. 163-84.

14. W. A. Lewis, 'World Production, Prices and Trade 1870-1960', *Manchester School of Economic and Social Studies*, Vol. 20 (1952), No. 2, pp. 105-38.

15. T. Wilson, R. P. Sinha and J. R. Castree, 'The Income Terms of Development and Developing Countries', *Economic Journal*, Vol. 79 (1969), No. 316, pp. 813-32.

16. See also Lloyd G. Reynolds, 'The Spread of Economic Growth to the Third World: 1850-1980', *Journal of Economic Literature*, Vol. 21 (1983), No. 3, pp. 941-80: '. . . there is no clear evidence that the terms of trade between primary products and manufactures have moved appreciably against primary products since 1945'. In fact, considerable statistical endeavour is needed to determine how the terms of trade have moved: see J. Spraos, 'The Statistical Debate on the Net Barter Terms of Trade Between Primary Commodities and Manufactures', *Economic Journal*, Vol. 90 (1980), No. 357, pp. 107-28; D. Sapsford, 'The Statistical Debate on the Net Barter Terms of Trade Between Primary Commodities and Manufactures: A Comment and Some Additional Evidence', *Economic Journal*, Vol. 95 (1985), No. 379, pp. 781-88; and J. Spraos, 'The Statistical Debate on the Net Barter Terms of Trade: A Response', *Economic Journal*, Vol. 95 (1985), No. 379, p. 789.

17. See the related discussion in Chapter 2, p. 40.

18. Harry G. Johnson, 'Tariffs and Economic Development, Some Theoretical Issues', *Journal of Development Studies*, Vol. 1 (1964), No. 1, p. 6.

19. See Ghulam Mohammad Radhu, 'The Rate Structure of Indirect Taxes in Pakistan', *Pakistan Development Review*, Vol. 4 (1964), No. 3, Table 6, p. 551.

20. International Labour Office, ILO, *Growth Employment and Equity: A Comprehensive Strategy for the Sudan. Report of the ILO/UNDP Employment Mission, 1975*, ILO, 1976. Chapter 12 and Technical Paper 17.

21. This scheme was designed to reward exporters of specified products with import licences. Since imported goods were scarce they could be sold very profitably at a premium over landed cost; alternatively, the licences themselves could be sold at the ruling market price for such import entitlements.

22. It has been estimated that the effect was that Bangladesh agriculturalists had to pay 8 rupees for one dollar's worth of manufactures, against the official exchange rate of 4.75 rupees to the dollar, whereas Pakistan's manufacturers

were selling manufactures at 7 rupees to the dollar. See Stephen R. Lewis, Jr., *Economic Policy and Industrial Growth in Pakistan*, London, Allen & Unwin, 1969.

23. For a discussion of some aspects of this, see Henry J. Bruton, 'The Two Gap Approach to Aid and Development: Comment', *The American Economic Review*, Vol. 59 (1969), No. 3, pp. 439-46, and 'Reply to Bruton' by Hollis B. Chenery, ibid., pp. 446-49.

24. See Jack Parkinson, 'The Role of the Fund', in Just Faaland (ed.), *Aid and Influence: The Case of Bangladesh*, London, Macmillan, 1981.

25. In 'Should Developing Countries use Currency Depreciation as a Tool of Balance of Payments Adjustment: A Review of the Theory and Evidence and a Guide for the Policy Maker', *Journal of Development Studies*, Vol. 19 (1983), No. 4, p. 461. See also A. Bhagwat and Y. Onitsuka, 'Export-Import Responses to Devaluation: Experience of the Non-Industrialised Countries in the 1960s', *IMF Staff Papers*, Vol. 21 (1974), No. 2, pp. 414-62; and Donal J. Donovan, 'Real Responses Associated with Exchange Rate Action in Selected Upper Credit Tranche Stabilization Programs', *IMF Staff Papers*, Vol. 28 (1981), No. 4, pp. 698-727.

5 Policies for agriculture and industry

As we discussed in Chapter 1, very large changes in the structure of an economy take place during development. Agriculture declines in relative importance as industry expands, the provision of services takes new forms and a vast infrastructure of facilities has to be created. Many of these changes will be brought about by the actions of individuals or institutions working independently and responding to the situation and opportunities as they see them, and within the framework of fiscal, monetary and trade policies described earlier. Some things must of necessity be carried out by government and public bodies, and these ought to be part of well-planned programmes consistent with the evolution of the economy and the need for public services. Part of these programmes will be concerned with the provision of infrastructure as an adjunct to private sector development, but not all will be so, particularly if the state is interventionist in character and set on entering the field of production itself. Some of the state's activities will be concerned with the population itself, with its growth and location, and with the provision of services for it, including education and health care, as will be discussed in Chapter 7. It will also be anxious to create opportunities for employment as part of the mobilisation of the country's resources and as a means to providing full opportunity to individuals. For all these activities, policies will have to be devised and put into effect.

In sectors where the state does not intend to be directly involved, some intervention may also take place and, at the very least, it will be necessary to consider how far activities in these sectors should be guided by adopting specific policies for them. The less direct intervention is involved, the more important it will be to consider this and how policies should be put into effect.

In a comprehensive plan, policies would be laid down for the development of all the major sectors of the economy: for agriculture, industry, power, transport and other means of communication, in directly productive sectors; for housing, towns, education, health and family planning, as part of efforts to improve the quality of life. However the business of government is conducted, plan or no plan, the government has to consider what its attitude should be to the changes taking place in the various sectors, whether it should seek to accelerate or retard them, to control or modify them.

In what follows we do not attempt to examine every sector of the economy and consider how it should be encouraged to evolve and what policies would be most likely to achieve the government's aims, for this would take too long. In this chapter we restrict ourselves to discussing the agricultural and industrial sectors and considering what their development is likely to entail for the shift of manpower between them. The choice of the agricultural sector for discussion rests on its importance in the early stages of development, contrary to that of industry, which may be of small dimensions but destined in the longer run, in many countries, largely to eclipse primary production. The discussion of the industrial sector, in particular, allows us to consider some of the effects of direct controls which in developing countries, as elsewhere, may be used as an alternative or supplement to fiscal, monetary and trade measures designed to influence economic activity.

AGRICULTURE

Amongst the lowest-income countries, only Benin has less than half its population engaged in agriculture; in many of them more than 80 per cent are occupied in this way. The proportion of population living in rural areas, including those gaining their livelihood in non-agricultural pursuits, is, of course, even higher; in Bangladesh over 90 per cent. In traditional societies, people gaining their livelihood in rural areas are not just agriculturists. The division of labour has not evolved very far; most families are their own farmers, builders, hewers of wood and carriers of water, they provide their own transport and health care, such as it may be, and make many of the things they use in the ordinary way of life. In short, they are often largely self-sufficient, in self-contained communities if not as individuals. For most of these people the opportunity to improve their lot will depend to a large extent on whether they can grow more food or raw materials. Employment opportunities in rural industry, construction and services will increase only slowly to begin with as development proceeds and, therefore, few people will be able to earn their living outside agriculture itself.

In some countries, but not all, starvation is a constant threat: a continuously increasing population may press on land resources; bad harvests may reduce food output severely, sometimes over prolonged periods; climatic shifts may inflict permanent damage on agricultural prospects; food supplies imported from other countries may be cut. In such cases improvement in agricultural practices is desperately needed.

Even when starvation is an unlikely event, an increase in the output of food of appropriate kinds is needed to improve dietary standards. Malnutrition is prevalent in most underdeveloped countries, but could be overcome in many of them if better use were made of agricultural opportunities. In Bangladesh in the mid-1970s, the intake of calories was little more than 90 per cent, and the protein intake per capita only 60 per cent of that needed for adequate nutrition. These are average figures and so conceal marked differences between individuals: the poor and the rich and those that live in the towns or in the countryside. In the Sudan even with normal rainfall and in spite of vast areas of uncultivated land, malnutrition is also very evident, particularly amongst children. At the time we write, Mozambique and Ethiopia are in the throes of famine and even the Sudan is threatened. In developing countries throughout the world, and in the poorer ones in particular, food supplies and effective demand for them are inadequate to a life-threatening extent for large numbers of the populations.

There are many other reasons for attaching importance to agricultural development. Agricultural raw materials often provide the means to establish agro-based industries: cotton, jute, sugar, rubber and many others. Many of them can also be exported and so provide the means to make purchases overseas. For better or for worse, Bangladesh has been highly dependent on exports of jute in raw or manufactured form, and the Sudan on cotton, to obtain manufactured goods. Even when countries have not established an export trade they may still have the potential to do so if yields can be increased, new crops produced or new markets opened up.

Other reasons, evident in the historical pattern of development of countries discussed in Chapter 1, can be advanced for improving agricultural productivity. The pattern of output and employment changes as development takes place: as industrialisation accelerates, workers are needed for factory employment and in service occupations; once underemployment in agriculture is overcome, it must improve its productivity to release the workers needed in other sectors. At the same time, sufficient food must be produced so that workers in the towns can be fed; they, in turn, must produce a surplus of goods or provide services to pay for the food they eat. In this way mutually supporting and growth-creating activity results.

Another aspect of this interdependence is that much of the saving initially needed to finance development and industrial investment must come from agricultural incomes if capital is to be accumulated sufficiently rapidly to give a high rate of increase in output. This means that part of the agricultural surplus must be made available to provide for development elsewhere. This might be brought about by 'unfavourable' terms of trade between agricultural and industrial products. Low prices for agricultural goods and high prices for industrial ones could enhance the profits of importers and industrialists, both directly and by keeping down the price of labour. In circumstances where, to the contrary, agriculture provides a surplus over and above subsistence needs for those engaged in it, resources may be transferred for investment in industry directly out of the sales of agricultural products, as the better-off farmers in Bangladesh are thought to do. This does not necessarily entail any pressure for financial flows through banks or other intermediaries. The better-off farmer may be investing the proceeds of his farming in his own industrial, constructional or merchanting activities. However the transfer takes place, rural consumption is reduced and investment elsewhere enhanced unless, of course, the surplus is simply consumed elsewhere.

Increasing agricultural output and improving productivity requires different measures in different countries, depending on the availability of land, the way that it is distributed between those who cultivate it, the technical opportunities to increase output, and the social constraints that affect the totality of rural development as well as agricultural performance. In the following sections we deal with some aspects of these factors affecting development and underline their importance in the countries to which we refer.

Landholding and agricultural efficiency

The systems of landholding vary greatly from country to country throughout the world. For the sake of illustration we draw on Bangladesh, the Sudan and Mozambique in turn and describe how farming efficiency is affected by the system of landholding in force.

In Bangladesh the amount of land owned or cultivated by individual farmers tends, as we have seen, to be very small and frequently the total holding may be made up of scattered plots. Inheritance has the effect of dividing family holdings between the heirs and, as time goes on, they may dwindle to little more than garden plots. At the same time, relatively large landowners emerge, perhaps by purchasing land from their less fortunate brethren made destitute at a time of harvest failure. What effect may this be expected to have on farming efficiency? Several possible consequences may be detected. In the first place, 'strip' farming is not conducive to efficiency and wastes some of the land when baulks are left to define ownership.[1]

Secondly, large landowners may not cultivate their land, or all of it, themselves, preferring to put it out to tenants; smallholders may also do this if they see other ways to make a living. Tenancy is frequently conducive to inefficiency. In Bangladesh the product is shared, often on a fifty-fifty basis, between tenant and landlord with the tenant providing the inputs. The effect of this is that too little is likely to be provided in the way of inputs, since part of the consequential increase in output would go to the landlord who pays nothing. It may also be that the tenant purchases his inputs from his landlord as a part of the leasing agreement and at higher prices than he might have to pay elsewhere, with the result that the amounts of inputs used is too small.

As the 'green revolution' takes hold and yields increase, the landlord may take a tighter grip and demand, say, two-thirds of the crop, thus continuing to accord the tenant no more than a subsistence return from his activities.[2] But it may also happen that the landlord, realising that there are opportunities to increase output profitably, will take the land back into his own hands and farm it more efficiently with the aid of modern technology. In either case the would-be sharecropper tends to lose.

Efficiency of cultivation is also influenced by the size of agricultural holdings. When a holding is too big to be worked by a family group, or whenever hired labour is used, the marginal product of labour will be equated not with the opportunity cost of the labour employed, which may often be zero, but with the subsistence wage that must be paid if labour is willing to accept employment in the first place. Thus it is to be expected that output per acre would be less in the case of land farmed by large landowners, using hired labour, than by owner-occupied farms of smaller dimension which can be worked by the family. Within the technologies with which they are familiar, small farmers generally appear to be able to make good use of their opportunities. There is considerable evidence for this, but there may be some exceptions. For example, a study by Dasgupta on the production of rice in six areas showed that in three of them there was a negative relationship between size and yield per unit of land, while the reverse was true in the case of the other three.[3]

In a famous book, *Transforming Traditional Agriculture*, Professor Theodore Schultz argued that farmers within traditional agriculture allocated their resources in an efficient manner born of generations of experience. Attempts have been made to test this assertion. One way to do this is to check whether farming inputs are being used in the right quantities so that the marginal value products of the different inputs are in proportion to their prices and that the marginal value product of each input is approximately equal to the cost of the input at the margin.[4] If this were not the case, farmers would be able to increase output by purchasing more of one input at the expense of another, or by increasing purchases of one or more inputs.

One way to test this is to try to establish production functions based on (typically) cross-section data.[5] A production function shows in the form of an equation how the quantity of output is related to the combined quantities of inputs and it may be used to show how output will change as the quantity of one (or all) input(s) are varied. If the price of the input and the price of the product are known, it is possible to calculate whether the cost of an additional unit of an input is approximately equal to the increase in the value of output that it brings about or, in cases where complementarity is involved, whether a combination of inputs would have the same result. Several studies have seemed to show that this is indeed the case, indicating that further applications would not be worthwhile, but some doubts have been voiced.

J. M. Wolgin has suggested on the basis of an econometric analysis that farmers may be averse to taking risks.[6] Thus, even if increasing an input or inputs would increase output profitably, taking the good years with the bad, but also allowing for the possibility that in any year the harvest might fail because of climatic or other conditions, then farmers may be reluctant to increase their use of inputs for fear of having a bad year and failing to recoup the additional expenditure involved. His analysis seems to suggest that insufficient amounts of inputs are used so that the marginal net value product tends to be in excess of the cost of the inputs, implying that more of them should be employed. Such econometric analyses are far from conclusive and give only part of the story. Farmers living in small communities might be expected, as Schultz maintained, to learn from what they and their neighbours have experienced over generations; but not all farmers are good farmers. There is almost certainly room to improve the performance of some farmers and many factors other than risk govern their use of inputs.[7]

Other aspects affecting output per acre of land also require consideration. Small farmers find it difficult to get the resources they need to improve their farming practices, sometimes for lack of credit and at other times because their scale of operation is too small to justify acquiring some capital asset with an element of indivisibility. Here large farms are at an advantage. In West Pakistan in the 1960s there was a large increase in the number of tubewells installed for irrigation. Most of these wells were installed by cultivators with 25 acres or more who had sufficient land to justify the installation of a small well and the ability to sell any surplus of water to other farmers in the neighbourhood.[8] With different factors working in different directions, it is scarcely surprising that evidence collected in the field of the relation between size of holdings and yields is often contradictory.

It is not much easier to generalise about the readiness of small or large farmers to innovate. Sometimes the initiative may come entirely from outside farming. Thus in the case of the tubewells referred to above, perhaps 20 per cent of those in the Gujranwala area were provided by town investors who had little or no land. While large farmers may be in a better position to innovate than small farmers, they may not be under the same pressures to do so or they may not have an innovative turn of mind. A detailed study of the Noakhali District (in Bangladesh) by Aksel de Lasson examines the many factors that might affect leadership or contribute towards tardiness in making innovations.[9] The innovators seemed to be those who were short of land because of their small holding but with access to water for irrigation–so necessary for the adoption of improved systems of cultivation. It was also evident that the innovators were active members of organisations and had a positive attitude to modernisation.

It is not disputed that the size of farming operations is a factor affecting their performance, but it is evident that the size and form of agricultural operations most conducive to efficiency are highly dependent on circumstances. It may also be added that if initially there is some virtue in smallness, the units of operation in advanced countries tend to be large in acres and small in men. This tendency already seems to be in evidence in the Punjab in Pakistan where small farms (1-5 acres) and large farms (50 acres) have higher output per acre, reflecting greater use of inputs in both cases.[10]

If, to take another country, attention is centred on the Sudan it is evident that very different considerations affect the efficiency with which land is utilised. Size of landholding is not an issue in the same way as it is in Bangladesh because there are reserves of uncultivated land which could be used to feed a much larger population. Away from the areas irrigated by the Niles, shifting cultivation is the rule with the land being cleared by the men and cultivated by the women. There is thus no tenant-owner relationship involved.

Traditional agriculture in the Sudan is not an efficient or very productive form of farming in terms of per acre yield and it is supplemented by other systems. There are, for example, some large-scale operations in which a thousand or more acres may be farmed using tractors, either by a private operator or a government corporation. Of even greater interest is the organisation of irrigated cultivation in the area known as the Gezira, which became possible when the Sennar Dam across the Blue Nile was completed in 1925 to provide the water need. The initial purpose of the development was to grow cotton for the Lancashire market; subsequently the irrigated area was enlarged and other crops were added. The scheme is under national control and run by the Sudan Gezira Board, which, including other areas, is responsible for over 2 million acres. Still other irrigated areas bring the total irrigated area under corporate control to about 4 million acres.

It might have been expected that these very large irrigated areas would have been operated as state farms with labourers employed by controlling bodies. In fact this is not what has happened. The scheme adopted by the Gezira Board has served as a model for a new type of agricultural organisation, a tripartite arrangement between the government, the Board and tenant farmers of the Board. For the main crop, cotton, the Board decides how much acreage to cultivate, manages the planting programmes for the tenants, specifying when to sow, when to fertilise, etc. It provides many services such as irrigation, ploughing, spraying, part of the cost of labour, and ginning and marketing of the cotton crop. The tenant supplies his own labour, as well as hiring additional labour where necessary, and arranges for the marketing of other crops that he may choose to grow. A joint financial account, for the cotton crop only, is established, out of which the Gezira Board and the government take their share, with the tenant getting roughly half. The rather arbitrary division of costs and returns between the tenants and the Board might not seem to be ideally adjusted to the most efficient use of resources relative to the returns from them. Nevertheless, this may have been outweighed by improvements in cultivation. Yields rose in the past, although not to the levels attained in other cotton-growing countries. In recent years there has been some setback to yields partly as a result of less stringent supervision.

Efficiency is only one aspect of the operation of such schemes. The tenants are able to earn rather high incomes compared with other forms of cultivation in the Sudan, as might be expected to occur with irrigated agriculture. In effect the Gezira tenant is a rather superior type of farmer benefiting from being able to exploit a productive facility in limited supply. A traditional farmer in the western part of the country cannot aspire–other than in very exceptional cases–to be taken into the ranks of those occupying the land controlled by the Gezira Board. His option for participation is limited to working on the Gezira land as a migrant worker, mainly during the picking season, which helps him; but the experience also clearly demonstrates to him the extent of relative deprivation that he suffers by comparison with his more fortunate compatriots.

Nevertheless, the system of farming adopted in Gezira-type

schemes has a great deal to commend it. It can be conducive, and can be made more so, to efficient farming, with the opportunity of taking advantage of modern plant strains and cultivating them in a way that makes the best use of water and modern technology. At the same time, some of the character of individual farming is preserved. Markets are also organised by the Board so that the tenant farmer is relieved of this responsibility, although he is dependent on the good judgement of the Board in marketing at the right time and right price in the face of a fluctuating market. In principle, the Board ought to be able to do this more efficiently than individual tenants with small crops to market and little knowledge of marketing conditions.

We turn now to another aspect of the effect of landholding systems on farming efficiency and equity as illustrated from the Sudan. This concerns the herding and ownership of cattle and shows how the absence of property rights in land can give rise to inefficient husbandry. Land in the Sudan is not generally owned by individuals; it is in effect free for all with consequences that might be expected. In much of the Sudan the grass is sparse and the rainfall uncertain. The cattle have to be moved to where food and water are available and this involves treks over great distances. There are many competing cattle owners and so there is no incentive for any of them to consider how the total grazing area of the Sudan should be exploited or protected in the interest of getting the best overall results. Moreover, cattle in the Sudan are regarded as a store of wealth as well as a means to obtain a livelihood. One consequence of these complex factors is that the number of cattle tends to exceed the optimal number that should be kept in Sudanese conditions. This is most noticeable at water places, where every blade of grass may have been consumed for some considerable distance around; one result of this is that a cultivable area is in danger of returning to permanent sand and desert.

Finally, we comment on some aspects of landownership in Mozambique. It will be recalled that when Mozambique gained her independence, the Portuguese settlers left and the large farms they operated were taken over by the state. This has encouraged a two-pronged drive towards agricultural growth. The first centres on the operation of state farms of spectacular size. Large farms, when land is in sufficient supply, do offer some advantages: opportunities to exploit the most efficient methods of farming, the productive use of machinery and the development of efficient marketing arrangements, including the possibility of arranging long-term contracts. Nevertheless, areas of this size present considerable management problems. The gradual build-up over decades of the Gezira Board's operations made it possible to recruit and train managers and to develop management systems tested by experience. Attempting to run very large farms without the opportunity to learn gradually clearly presents considerable problems. The utmost dedication on the part of officials is required, as well as training schemes for managers, if state farms are to function successfully in Mozambique.

The second prong of the programmes for modernising agriculture in Mozambique was aimed at improving the performance of traditional agriculture through cooperatives, often operated as a sideline to the cultivation of private plots by members of the cooperative. The areas operated by cooperatives were intended to be large enough for some economies of scale to become evident in time, including the wider use of the skills of gifted farmers exercising their influence over the whole of the cooperatives' operations rather than only over the small plots that they would be able to farm individually. It was also planned to aid the cooperatives with the supply of seeds, fertilisers and pesticides, as well as machinery. In other respects, it was hoped that the expertise that might be displayed in the state farms would rub off on to co-operatively organised farmers. Cooperatives always seem attractive in principle as organisational forms, but the reality often belies the good results that are expected from them. Mozambique's present situation has been too precarious to allow the cooperative movement to gain momentum and its future must be regarded as uncertain.

A Nordic view of the organisation of agricultural production in the developing countries of Southern Africa goes against private commercial estates or state farms as institutions of agricultural and rural development because at this point these forms of organisation are thought to be inefficient in terms of output growth and to endanger equity while ignoring the mass of rural dwellers.[11] Here the role of agriculture is being placed in a wider setting than that of production alone, although emphasis is placed on providing the means to increase output and market it, and to improve the relevance of agricultural research and training. A realistic observation is the need to concentrate on the farming activities of women who are the major cultivators in many African countries but who tend to be disregarded in schemes to improve agricultural productivity.

The practical reality is that in most countries family farms are likely to constitute the major source of food and employment in rural areas, where most people live. At present, productivity is too low to provide an acceptable standard of living and meet the needs of a developing country for agricultural products as described above. Nevertheless, in most countries the means of support and communication needed to help family farmers have yet to be found and put into operation.

The right to own or cultivate land may be established by custom, conquest or law, but it is not necessarily settled for all time. Demands for reform of landownership are always likely to occur when land or the better land is scarce. The case may be made either in terms of equity or efficiency, with equity generally being uppermost in the minds of the protagonists. As we have seen, greater equality in the distribution of land is not necessarily conducive to efficiency. In countries like Bangladesh, land reform is not likely to get very far. Efforts to reduce the holdings of the wealthier landlords are likely to be countered by putting the land out to relatives; efforts to move towards greater equity in holdings might lead to areas too small to yield a living; the process of land reform is exceedingly complicated and long drawn out, with the result that reform, even if it were accomplished, might soon be put into reverse as holdings were once again acquired by the wealthy. If land reform could be effected it might ultimately increase production but there would inevitably be some serious dislocation as land changed hands.

There are, however, circumstances in which land reform can be beneficial; that of South Korea is often cited as an example. Here, in 1953 at the end of the Korean war, steps were initiated to reduce the high concentration of landownership with the intention of giving the many small tenants ownership of land and freeing them from the payment of extortionate rents. After reform, only 7 per cent of the farm households remained exclusively as tenants. Subsequent progress was impressive. The yield of paddy increased from the already high level of 3,340 kilograms per hectare in 1952-56 to 4,700 kilograms in 1974, with the adoption of new varieties. Between 1963 and 1975 the income of rural households increased by 50 per cent. Since landlords were not generously compensated for the expropriation of their land the result was a substantial redistribution of assets and income.[12]

The above cannot do more than illustrate some of the relationships that emerge from a consideration of landholdings and farming efficiency. In many countries, and particularly in the most highly populated, low-income countries, typical landholdings are small. This may still be the case where land is more plentiful because of lack of means to cultivate large areas or to market the output from them. For China, it has been commented, the pressure on the land is such that farming has become an extended form of gardening and the intensive application of labour has become, in an exaggerated yet graphic illustration, equivalent to manicuring the lawn with a pair of scissors. Where the pressure on land is great and holdings small, improving agricultural output involves the difficult task of attempting to reach and influence the performance of a multitude of individual farmers. The alternative of creating larger farming units is unlikely to be attempted, in most cases, because of the social disruption involved and perhaps uncertainties about how larger units could be managed.

In the Sudan and Mozambique, as we have seen, different forms of landownership are much in evidence and related to the amount of land these countries have and to their social and political structures and stage of development. Colonial influence in Africa, as well as in other parts of the world, was instrumental in building up large holdings of land. The efficiency with which these were managed varied. Farming practices were highly developed in the Gezira, as they were in parts of Kenya and Zimbabwe, less so in Mozambique. The traditional agriculture, lying alongside the large tracts of colonial-owned land, although efficient in the use of its own technology, could not emulate the results that could be obtained by modern technology. Moreover, as the population grew, many traditional farming areas became heavily overpopulated. Great inequality of income and wealth emerged from such different methods of cultivation, which reinforced the enormous initial advantage of having gained possession and access to large tracts of fertile land. There was a dual economy in agriculture, the one rich, highly productive, relatively capital-intensive, using hired labour; the other poor, relatively unproductive, labour-intensive and self-sufficient. The inequalities that arose in arable farming were as evident in cattle rearing for which the use of land was of overriding importance.

In plantation agriculture the picture was different in that operations were labour-intensive, as in the tea gardens of Bangladesh. Here access to markets on the part of expatriates and their ability to build up the labour force they required from within or without the country were all-important. Plentiful supplies of land make all the difference to the organisation of agricultural production and provide leeway for the adoption of different systems of farming, for extensive rather than intensive farming, and for higher rewards for those engaged in farming operations.

Opportunities to increase agricultural output

There is a great gap between what is being accomplished by traditional agriculture and what the people and the land they farm ought to be capable of producing. Agricultural conditions differ greatly from area to area and may often account for differences in yields, but certainly not for all the differences that are observed. The yield of rice in the developing world in the years 1977-9 was less than half of that of the developed world; the yield in Bangladesh was only one-third that of Japan and an even smaller proportion of that of South Korea. For China the comparison comes out better; nevertheless, the average yield falls far short of that of the best producers. For wheat the comparisons are generally more favourable, but even here the highest yields produced in the Netherlands and the United Kingdom, with the aid of high inputs, are on average three to four times those obtained in the developing world.

The very highest yields reflect radical changes that have taken place in the cultivation of major foodgrains in the postwar period. The yield of rice grown in Japan today is about 80 per cent greater than it was in the mid-1930s; yields in China are about 50 per cent greater, and the same is roughly true for the world as a whole. In the case of wheat the story is similar. For the world as a whole yields are now about 80 per cent greater than they were before the war; in Mexico, the home of the modern wheat technology, yields are three to four times as great. In the United Kingdom, where yields were already high before the war, they have roughly doubled by now.

Yields in developing countries also can be greatly increased and the cost of doing so is frequently small in relation to the

Table 5.1 Some significant innovations in crop
production and dates of widespread use

Chlorinated hydrocarbons for insect control	1945
Minimum tillage	1945
Foliar feeding	1945
Direct applications of anhydrous ammonia	1947
Chemical weed control	1951
Systematic biocides	1953
Hybrid sorghum	1957
Dwarf wheat	1962
Dwarf rice	1965
Opaque 2 maize (high lysine)	1965
Hybrid barley	1969
Hybrid cotton	1970

Source: Andrew Pearse, *Seeds of Plenty, Seeds of Want,* Oxford,
Clarendon Press, 1980, p. 8.

increase in output that can be brought about. Some ways in which
this can be done are discussed below.

New strains and other innovations
One of the most significant innovations in plant breeding was the
development of hybrid maize in 1933. Table 5.1 brings together
some of the major technological developments that have greatly
changed production in the postwar period. Although the table
stops at 1970, agricultural innovation continues: for example, the
development of triticale, a cross between wheat and rye, capable
of producing high yields on acid soils short of phosphorus, such
as those of East Africa, and attempts to develop plants capable of
fixing nitrogen themselves.

The new varieties of grains were man-made and were designed
to improve the response to nutrients and to concentrate it in the
production of the grain itself, rather than in the structure of the
plant. One consequence was that the plants needed to be shorter
in order to achieve the robust quality necessary to support the
weight of the grain and to prevent them from lodging in the
ground if they were roughly treated by wind or reaper. By this
means greater amounts of fertiliser could be given without running the risk of loss that results with traditional varieties. Another
characteristic of the new grains was that they had more grain-
bearing stems. The greater leaf surface that resulted increased

exposure to light and facilitated photosynthesis, involving a much larger take-up of fertiliser. The photosensitivity of the plant also received attention in relation to its growing cycle and its synchronisation with seasonal weather conditions. With further technological advance in the control of the plant's photosensitivity, multiple cropping may be possible, although this may increase the risk of poor yields if the weather turns out to be abnormal.

The new varieties of plant often require different and more complicated systems of cultivation. Weeding, watering, fertilising, transplanting and plant spacing have to be carried out in a stipulated manner, which is more demanding of accuracy and labour than traditional methods of cultivation. The inputs required for cultivation are often complementary, so that the absence or inadequate representation of one or another of them can have disproportionate results. Hybrid varieties are not self-germinating, so that fresh seed has to be provided for each crop.

The performance of new varieties of plants depends on the conditions in which they are grown. It is often necessary to modify new strains if they are to do well in different environments, and sometimes entirely different plants may have to be developed because those that do well elsewhere fail in different growing conditions. Since improved seeds may fail after a time, because of disease or pests, it is also necessary to develop new resistant varieties. Needless to say, there is still great scope for improvement.

Some of the most important developments in the breeding of different strains of foodgrains have resulted from the creation of international research centres, including the International Maize and Wheat Improvement Centre (CIMMYT) established in Mexico and the International Rice Research Institute (IRRI) in the Philippines. The strains that they have developed have had far-reaching effects on many countries and Bangladesh has benefited from several new strains of rice, initially the strains with the code numbers IR 8 and IR 20. In the Indian sub-continent the planting of new varieties is evident in the changing landscape.

International research stations, however successful, do not obviate the need for national research establishments because certain varieties of plants have to be adapted to local conditions. It may be that, in the future, national research stations should be established in developing countries, rather than relying on a handful of particularly well-endowed institutions in restricted locations. They might prove cheaper to run, and the fact that the benefits of the introduction of new strains tend to accrue first to the areas in which they are developed is a further argument for this. It is not always possible, however, either to provide the highly skilled scientists and special facilities needed to engineer innovations requiring special techniques, or to ensure that their research is directed to grass-roots needs. As is often the case, the temptation is to engage in fundamental research rather than to concentrate on the immediate needs of farmers to improve their performance. What contribution, it may be asked, has the Agricultural University at Mymensingh made to the improvement of agricultural performance in Bangladesh?

Adoption of innovations

It would be wrong to think that just because high-yielding strains have been created they would be instantaneously adopted. They are not suitable for all locations; small farmers (as we have seen) may fight shy of the risks involved; the complementary inputs needed may not be readily available; too few experts may be available to introduce new practices or man experimental farms. Moreover, where women carry out farming operations, extension work and workers may be inadequately orientated to the needs of women cultivators.

In developed countries, large firms with their own research departments introduce new strains of plants, manufacture fertilisers and provide the technical advice needed. In the less-developed countries, the picture is quite different and the market forces facilitating the acceptance of new methods of cultivation are often totally absent. Ignorance, poor infrastructure, bad communications, small scale of operation and other factors may all intervene to prevent any spontaneous movement to the adoption of improved practices.

Where it is unlikely that private enterprise can be relied upon to bring about changes in agricultural techniques, government policies may be devised to accelerate the process. In Bangladesh, as in many other developing countries, the government has tended to take a leading role in trying to promote the use of new technologies, but for the most part with only moderate success, partly because the introduction of new methods requires a package of measures if it is to succeed. These include, amongst others, provision of inputs, price support and measures to promote rural development.

The inputs needed are supplies of seeds, fertilisers, pesticides and water. Of these the provision of water is likely to be the most costly and difficult to organise. In terms of the increase in output they can engender, the costs of seeds, fertilisers and pesticides may be quite small; nevertheless, they may lean quite heavily on a balance of payments that is precarious. Bangladesh, for example, is fortunate that it has supplies of natural gas that can be converted into urea, thus providing the nitrogenous fertiliser needed for efficient cultivation. Manufacture, however, is costly, because a large amount of capital has to be invested in the plant needed for conversion of the gas. Moreover, means have to be found to distribute fertiliser and other inputs and to arrange credit for their purchase.

The cost of securing supplies of water for irrigation in Bangladesh during the dry season varies according to the source of water. If surface water is readily available the cost may be quite small, but most such opportunities have been exploited, and so tubewells, an expensive operation, need to be drilled. As tubewells often have to be sunk to considerable depths and the water has to be pumped out, economy dictates that they should be used over as large a command area as possible so that costs may be spread along with the water. This requires considerable organisation: irrigation channels have to be dug and land surrendered for the purpose, the flow of water has to be regulated between the plots, the tubewell has to be kept in repair and its pumping elements periodically overhauled, and above all, costs have to be met and apportioned. When perhaps fifty farmers might be involved in this process there is plenty of opportunity for dispute, neglect and consequent inefficiency. We discussed above how it was possible to overcome these problems in West Pakistan. Another standard answer is to form a cooperative, but cooperatives are often badly run and may favour the larger farmers at the expense of smaller farmers.

It is sensible to exploit the easy and relatively less costly means of raising output first, such as using surface water and small and medium-size tubewells. However, in the case of Bangladesh, they will not be enough to feed a growing population adequately and further, progressively more expensive, methods of increasing production will have to be used. These involve attempts to regulate flooding, to improve drainage and to change the topography of the land. With a reasonable amount of success, the addition of such measures to the basic package of inputs described above might enable output of rice in Bangladesh to be quadrupled within, say, a quarter of a century.

In most other developing countries there is considerable scope to increase agricultural output. In the Gezira, for example, irrigation practices could be greatly improved, and with the construction of the Jonglei Canal to ease the passage of the White Nile through the marshy area of the Sudd, where loss from evaporation is high, more water should be available to extend the present irrigated area both in Northern Sudan and in Egypt. It would also be possible to increase the area devoted to rain-fed agriculture if private operators felt it profitable to do so and could move the produce to market. Improvements in agricultural practices and the introduction of new crops should also be possible. In Mozambique, as we have seen, agricultural output could be greatly increased. In Botswana, to take another example, the opportunities to increase agricultural output are much less, but here again irrigation in the form of the Malapo system, in which bunds or areas of land enclosed by an earth wall are constructed to retain flood waters emanating from the Okavango Delta, offers the possibility of extending traditional methods of irrigation used in the delta.[13] Other improvements in techniques are possible but are limited by the scarcity and irregularity of rainfall. Improvements in cattle management also provide opportunities for an increase in output.

Agricultural price policy
In developed countries supply seems to be very responsive to increases in government guaranteed prices and this has been advocated as a way to increase output in developing countries, too. However, it cannot be presumed that an increase in price will invariably result in an increase in marketed output. Some supply curves may be backward-sloping so that an increase in prices might not have favourable effects.[14] In Mozambique, for example, the availability of consumption goods is so limited that there is little incentive for farmers to increase output beyond their own consumption needs. While economic studies seem to have shown that the supply response to an increase in price for individual crops is to increase output, this does not necessarily mean that a general rise in agricultural prices will lead to any considerable increase in output.[15] In Bangladesh, for instance, it seems that an

increase in the price of rice relative to that of jute has the effect of increasing the acreage put down to rice and thus in its supply. However, since the cultivable area is almost fully utilised, total output of all crops may not expand because the amount of land committed to crops other than rice is liable to be reduced. Where the constraint of land shortage does not operate, support for agricultural prices is conditional on the government having the money to boost market prices, which is often not the case. Furthermore, if the government has money to spend, it may, as in the case of Bangladesh, be more inclined to use it to subsidise urban consumers in the interest of getting political support. Thus price support may not be a feasible action. In some cases, for example, in the Sudan, the profitability of agriculture may be reduced by the imposition of export taxes. Again, the government's need for revenue has to be weighed against the need to increase agricultural output for export.

The above are only some of the reasons why price support for agriculture has not been vigorously pursued in developing countries. Nevertheless, in conditions of food shortage plus a recognition of the impediment that a slow growth of agricultural output imposes on development, there is a growing conviction that greater incentives for agricultural production may be a necessary condition for raising output. So far as prices are concerned, such incentives may take the form of a shift in the terms of trade between agriculture and other sectors of the economy, including import and export sectors. Overvalued exchange rates tend to encourage the import of agricultural products and make the export market for them less profitable. This in turn affects the balance of payments and if it leads to severe restrictions on imports, as happened in Tanzania in the 1970s, the economy may suffer severely. A similar effect may be precipitated if agricultural prices are supported in such a way as to place prices of export crops at too low a level compared to output for domestic consumption. In this case exports will be discouraged as cultivation shifts to more profitable opportunities.

Still another aspect of the same syndrome may be marketing inefficiencies, perhaps on the part of state marketing boards. These have the effect of reducing farm gate prices and thus discourage production. This emphasises the importance of looking at the totality of the package that may stimulate agricultural output. If costs can be reduced using new methods of cultivation, if marketing and access to markets can be improved, and prices maintained at profitable levels with the opportunity to purchase consumer goods, there is a much greater chance of stimulating output than if any of these measures are taken individually.

Integrated rural development

We have just stressed the need to consider a package of measures directed at increasing agricultural output. But does the matter end here? Ought not improvements in agriculture to be seen as one of many aspects of rural development which ideally would combine to form an integrated programme for development? The purpose of an integrated programme might be simply to ensure that improvements are not impeded because some important complementary activities are missing. However, it may go much further than this and take as its primary objective the awakening of a rural consciousness of the need to progress and the importance of generating community action to improve the way of life. In practice, both these aspects of rural development have to be considered, but the relative importance accorded to them in the minds of those responsible for devising rural development programmes may have a profound effect on the approaches advocated. B. Lecomte, for example, with a wealth of experience of rural development activities, is strongly of the opinion that it is very hard, if not impossible, to achieve rural development of a lasting and significant kind through government or other outside initiatives and actions or projects and programmes designed to improve productivities or living conditions.[16] The starting-point for rural development in his view lies with the people themselves and it is not until they themselves establish their 'felt' needs, and achieve the leadership and organisation necessary to go at least some way to meeting them, that they can be assisted by outside complementary activity.

Others, perhaps on less sure ground, have felt that rural development could not be left until leadership emerged in the locality and that some form of outside prompting, as a very minimum, was necessary to set things in train. This is the approach that has been attempted in Bangladesh, not, it may be said, with conspicuous success. The approach of Bangladesh to rural development is particularly associated with the work of the Comilla Academy for Rural Development and its first director, Akhtar Hameed Khan. In this approach, cooperatives were organised to overcome the inertia and isolation of villages. Many of them were agricultural cooperatives, but others were concerned with non-agricultural occupations including cottage industries, women's interests and housing. There was also a youth programme with provision for schools. The agricultural cooperatives were involved in extension work, with a model farmer demonstrating and explaining how agricultural practices could be improved.

In many ways the Comilla model continues to be central to present-day rural development programmes in Bangladesh, but many other complementary development activities are also required. These include the construction of rural roads, large scale irrigation and drainage projects, attempts to improve health care and education, and the construction of living quarters and buildings for civil servants who guide the programmes in the rural communities. Not much of the finance for these activities is raised locally and the main source of support, directly or indirectly, is that of foreign aid, including the food-for-work programme whereby food provided under aid is used to pay casual labour employed in construction, mainly at times when other employment is more than usually difficult to find.

The above might appear to suggest that rural development is highly advanced in Bangladesh but this is not really the case. A great many of the cooperatives function badly although they are still the main hope of organising rural society for collective action, but they cannot undertake many of the complementary activities listed above which often depend on the coordination of the activities of multifarious government and other agencies, which is hard to accomplish. To assist in this, local government institutions need to be built up and perfected. The obstacles to rural development are great: employment opportunities are very hard to create; money for the maintenance of structures is hard to come by and new roads and buildings may not be kept in adequate repair; resources for other purposes, health, education and training, including trained manpower, likewise are totally insufficient.

An interesting example of self-help is the Harambee movement ('Let's all work together. Get up and go.') in Keyna with emphasis on development projects. The self-help movement in Kenya has a long history with roots in the pre-independence period. Harambee activities include projects carved out by the communities alone, as well as projects with outside and government involvement.

These may include the construction of social infrastructure such as schools and health facilities, and also roads, cattle dips and production activities undertaken by women's groups. In 1981, these local initiatives were estimated to cover 30 per cent of total rural development investment.[17] The effects in providing primary and secondary education are noteworthy, with all of the capital costs of primary education being met through Harambee efforts. Contributions may be made in cash or kind. This has been so successful that the government appears to be looking at it as a source of revenue. Thus in the case of Kenya we see local initiatives at work.

Mozambique might be able to develop similar activity operating through the party system. In principle, leadership can be organised, cadres trained and pressures applied. Some changes in society can be consciously engineered. The communal villages were conceived of as political and social units with an autonomous administrative and political entity, responsible for justice, security, finance, production and basic services. Production was to be organised by cooperative activity closely linked through its managing committee with the governing body of the village, so ensuring some overlap in the direction of affairs. Again, as in Bangladesh, cooperatives were to extend beyond cultivation: fishing, industrial activities, handicrafts, housing, consumers and service cooperatives could be similarly organised.

Finally, we stress again that the purpose of integrated rural development is to secure mutually reinforcing activities, in this respect being akin to the 'big push'.

FROM AGRICULTURE TO INDUSTRY

In a much quoted article, Sir Arthur Lewis explained how, as development proceeded, labour would move from agriculture to industry.[18] His model assumed that there was surplus labour in the countryside which could be dispensed with without affecting agricultural production because there was both open and concealed unemployment. Industry would be able to take up initially small, but gradually increasing amounts of labour as it accumulated capital with which to provide employment. Eventually, it was supposed, all the labour not required in agriculture would be absorbed into industry (and increasingly in service employment), and the proportion of the population living and working in the countryside would be considerably reduced.

Other authors have elaborated the model and raised a number of questions about it. Some of the underlying considerations can be exposed, following Ashok Mathur, by describing how the output of a family farm of given size would increase as more labour is employed with the effect of increasing the man-land ratio.[19]

At first the marginal product is assumed to increase as more labour is used, but this movement is gradually reversed and decline sets in. As the man-land ratio rises, a point will be reached where the marginal product of labour is just equal to the subsistence wage which may be assumed either to be conventionally determined or, alternatively, to be just enough to meet minimum dietary requirements. At this point landlords would certainly not wish to hire any additional labour because they would have to pay more in wages than they would get in increased product, and in fact they might stop doing so at an earlier point, since they are—in a different degree—adverse to risk.

Families farming their land with their own labour would not necessarily limit the labour they use to the amount for which the marginal product is equal to the subsistence wage. If outside employment were difficult or impossible to get, it would pay to increase the amount of labour employed until the man-land ratio was such that the marginal product became zero, at which point no addition to the labour input would increase output any further. It might be, however, that with outside employment hard to get, the number of family workers attached to the farm would exceed the numbers for which the marginal product was zero. In this case the work might be divided out with each member doing less than he would be prepared to do if labour were scarce. This is possible because as long as the man-land ratio does not exceed that at which the average product equals the subsistence wage, all can live off the produce of the farm. Beyond this point, any additional labour could not be fed and it would be essential to find some supplementary employment elsewhere.

In the terms of this scheme we can classify the amount of labour that might be available for non-farm purposes in three ways. First, any labour used in excess of that giving a marginal product equal to the subsistence wage can be regarded as underemployed in the sense that, if employment were available, it could earn more elsewhere; second, any labour in excess of that for which the marginal product is zero, while still remaining on the farm and sharing work, is effectivelly totally unproductively employed; while, third, if the labour available is so great that output is insufficient to provide a subsistence wage, there is open unemployment and presumably an active search for work elsewhere.

Ashok Mathur used his model to estimate how much disguised unemployment there was in West Bengal (contiguous with East Bengal, now Bangladesh) and the Punjab in the 1950s. Data of man-land ratios was available for farms in these areas and there was also information showing at what man-land ratios labour was 'hired in' and 'hired out'. The man-land ratio at which labour ceased to be hired by commercial farms indicated where output per man was equal to the subsistence wage; the man-land ratio at which family labour sought employment elsewhere indicated the beginning of open employment. Between these two land ratios there was excess labour operating in a state of disguised un-employment and this could be worked out. In so far as some of the workers within this category of disguised unemployment do produce some output, it might seem that the extent of disguised unemployment is exaggerated to some degree. Clearly a great deal of judgement is called for in carrying out such calculations based on uncertain figures. They did suggest, however, that the extent of disguised unemployment appeared to amount to almost one-third of the labour force in the case of West Bengal, but only about one-twentieth in the Punjab.

Most visitors to countries in the Indian sub-continent would have little doubt about the existence of disguised and open unemployment in agriculture and elsewhere, but some research has suggested, nevertheless, that there may not be a great deal of agricultural labour that would readily be available for employ-ment elsewhere. A study by Iqbal Ahmed throws further light on the nature of disguised unemployment and the availability of labour for work.[20] He examined the Shahbazpur Union in the Brahmanbaria subdivision of the Comilla district by means of a carefully administered questionnaire. The cultivators of plots of land were asked how many man-days of labour had been used for various types of cultivating activities. This enabled a picture of manpower requirements to be built up.

The next step in the investigation was to establish the amount of labour actually available. Not all the inhabitants of the union could be considered as available for employment. Those with large holdings of land or other sources of work or income and those with education did not wish to accept any kind of work because of the class structure and social and economic conditions. In modern terminology they might be regarded as voluntarily unemployed. There was also a class of voluntary underemployed. For them working on their own farms was respectable but working on other people's land was simply not done, unless it was in the form of mutual cooperation with no payment involved, each helping the other as the need arose. Combining the concepts of voluntary unemployment, voluntary underemployment and involuntary unemployment gave total unemployment.

With the aid of the survey and the number of days that were to be regarded as available for work per year it was possible to establish quantitative measures of unemployment following the definitions given above. If it is assumed that there are 275 working days in the year, voluntary unemployment came to 8 per cent, voluntary underemployment to 26 per cent, and involuntary unemployment to 8 per cent. The rate of involuntary unemployment appears to be remarkably low. Even on the assumption that 365 days would be worked per year, the extent of surplus labour comes to only some 13 per cent.

The above are ratios of annual aggregates. Another factor affecting manpower requirements in agriculture, and so the extent of unutilised labour, is that the pattern of labour employment for most crops is highly seasonal depending on the times of sowing, weeding and harvesting. Using the crop calendar and the number of man-days needed for different operations it is possible to build up a picture of monthly employment requirements. This is depicted in Table 5.2 for 147 farms in Dinajpur for major crops cultivated in Bangladesh. The table shows the amount of labour needed to cultivate the various crops of rice, jute, tobacco, pulses, etc, on plausible assumptions. In the case of Dinajpur it was estimated that 193 labourers were available. It was also assumed that care of livestock would require the equivalent of 29, leaving the equivalent of 164 for cultivation of crops. Comparing this total with monthly requirements it may be seen that in many months the available labour is considerably in excess of that required, most notably in September and October where there seems to be no cultivation work to do in Dinajpur. In the peak month of March, however, it appears that the amount of labour available is barely sufficient for requirements.

Table 5.2 Number of man-months of labour required for crop cultivation in Dinajpur, 1969-70

J	F	M	A	M	J	Jy	A	S	O	N	D
14	89	166	151	84	66	139	139	0	0	99	99

Source: Taken from M. Muqtada, 'The Seed-Fertilizer Technology and Surplus Labour in Bangladesh Agriculture', *Bangladesh Development Studies*, Vol. 3 (1975), No. 4, p. 420.

Such calculations can give very different impressions of the amount of labour that is available. Unemployment, whether open or disguised, varies from nil in March to 78 per cent in January and 85 per cent in September/October. The latter figures, on the assumptions made, almost certainly exaggerate the degree of unemployment, since the 'off months' will be used to carry out other types of work, such as repairing the house, which must be done regularly given the flimsy nature of a bamboo construction.

It is evident that if labour is to be more fully utilised, either a reverse seasonal pattern of employment will have to be devised or the seasonal labour requirements of the agricultural rotation modified in some way, perhaps by adopting different crop rotations or partial mechanisation. Nevertheless, the opportunity to divert labour from agriculture to other occupations may be much less than is generally supposed, given the low rate of agricultural productivity.

In the light of the above discussion it can be seen why the Lewis model of the transfer of labour from agriculture to industry requires qualification and modification. Thus Ranis and Fei have suggested that it is useful to distinguish stages in the transfer of labour to industry.[21] The first stage corresponds to that postulated by Lewis with surplus labour gradually being transferred to industry; as all surplus labour is eliminated, the second stage commences with the marginal product of labour rising towards the subsistence wage; when the subsistence wage is reached, commercialisation of agriculture may be said to be attained and the second stage accomplished. In the third stage, labour will continue to be transferred to industry, and agricultural wages will rise still further. Labour is now scarce and various consequences will follow. In the first place, labour's share of agricultural output will increase (the marginal product of labour will rise as its quantity diminishes in relation to the limited amount of land) and landlords' returns will fall. Thus there will be less to invest in industry, or elsewhere. Furthermore, so long as technology remains the same, the output of food will fall and so less will be available in total. It is sometimes argued that this may take place quite early in the transfer of labour depending on how leisure is regarded. It makes some difference as to whether accessible land is scarce or plentiful. If land is plentiful so that all who wish have some to farm, loss of labour is likely to lead to reduced output and to higher prices and rewards to labour, unless the reduction in production is replaced by imports. Where land is scarce it is less certain that output will fall as workers transfer to industrial or service employment. As workers leave, the incomes of those left behind will increase and they may decide that they will work for a shorter time or less intensively. This may not happen if they already have more leisure than they know what to do with and are in a state of enforced idleness for lack of land; in these circumstances leisure will be given up as long as any increase in food can be produced. There will also be no reduction in food output if leisure is an inferior good so that although leisure is valued, opportunity to increase income will be taken even if some leisure is sacrificed. Finally, if leisure and increased income are regarded by the farm-worker as perfect substitutes (so that one unit of income is always regarded as equal in subjective satisfaction to a given amount of leisure), the same amount of food will be produced as before.[22]

Clearly, theoretical discussions do not lead us very far. Nevertheless, there may be a danger of a contraction in supplies as workers leave agriculture for industry and other employment. In practice this might be counteracted in several ways. Agricultural prices might increase and production might respond to this; changes in farming practices may be induced or occur spontaneously. In some circumstances (for example in Britain in the nineteenth century) a deliberate decision might be made to replace domestic with imported food.

An improvement in agricultural productivity could have the effect of increasing savings if it increased landlords' returns, or if it increased agricultural wages and part of these were saved. It is likely, of course, that agriculture will increase its own investment, so reducing transfer of savings to industry, but it is uncertain how far this will go. In Bangladesh, for instance, it is thought that landlords may prefer to invest outside agriculture, perhaps to spread their risks. In other cases the transfer of savings from agriculture to industry might be reversed, with industrialists investing in agricultural operations or in the provision of agricultural inputs for industry.

INDUSTRY

As development proceeds it is to be expected that industrial activity will increase. Although this may seem to have occurred spontaneously in the industrialisation of previously low-income countries such as South Korea or Taiwan, this is not entirely the case; in most developing countries government seeks to promote industrial development. It may justify such action on many grounds, for example, by pointing to a shortage of entrepreneurs (as in Pakistan in the 1950s), to difficulties in raising finance, and the reluctance of individuals to take risks. Such arguments may be supplemented with reference to the need to assist infant industries, the exigencies of the balance of payments, movements in the terms of trade, and so on. In short, it may be argued that economic and social considerations require a more rapid development of industry than would be brought about without government assistance. It is quite possible that this will favour industry over other sectors of the economy to the detriment of overall development, but for the moment we shall assume that without active encouragement industrialisation would not proceed fast enough. What, in such a case, might government seek to do in order to promote industrialisation? In the first place, it is likely to consider whether the state should take it upon itself to establish and own industrial enterprises with this and other objectives in mind.

Public or private ownership?

The role of the private and public sectors of the economy in industrial operations is a much debated issue. Some of the arguments for one or the other are rehearsed here. Stalin's Russia would never have contemplated private enterprise as an instrument of economic development. Mozambique's development is also likely to be publicly owned for the most part for similar ideological reasons, although there may be scope for some development in private hands. India's approach might have been to confine industrial development to the public sector, but Nehru's philosophy, as illustrated by the following quotation, won the day:

I have no shadow of doubt, if we say 'lop off the private sector', we cannot replace it adequately. We have not got the resources to replace it, and the result would be that our productive apparatus will suffer. And why should we do it? I don't understand. We have our industries, there is a vast sector, and we have to work it. Let the State go on building up its plants and industries as far as its resources permit. Why should we fritter away our energy in pushing out somebody who is doing it in the private sector?

There is no reason except that the private sector might build up monopoly, might be building economic power to come in the way of our growth. I can understand 'Prevent that, control that, plan for that'; but where there is such a vast field to cover, it is foolish to take charge of the whole field when you are totally incapable of using that huge area yourself. Therefore, you must not only permit the private sector, but, I say, encourage it in its own field.[23]

In Bangladesh the same issues were fought over in the 1970s by the politicians (not to say their would-be counsellors from the donor countries and agencies). It was felt there that, irrespective of the usual Marxist reasons for public sector ownership, there was little alternative to nationalisation of industry; many of the industrial owners had been Pakistanis who fled the country during the war of independence in fear of their lives. Initially, as a practical compromise, it was decided to leave a place for private enterprise in the industrial sector, but only for relatively small-scale operations; in this way, it was thought, the dangers of exploitation of man by man might be avoided. As time has gone on, the original restrictions on the private sector have been modified and it has been allowed much greater scope. The Sudan also seems to have passed through an initial phase of wishing to reserve industrial development for the state, later modifying its approach to enlarge the scope for private enterprise.

In India the state assumed a monopoly not only in atomic energy, arms and the operation of the railways, but also the responsibility for setting up new establishments in iron and steel, shipbuilding, mineral oil, coal, aircraft production and tele-communication equipment. Often, large-scale projects in the industrial sector require foreign assistance in the provision of capital or expertise, and foreign companies may be involved as partners in the development. Without state support it is doubtful if outside interests could be attracted to participate in the planned build-up of the industrial structure; also, government involvement may well be needed to regulate and monitor the operation of companies, particularly those that are foreign-based.

The net effect of these various influences, except where there is total commitment to public ownership, is that a mixed industrial sector emerges, partitioned (but not always neatly) between public and private operation. Many strong beliefs are held about the relative efficiency of the two types of organisation. Protagonists of private industry maintain that public industry is bound to be inefficient and wasteful, subject to political control and bureaucracy and incapable of being commercially minded; moreover, it is liable to be forced to meet various conflicting requirements related to profitability and social objectives. Against these views are those of the protagonists of state endeavours who regard private industry as having no regard for social needs, exploiting the workers and generating acute inequalities in income distribution. An alternative to both these systems of organisation, that of cooperatives, is sometimes thought to blend the best of both worlds, and succeeds if the climate is right. But democratic control of an activity is no guarantee of efficiency and may not ensure that the best selection is made to executive positions. On the advantages and disadvantages of state and private industry it is probably best to keep an open mind and to approach the question in the knowledge that a variety of organisational structures can be made to work well, if the will is there.

If public industry, including public utilities, is to work effectively, the outlook of those engaged in it must approximate more closely to that of private entrepreneurs than to that of civil servants. This is the issue of how nationalised undertakings should be run and the nature of their relationship with government and the civil service of the country. These issues became very apparent in Bangladesh shortly after the nationalised industries were established. Many questions arose: who should be responsible for appointing the chairman and board of directors of a public corporation; how were salaries to be fixed; would the plans of the industry have to be approved by government; should an attempt be made to maximise profits, or should prices be fixed at a level that is expected to give a suitable return on capital, or at a level that would permit ordinary people to avail themselves of the supply of output produced? As a general rule, it might be best to seek, to insulate the nationalised industry from day-to-day interference from government, although it would be unrealistic to think that government can be kept out of an industry's affairs entirely.

The most crucial aspect of administering nationalised industries probably lies in the appointment of managerial personnel. Many criteria can be advanced for judging the quality of appointments to senior managerial positions. A study by Professors Rehman Sobhan and Muzaffar Ahmad of appointments made to nationalised corporations at the time of Bangladesh's independence in the early 1970s concludes that the record of appointment was far from unsatisfactory.[24] It is often maintained that far too few technically qualified people are appointed, both in developed and underdeveloped countries; yet, in Bangladesh, by one criterion, selection had clearly reflected a fair balance between technically qualified management and generalists. There was little evidence of personal patronage. The real problem seemed to be not so much unsuitable appointments, as the constraints imposed on people of established ability in using their talents.

Encouragement and control

If the state wishes to accelerate industrialisation in the private sector of the economy it may consider first what impediments are present. Frequently the infrastructure requires improvement. This ranges from the provision of communications, roads, railways, public utilities, telephone service, etc., to the establishment of industrial areas with such facilities, and it may extend to training workers and establishing free-trade zones. In the case of Pakistan, government's efforts to encourage industrialisation went much further and included setting up industrial establishments in the public sector with the intention of selling them off later to private industrialists so as to provide a nucleus for further expansion. This is an extreme case, but it will be quite usual for government to exercise pressure on industrialists to expand their activities in particular directions and to try to attract industrial investment from other countries.

A common way of increasing the incentive to industrialise is to impose protective tariffs. As was discussed in Chapter 4, there are theoretical objections to the imposition of tariffs designed to protect a particular sector of the economy, and prices and incentives may become severely distorted in the process. Subsidies may also be given, although this is not likely to be greatly favoured because of the cost. A country bent on speedy industrialisation is likely to facilitate the flow of investment funds in this direction, frequently at the expense of other sectors of the economy. Sometimes such funds may be channelled through financial institutions established for the purpose.

If fiscal and monetary policies are functioning well and if the balance of payments is sound, it may be possible to leave private industry to go its own way, responding to market price signals to regulate its output, and acquiring capital resources for expansion from profits, new equity or loans. Many countries are not prepared to do this and seek to control industrial development. This was markedly so in the early years of independent Bangladesh and Mozambique, both of whom were experiencing balance of payments difficulties and both of whom, in different ways, were interventionist in outlook. It was also characteristic of the industrialisation of both East and West Pakistan in the 1960s. At this time imports, at the ruling rate of exchange, were scarce. Rather than raising the price of imported goods by devaluation and leaving market demand to determine what was imported, it was decided to ration imports by an import-licensing system which, of course, had to be operated by civil servants. This limited the amount and types of goods that importers could buy.

In addition to the operation of this system, controls were exercised on industrial investment and, at times, on prices. The result was great inefficiency and waste. This is what Professor Papanek had to say about controls:

The system of detailed direct controls was very costly. It introduced inequalities of its own, created political difficulties, was accompanied by economic inefficiency, and undermined the efficiency of government. The few civil servants who made the crucial decisions could not know enough to avoid serious mistakes, and sometimes could not get their decisions carried out. At the same time, private decision-makers, thanks to the control system, had an incentive to make decisions that were not desirable for the economy ... there is the story of an investor given licences to import most, but not all, of the machinery he required, and who was thus unable to produce anything. The coal mines produced at far less than capacity because they could not get foreign exchange to purchase safety lamps, though the cost of lamps was a tiny fraction of the mines' output. Decisions that should have been made in hours or days sometimes took months if they required governmental approval.[25]

A further effect of the restrictive controls is that the attention of managers shifts from trying to improve the efficiency of production to trying to secure supplies of imported goods and materials that can only be obtained under licence. It also gives rise to the danger of bribery and corruption, which may tend to prolong the retention of such systems even when they can be dispensed with. Matters are made worse when the amount of investment that is licensed and executed results in much more capacity than can be used, given the limited supply of imported inputs needed for production. This, again, was a wasteful characteristic of industrialisation in Pakistan.

In the face of these strictures it may be wondered why controls were adopted in the first place. There were some bad reasons, for example, the irrational continuation of wartime controls already in existence, or the desire of bureaucrats to exercise their own areas of influence and sometimes to gain from 'sweetners'. More positively, controls were seen as a means to exercise social priorities that could not be enforced if most economic decisions rested on market prices. There were also considerations related to the balance of payments and economic fluctuations transmitted from outside. In 1974, Bangladesh's imports increased so much in price that severe cuts had to be made and it was perhaps thought possible to effect these more equitably through controls than through scarcity reflected in high market prices. Again, it is sometimes possible to adapt to shocks more quickly by direct action than market forces. Nevertheless, it has to be recognised that the efficient use of controls requires a high standard of administration in circumstances where this is a scarce factor, so that a controlled economy may work less satisfactorily in most respects than one in which government interference is kept to a minimum

Social consequences

The effects of controls and protection on the functioning of the economy are not the only consequences that require consideration. In Pakistan the two combined together to produce a very considerable concentration of industrial power. The underlying reason for providing incentives for industrial operations was to foster an expansion of the industrial base. In this the measure succeeded, in spite of the inefficiencies described above, and industrial output in Pakistan expanded rapidly. As might be expected, the growth of individual firms varied greatly. This was not just a reflection of their efficiency; growth depended on mobilising support from government, on the ability to raise cash for old and new ventures and to build up diversified, but inter-locking, ventures in which the common factors were finance and family. In the industrial revolution in Europe such enterprise would have been welcomed and the criticism of its social effects would have been subdued, but at that time business owed much less of its success to the facilitations of the state than did the expanding businesses of Pakistan two hundred years later.

It is natural to regard the concentration of power that resulted in Pakistan as being an unexpected as well as an unwelcome con-sequence of development. This view is mistaken. The planners who prepared the second five-year plan for Pakistan were not unaware that the growth of the industrial sector would lead to a concentration of industrial power. This was regarded as a price that would have to be paid in the short run if industrial develop-ment were to take off. The view that, in suitable circumstances, development can best be fostered through industrialisation does not find great favour amongst development economists today, perhaps mistakenly. One of the reasons why it is fashionable to place emphasis on other forms of development is that they are thought less likely to lead to concentration of economic power. Pakistan's experience may seem to provide some justification for this shift in approach. In terms of family ownership, industry became highly concentrated in the 1960s, as a study by Lawrence J. White has demonstrated.[26]

The issue of concentration was raised by Dr Mahbub ul Haq, at that time the chief economist of the Planning Commission, at a management seminar in Karachi in April 1968, where he noted that economic power in Pakistan was concentrated in the hands of twenty families.[27] This was probably no more than the Planning Commission had expected from the development strategies that had been devised in 1960, but the time had now come to start to deal with the inequalities that had emerged from that approach. In fact, the concentration of industry as measured by White appears to have been close to that indicated by Haq. Table 5.3 summarises White's findings and gives a measure of comparison

Table 5.3 Comparison of control of assets of privately
controlled industrial firms, India and Pakistan

	India 1958 %	Pakistan 1968 %
Largest 4 groups	17	16
Largest 13 groups	26	34
Largest 20 groups	28	42

with India, taking figures for India ten years earlier than for
Pakistan, which is not inappropriate, given that the Indian
economy was more advanced than that of Pakistan.

The figures seem to confirm that industry was highly concentrated in Pakistan. Many processes of growth are likely to give rise
to high concentration. In Germany, for instance, the fifty leading
industrial companies accounted for about 40 per cent of the sales
of all industry in 1966. In other countries industrial control also
tends to be highly concentrated. It might be reasonable to expect
that the control of industry in Pakistan would be more concentrated than industry in Western countries, because of the small
size of Pakistan's industrial sector. There is, however, one essential difference; although in industrialised countries small
numbers of companies may carry out a high proportion of industrial production, sharcholding in them tends to be fairly widely
diffused. When families in developing countries are in control of
what, by Western standards, would be regarded as modest enterprises, benefits tend to be much more concentrated in family
hands in terms of jobs, remuneration, dividends and the opportunity to expand activities still further. Power may also extend
well beyond the walls of the enterprises themselves, with representation on the boards of publicly owned companies and close
contacts with officials and politicians.

In a country such as Pakistan it is not easy to redress the
balance of economic inequalities by progressive taxation. This
would matter less if the profits of the enterprises were largely used
to extend industrialisation through reinvestment. It is said of the
great merchants of Glasgow that they lived modestly until they
had built up their capital resources and only then moved to large
houses on Great Western Road. In Pakistan the rewards from the
protected industrial system, however inefficient that system may

have been, were sufficient both to accumulate the capital that was needed and after a short time to permit luxury living.

The reaction of Mr Bhutto's populist government, which came to power in late 1971, to the revelation of the concentration of industrial power was to pass nationalisation measures, covering large-scale industry in all major sectors. At first sight this might have seemed to bring the issue to an end. In fact it did not do so. The nationalisation measures were perhaps less than thorough-going, but the threat of further nationalisation extended also to small industry with the result that businessmen were put in a position of great uncertainty and discouraged from starting new businesses and investing further capital.

Small industry

In developing countries small industry is very important in providing for domestic needs and merits some discussion. It is generally labour-intensive and geared to the use of domestic resources and might seem to provide a basis for growth of industrial output. There is, however, often not the same conviction in developing, as in developed, countries, that small industry can play a leading role in economic development. Administrators regard the effort to encourage small industries as too great and costly in administrative time. The establishment of large industries is in some ways more easily organised and the immediate impact is, of course, much greater than the establishment of a heterogeneous collection of firms, each employing at the most a handful of workers. It is difficult to devise suitable bodies for helping small industrialists and, as we have seen, such bodies may operate very inefficiently. In its relations with small industry, officialdom is at some disadvantage; government has often little expertise and lacks the judgement about budding entrepreneurs and industrialists which local backers, friends and relatives may have. In their turn, small local industrialists may also feel at a disadvantage in dealing with officials, especially if there are government regulations to circumvent or favours to be asked. A local official can be in a strong position to exact his toll.

The view of small industry as an instrument of transformation owes something to historical interpretation of the industrial revolution. Manufacturing is seen as progressing from household handicrafts to small workshops and factories and further to the eventual predominance of large-scale production. Similar observations show an increasing sophistication in industrial products and their method of manufacture. Something of the same progression may be expected to take place in the case of developing countries, but the progression is likely to be mixed and in many respects overlapping. In the early stages developing countries are at a considerable disadvantage in industrialising. Experience is limited and managerial ability scarce. Capital is hard to come by and a plentiful supply of largely unskilled labour is a poor substitute. However, this would seem to point to concentration on industrial activities that are labour-intensive. Limited acquaintance with processes requiring advanced technologies may also seem to point in the same direction, particularly as they require large amounts of capital and skilled labour. Again, while opportunities to export may make it possible to sell goods for which domestic markets may be small, difficulties in organising such production and securing export markets, as well as other inadequacies, may make it desirable to concentrate on meeting domestic needs. In some cases it may be possible to exploit primary products available locally and use them as a basis for manufacture, but experience suggests that such activity may be slow to grow.

The above considerations tend to reinforce each other and suggest a certain pattern of industrialisation. In the early stage, food processing seems to provide a natural avenue for expansion, although not always with the best results. At the height of the sugar crisis in the middle of the 1970s, it seemed to be sensible to involve the Sudan in sugar production with world, as well as domestic, markets in mind; in retrospect the decision to do this seems to have been dubious as difficulties and delays were encountered with the programme. In Pakistan, on the contrary, the availability of locally grown cotton offered opportunities both to provide for domestic needs and to develop an export market, as did the supply of jute grown in Bangladesh. Textile production still tends to be labour-intensive and large amounts of capital are not needed in order to get started and cater for domestic demand. Similarly, as incomes increase, demand becomes apparent for a variety of goods that can be produced locally, such as pots and pans, furniture, cooking stoves, agricultural implements and basic engineering products. Such goods can often be produced by a variety of techniques, and those that minimise the use of capital can be selected. This would attract the approval of those who have emphasised the desirability of providing as much employment as possible and using production techniques appropriate to the resources available in developing countries. We discuss this aspect of industrialisation in greater detail in Chapter 7 in the context of employment creation. Desirable though it is to select appropriate technology and increase employment opportunities, it would be wrong to determine the pattern of industrialisation solely with an eye to these criteria.

Some highly capital-intensive industrial operations are unavoidable. The conversion of natural gas to nitrogenous fer-tiliser in Bangladesh is a case in point. Highly capital-intensive operations may also be defensible if they provide the means to create employment in other sectors with low capital-labour ratios. There may also be something to be said for introducing modern technology if other forms of spin-off are to be expected, such as growing realisation of the potentialities of new techniques.

While trends from the manufacture of simple domestic pro-ducts to sophisticated international ones are observable, there is a good deal of overlapping in practice. Primitive methods for the extraction of oil from seeds in the villages exist side by side with more advanced solvent-extraction methods; the tribal arms factories in the North West Frontier in Pakistan are physically not far removed from ordnance factories capable of producing modern weapons; the children compressing dung into cakes to be burned as fuel in India might be surprised to hear of that country's atomic capabilities. There is no inevitable and systematic pro-gression in moving through stages from one type of production to another, or from domestic to international products. It is the experience of many countries that it may be possible and desir-able to leave out some or all of the intermediate stages of develop-ment experienced in advanced countries.

It is instructive to consider the industrialisation experience of South Korea. The success of that country in industrialising is attributed to a number of special factors, as well as to the govern-ment policies followed. Contrary to Pakistan, rapid industrial expansion in Korea was not associated with excessive protection, although at times exports were quite heavily subsidised. This did not stop a very rapid growth of output, varying between 15 and 30 per cent for a number of years.[28] The expansion, based on light manufacturing initially, was followed by diversification into chemicals, petroleum and basic metal industries. Small and medium industries contributed substantially to exports, helped by measures to improve their financial position. Nevertheless, industry is dominated by large firms employing at least 200 workers which, in 1971, produced over 70 per cent of output and employed more than half of the workers in industry.

The development in Korea of the electronics industry owes a great deal to foreign firms. Not only do these operate on a large scale, producing as subsidiaries of multinationals based in the United States or Japan, they also provide market outlets for domestic firms using their brand names. In the shipbuilding industry Korea has taken advantage of its highly disciplined and relatively cheap domestic labour to sell ships on international markets.

The benefits to be obtained from industrialisation are more clearly seen in an international than a domestic context. In deciding on the balance of emphasis between industrial and other economic activity, one of the considerations may be that very great difficulties are met in trying to increase agricultural output, particularly if, as in Bangladesh, there is little additional land to bring into cultivation and the typical holding of land is small. The alternative of industrial development within domestic markets may also seem unattractive, once the immediate opportunities for import replacement are used up. The amount of capital needed to create new jobs in capital-intensive industry may often be beyond the reach of a developing country, at least if it is planning permanently in terms of home demand alone. Many criticisms are advanced of the role of multinational corporations in development, but in suitable circumstances they can be the means of matching production possibilities to market opportunities through the provision of capital, know-how and market outlets. At one and the same time it is possible to solve many of the bottlenecks that impede development. Such possibilities are not, however, unlimited. Small countries with specially favoured relationships can succeed in pinning their industrial development on world companies with ready markets. Their impact on the markets of other countries, while not unnoticeable, are assimilable. On a larger scale, this process by which developing countries supply manufactures to developed countries in exchange ultimately for supplies of food as well as other types of manufactures, could represent such an inversion of existing comparative cost advantages as to be politically unacceptable in the developed countries. Nevertheless what Korea, Singapore and Hong Kong have been able to demonstrate in a way that has so far escaped Pakistan and Bangladesh is that labour costing one-fifth or even one-tenth that of industrialised countries (even of Japan) offers enormous competitive advantages on world markets, provided, of course, that productivity comes near to Western levels and quality can be maintained.

Lessons and options

Are there other lessons to be learned about industrialisation? Perhaps the first is rather obvious; the industrial structure that is adopted by any country has to be compatible with its political and social structures. It is not to be expected, for instance, that Mozambique will be prepared to see private enterprise in charge of large-scale and basic industries; it is to be expected that other countries will also want to see substantial parts of industry under public control, irrespective of any considerations of efficiency; and there will continue to be bastions of private enterprise in Hong Kong and other places. Where private enterprise is to be relied upon to operate substantial sectors of the industrial sector, it is necessary to set a framework that will enable it to function, while at the same time requiring efficiency in operation. In many cases this is likely to involve close cooperation between the state, private interests and, in some cases, foreign companies.

Primary consideration must be given to the relationship between private enterprise and the state. The preoccupation with incentives in Pakistan went too far. This was one reason why the system of licensing industrial development had to be maintained. If there had been a greater emphasis on properly engineered market forces, the concentration of industry might have been less marked, although it would still have existed. Although the government may play a major role in helping to establish industry and create conditions in which it can be profitable, it does not always benefit sufficiently from this in the form of taxation yields. This applies to international as well as local companies and raises the question as to whether companies should be required at some time in the future to make shares available to local investors on pre-arranged terms, in the interests of spreading both ownership and benefits more widely. This could, of course, include or be confined to the government and in this case could be regarded as a form of taxation. Devices of this kind are more readily resorted to in relation to foreign corporations operating in a developing country. Botswana has concluded agreements with De Beers for the extraction of its diamond deposits, whereby the government is given a share of the equity capital without having to pay for it, and in addition the government may buy additional shares for a consideration. At the same time, profits attributable to the De Beers interest are moderated by the imposition of royalty payments and profit taxes and ultimately by modification of the initial provisions of the agreement. In this way the expertise of the foreign company can be harnessed to the needs of the developing country on a fairer and more equitable basis, which is still consistent with efficiency.

Both large and small industries have a part to play in industrial development; there should be no sense of exclusivity. Each has its own advantages and disadvantages. From the policy point of view, however, there is a danger that investment and other resources may be channelled to large industry to an extent that deprives small industry of the opportunity to develop, and measures may be needed to try to avoid this happening.

FURTHER READING

Agriculture

Philip H. Coombs and Manzoor Ahmed, *Attacking Rural Poverty*, Baltimore, Md., Johns Hopkins Press, 1974.

Subrata Ghatak and Ken Ingersent, *Agriculture and Economic Development*, Brighton, Sussex, Wheatsheaf Books, 1984.

Mahabub Hossain and Steve Jones, 'Production, Poverty and the Co-operative Ideal: Contradictions in Bangladesh Rural Development Policy', in David A. M. Lea and D. P. Chadhuri, (eds), *Rural Development and the State*, London, Methuen, 1983, pp. 161-85.

Michael Lipton, *Why Poor People Stay Poor: A Study of Urban Bias in World Development*, London, Temple Smith, 1977.

Industry

John Cody, Helen Hughes and David Wall, *Policies for Industrial Progress in Developing Countries*, Oxford, Oxford University Press, 1980.

J. B. Donges, 'A Comparative Survey of Industrialisation Policies in 15 Semi-Industrial Countries', *Weltwirtschaftliches Archiv*, 1976, pp. 626-59.

Parvez Hasan, *Korea, Problems and Issues in a Rapidly Growing Economy*, Baltimore, Md., Johns Hopkins Press, 1976.

Ian Little, Tibor Scitovsky and Maurice Scott, *Industry and Trade in Some Developing Countries*, Oxford, Oxford University Press, 1970.

Gustav F. Papanek, *Pakistan's Development, Social Goals and Private Incentives*, Cambridge, Mass., Harvard University Press, 1967.

Hubert Schmitz, 'Growth Constraints on Small-scale Manufacturing in Developing Countries: A Critical Review', *World Development*, Vol. 10 (1982), No. 6, pp. 429-50.

NOTES

1. In the Indian sub-continent, the Royal Commission on Agriculture in India (London, 1928, quoted by Ladejinsky in Louis J. Walinsky (ed.), *Agrarian Reform—an Unfinished Business*, Oxford, Oxford University Press, 1977, p. 377) noted that: 'In extreme cases the result is ludicrous: in Ratnagiri, for instance, the size of individual plots is sometimes as small as 1/16th of an acre . . . In the Punjab, fields have been found over a mile long and but a few yards wide, while areas have been brought to notice where fragmentation has been carried so far as effectively to prevent all attempts at cultivation' (p. 124 of the Commission's Report).

2. See Andrew Pearse, *Seeds of Plenty, Seeds of Want*, Oxford, Clarendon Press, 1980, p. 125 and Chapter 7.

3. Biplab Dasgupta, *Agrarian Change and the New Technology in India*, United Nations, 1977, UNRISD Report No. 77.3 (quoted by Andrew Pearse in *Seeds of Plenty, Seeds of Want*, op. cit., p. 108). For an extended discussion, see Anne Booth and R. M. Sundrum, *Labour Absorption in Agriculture*, Oxford, Oxford University Press, 1985, particularly Chapter 5 ('Scale of Production and Labour Intensity of Agriculture'). See also Michael R. Carter, 'Identification of the Inverse Relationship between Farm Size and Productivity', *Oxford Economic Papers*, Vol. 36 (1984), No. 1, pp. 131-45.

4. It will be recalled that, under conditions of perfect competition, the marginal value product of an additional (small) amount of an input is equal to the physical output resulting from the additional input multiplied by the price at which the output sells, or is valued.

5. Many forms of production function are possible. The Cobb-Douglas production function related to inputs of capital and labour is of the general form $Q = AK^a L^{(1-a)}$. Here Q stands for quantity, K for capital and L for labour. Regression analysis is used to establish the parameters A and a from the available data.

6. 'Resource Allocation and Risk, a Case Study of Smallholder Agriculture in Kenya', *American Journal of Agricultural Economics*, Vol. 54 (1975), No. 4.

7. See, for example, the study of K. Shapiro, 'Efficiency Differentials in Peasant Agriculture and Their Implementation for Development Policies', in *Contributed Papers Read at the 16th International Conference of Agricultural Economists*, Institute of Agricultural Economics, Oxford, 1977.

8. For details see Walter P. Falcon and Carl H. Gotsch, 'Lessons in Agricultural Development-Pakistan', in Gustav F. Papanek (ed.), *Development Policy—Theory and Practice*, Cambridge, Mass., Harvard University Press, 1968, p. 275.

9. See Aksel de Lasson, *The Adoption and Diffusion of Agricultural Innovations in Noakhali District, Bangladesh*, Dhaka, Bangladesh Institute of Development Studies and Copenhagen, Centre for Development Research, 1982, p. 43. (Integrated Rural Development Project in Noakhali, Bangladesh; CDR Project Paper A.82.4).

10. See Moazam Mahmood and Nadeem-ul Haque, 'Farm Size and Productivity Revisited', *Pakistan Development Review*, Vol. 20 (1981), No. 2, pp. 151-87.

11. This view was presented to the SADCC Conference at Lusaka, 1-3 February 1984, and represents the approach of Denmark, Finland, Norway and Sweden.

12. The above account is based on Eddy Lee's 'Egalitarian Peasant Farming and Rural Development, the Case of South Korea', in Dharam Ghai *et al.*, *Agrarian Systems and Rural Development*, London, Macmillan, 1979, pp. 24-71.

13. It is estimated that suitable water control would enable about 50,000 hectares to be cultivated in this area, yielding about 150,000 tons of food. See Just Faaland, *Notes on Development Potentials, Prospects and Policies in Botswana*, Bergen, Chr. Michelsen Institute, 1982 (DERAP Working Paper, A. 276).

14. See Gunnar Haaland, 'Dualistic Development: Issues for Aid Policy', in J. R. Parkinson (ed.), *Poverty and Aid*, London, Blackwell, 1983, pp. 63-78.

15. See H. Askari and J. T. Cumming, *Agricultural Supply Response: A Survey of Econometric Evidence*, New York, Praeger, 1976. Out of about 470 measured elasticities of supply, 85 per cent showed a positive relationship between price and output.

16. Bernard Lecomte, *L'Aide par Projet: Limites et Alternatives*, OECD Development Centre, 1985.

17. Frank Holmquist, 'Self-Help: The State and Peasant Leverage in Kenya', *Africa*, Vol. 54 (1984), No. 3, pp. 72-91.

18. W. A. Lewis, 'Economic Development with Unlimited Supplies of Labour', *The Manchester School of Economic and Social Studies*, Vol. 12 (1954), No. 2, pp. 139-91.

19. Ashok Mathur, 'The Anatomy of Disguised Unemployment', *Oxford Economic Papers*, Vol. 16 (1964), No. 2, pp. 161-93.

20. Iqbal Ahmed, 'Unemployment and Underemployment in Bangladesh Agriculture', *World Development*, Vol. 6, (1978), No. 11/12, pp. 1281-96.

21. John C. H. Fei and Gustav Ranis, *Development of the Labor Surplus Economy: Theory and Policy*, Homewood, Ala., Irwin, 1964.

22. This conclusion is reached as follows: the marginal product of labour declines as more of it is combined with a given quantity of land. The amount of output will be determined at the point at which the marginal product of additional labour is, in the farm-worker's estimation, equated with the marginal utility of leisure sacrificed. Since the rate at which leisure and output are exchanged is assumed to be fixed, irrespective of the worker's income, the same output will be produced as before. Note that in this case the marginal product of labour is not assumed to be zero. Rigorous proofs of the propositions examined above are to be found in R. A. Berry and

R. Soligo, 'Rural-Urban Migration, Agricultural Output and the Supply Price of Labour in a Labour Surplus Economy', *Oxford Economic Papers*, Vol. 20 (1968), No. 2, pp. 230-49, and in A. K. Sen, 'Peasant Agriculture and Dualism with or without Surplus Labour', *Journal of Political Economy*, October 1966, pp. 425-50. Underlying assumptions relating to returns to scale, etc. are also to be found there.

23. Jagdish N. Bhagwati and Padma Dessai, *India: Planning for Industrialisation*, Oxford, Oxford University Press, 1970, p. 141.

24. Rehman Sobhan and Muzaffar Ahmad, *Public Enterprise in an Intermediate Regime: A Study in the Political Economy of Bangladesh*, The Bangladesh Institute of Development Studies, 1980, p. 538.

25. Quoted from Gustav F. Papanek, *Pakistan's Development, Social Goals and Private Incentives*, Cambridge, Mass., Harvard University Press, 1967, pp. 116-19. His comments on the destructive influence of government control, which occupy many pages of his original text, are incisive and authoritative.

26. Lawrence J. White, *Industrial Concentration and Economic Power in Pakistan*, Princeton, NJ., Princeton University Press, 1974.

27. Ibid., p. 43.

28. See Parvez Hasan, *Korea, Problems and Issues in a Rapidly Growing Economy*, Baltimore, Md., Johns Hopkins Press, 1976, p. 67.

6 Population and family planning

There are three main reasons why a study of the growth of population is necessary to understand about development. The first of these is Malthusian, the fear that an increase in population will outrun increases in production. In the traditional form, this has relevance for Bangladesh; in a more modern variant, it is concerned with the depletion of non-renewable resources and damage to the environment, and so has world wide implications, some of which are examined in Chapter 8. The second reason is that population increase may have favourable or unfavourable effects on the rate at which economies develop, with the implication that population growth in some countries may have to be controlled. A third reason is to provide the understanding of the forces at work necessary to discover whether there is a case for a population policy; if so, what form should it take?

An analysis of these issues requires the preparation of forecasts of future population growth. Such forecasts are highly speculative if they are extended beyond the next decade or two, but they do to some extent illustrate the changing balance between population and available resources. They also throw some light on what rate of increase in per capita incomes may be achieved, as well as being an essential ingredient in planning economic development. This is why we start by considering the trend of population movements and discussing the use of demographic data.

WORLD POPULATION AND ITS ENUMERATION

Table 6.1 gives an impression of how the world's population may have changed since the birth of Christ; it also contains United Nations' projections of how it may change between 1980 and 2025. For our purposes it does not matter very much that the early figures are little more than guesses based on archaeological

Table 6.1 World population increase,
AD 1-2025

Year		Population (millions)	Average rate of increase p.a. since preceding date (%)
AD	1	256	
	600	237	−0.01
	1000	280	0.04
	1340	378	0.09
	1600	498	0.11
	1650	516	0.07
	1700	641	0.04
	1750	731	0.26
	1800	890	0.39
	1850	1171	0.55
	1900	1668	0.71
	1950	2525	0.83
	1980	4432	1.89
	2000	6121	1.63
	2025	8199	1.18

Sources: Up to 1900: Colin Clark, *Population Growth and Land Use*, London, Macmillan, 1968, p. 64.
From 1950: Leon Tabah, 'Population Growth', in J. Faaland (ed.), *Population and the World Economy in the 21st Century*, London, Blackwell, 1982, pp. 175-205.

material, occasional counts and other doubtful indications, because subsequent population movements are large in relation to the statistical uncertainties involved. World population increased hardly at all in the first millennium after Christ. Only by the first half of the nineteenth century had the rate of increase reached about 0.5 per cent per annum; thereafter it accelerated to reach a maximum of nearly 2 per cent in the post-World War II decades. When a population is increasing at that rate it doubles every 35-40 years. The estimate in the table for 2025 assumes that the rate of growth of population will slow down, but even so the world's population could well exceed 8,000 million in that year and continue to rise thereafter.

The growth of population differs greatly between countries and regions. As shown in Table 6.2, while in 1950 one out of every

Table 6.2 Population in the developed and developing world (millions)

	1950	1980	2000	2025
World	2,525	4,432	6,121	8,199
More developed regions	832	1,131	1,271	1,376
Less developed regions	1,693	3,301	4,849	6,822

Source: As for Table 6.1.

three human beings lived in the more developed countries, this proportion had declined to one in four by 1980 and may decline further to one in five by the turn of the century and to one in six by the year 2025. If these figures do in fact materialise, the effect will be very roughly to restore the geographical balance of the world's population to what it was in about 1750.[1]

Censuses provide measures of the size of a population and its composition. However, census enumerations in developing countries are far from reliable, much as our estimates of world populations in earlier periods of history. There is often under-enumeration in the first count, and a practice has been developed to make allowances for this with the help of subsequent detailed checks in selected areas by the most reliable enumerators. Still further checks will be made by demographers analysing the information published in census reports to see if it is consistent and compatible with other data and to pass judgement on how best to reconcile conflicting information. Sometimes censuses may be so badly done or distorted that the figures may not be credible. The census in 1963 for Nigeria, for example, was grossly distorted by inflated figures because it was known that it would be used as a basis for determining electoral representation.

MEASUREMENT OF POPULATION CHANGE

It is useful to know something about the various statistics in common use. The *crude birth rate* is the number of births in a year per thousand of the population. The *crude death rate* is similarly composed. The difference between the two provides a useful but crude measure of the increase (or decrease) in the population that is taking place. It is a crude measure because, in particular, no account is taken of the age distribution of populations. The same underlying fertility rates would show up differently in populations of different composition. Populations with many children or old people or both, for example, tend to show lower birth rates than those with a higher percentage in the reproductive ages. This suggests that other, more refined measures are needed to reveal underlying rates of change in a population.

One such measure, *the gross reproduction rate*, is designed to estimate how many female children a typical woman would bear in her lifetime, assuming that she lives long enough to pass through the whole reproductive age-span. The calculation is made by considering a succession of age groups within the reproductive age-span. Five-year groupings are often used, and for each of these an age-specific fertility rate is calculated by dividing the number of births in each age group (in a year) by the number of women in that group. If these age-specific birth rates are added up and then multiplied by five, to take account of the fact that it takes five years to pass through each age group, an estimate of the total number of females born on average to a women in her lifetime is obtained. In a developing country, however, with a high death rate such an indicator would be misleading because it takes no account of mortality. Many of the girls born will not reach maturity, others will not survive until the end of the childbearing age. Thus for a static population, that is, one that is not increasing or decreasing and maintaining its essential features, the gross reproduction rate would have to exceed unity by a considerable margin.

By carrying out more extended calculations allowing for mortality it is possible to provide a corrected indicator which gives a better picture of the population trend; this is the *net reproduction rate*. A net reproduction rate of one, if maintained over many years, would suggest that the population would just reproduce itself, a rate less than or greater than this would suggest decline or growth.

Still another indicator of fertility frequently used is the *number of children born on average per woman* completing her reproductive-life years. This to the statistically minded gives an indication of whether the population is likely to be increasing more or less rapidly. Clearly it is a much less precise measure than the net reproduction rate. In a developed country, with a low birth and death rate, the number of children ever born per woman is typically two; in a less-developed country it is often six or seven.

None of the indicators allows for the fact that long-term changes may be taking place. They are in effect compiled from a cross-section of different generations. The different cohorts moving through their lives may be behaving quite differently, reflecting perhaps a change in life expectancy or an improvement in contraceptive methods.

For what are now familiar reasons, death rates also require the most careful interpretation. The statistical probability of death varies greatly with age in developing countries; the infant mortality is generally high–ten times or more than is the case in advanced countries. Expectation of life at birth or crude death rates have their use as approximations and for rough comparisons, yet they may be very misleading if used uncritically.

Adequate population forecasts require detailed work. In principle the methods followed are straightforward. In practice there are many snags and difficult judgements to be made. The starting-point is the age and sex distribution of the population, at some given point of time and as accurately as it is known. Forecasting then proceeds by estimating births and deaths in future years. For this purpose, it is desirable to have age- and sex-specific birth and death rates, applying to fairly narrow age bands. Sometimes these may be compiled for each year of age, more frequently perhaps for the population grouped in, say, five-year intervals. If such rates are multiplied by the approximate populations in the age groups the number of births or deaths can be calculated. Assuming this to be done for each year of age, the population forecasted for the following year will be equal to the existing population plus the number of births and minus the number of deaths calculated, and the age distribution pattern will be moved on one year. Note, however, that allowance may have to be made for recorded or estimated migration into and out of the population studied.

The art of forecasting lies not so much in understanding the mechanics as knowing the appropriate assumptions to be made. Some population forecasts cover only a short period of time and may be reasonably accurate, while other forecasts may extend twenty-five or fifty years into the future and will be highly dependent on the assumptions made: Will the death rate fall over the next twenty-five years; and if so, at what ages and by how much? What will happen to the average age of marriage? Will the scope of education be extended and will there be greater opportunities for women to work; and how will this affect fertility? Will it be possible to introduce family planning and on what scale? Judgements about such matters are very difficult to make, and many factors, including advances in technologies for control of contraception, can throw population estimates very badly out. Several computer models have been developed for population forecasting which may be extended to take in many other aspects of the economy, as we shall see.

The process of population forecasting that we have been describing may be carried out without any great understanding of the underlying causes affecting fertility. To ask why parents have the size of families that they do is not a naïve question. The answers that are advanced can depend greatly on the discipline of the observer. Economists inevitably look for economic explanations and social anthropologists for those rooted in the structure of the society, family behaviour, beliefs and customs.[2] The two interact and, depending on the time-span considered, the one may be dominant or the other. Thus, it has been suggested that in many traditional societies demographic change (or lack of it) must be seen in terms of the dominant influence on behaviour exerted by the extended family and the benefits that children confer on parents and the family, both economically and politically, as a support in village councils, communal relations and maintaining influence in the outside world.[3] Time and economic forces may be expected to change these norms and allegiances, until perhaps family size appears to be dominated by material considerations.

Any list of possible determinants of family size is bound to be a long (and incomplete) one: the desire for children; the contribution of child labour to the work of the household; the cost of children's education in money or domestic help foregone; the burden of child care (if not undertaken by siblings); social and marriage customs, acceptability and availability of contraception; wealth, parents' education; child mortality; and many more. Attempts are often made to assess the importance of such factors with the aid of the familiar tool of regression analysis, and in other ways. Such investigations give some support to the view that the size of the family in developing countries is consciously determined to some extent. They may go further than this in pointing to the more crucial variables.

One such investigation attempted to explain the number of

births to a sample of women drawn from Pakistan's National Impact Survey conducted in 1968-69.[4] It was found that wealth (as represented by quality of housing and use of electricity) appared to be positively related to the number of children born; so was the husband's education, but not that of the wife which was negatively related; age at marriage also appeared to be negatively related (early marriage increased the number of children, not an inevitable conclusion); while child mortality had the effect of increasing the birth rate.[5]

Caution has to be exercised in drawing conclusions from uncertain evidence. Some commonly held views are that while wealth and higher incomes will at first tend to increase the birth rate (children are wanted), they may be expected, on historical evidence, eventually to have the reverse effect and, of course, the children of the wealthy may be less exposed to infant and other premature death. The World Bank maintains that the prevention of ten infant deaths yields one to five fewer births, depending on the setting.[6] Again, while education for women is a strong factor tending to reduce births, some of the effects work the other way: health is improved, with the effect of increasing fertility, and breastfeeding, with its associated reduction in conception, may be less prevalent.[7]

POPULATION AND ECONOMIC GROWTH

Views about the size of the family are primarily matters for the individuals concerned, but their decisions have consequences for the society in which they live. This may lead governments to operate population policies. Sometimes the object may be to bring about an increase in population, as the physiocrats thought desirable or as Nazi Germany intended to support its need for cannon fodder. In other cases the intention may be to limit population increase in order to provide a basis for more economic development. The relationship between population increase and economic well-being, however, is not a simple one. Many effects work in different ways.

An increase in population may be favourable to development, as well as the reverse. Too small a population makes it difficult to reap economies of scale; this may be true for Botswana, with a population of less than one million, for example, although some specialisation may be achieved through international trade. Transport systems are hard to develop economically; unless they can be used intensively, towns can be too small to provide a wide range of services cheaply, and local demand for many products may be too small for efficient production.[8] Although Myrdal has described the concept of the optimal population 'as one of the most sterile ideas that ever grew out of science', some of its implications linger on.[9] Of more importance may be the dynamic effects of an increase (or decrease) of population on economic activity.[10] This might come about, for example, if the response to having more children were for parents to work harder, of which there is some evidence. In subsistence economies there may be unused land to cultivate at the expense of leisure and this may lead to greater investment as well as greater output. Even in countries where agricultural land is limited, there may be scope to increase output through more intensive cultivation and greater effort. There may also be effects on innovation. With the pressures of supporting a large family, new methods of cultivation may be devised. A growing population is composed of a very high proportion of young people where vigour may increase economic activity and promote change. Historically, several writers have argued that growth depended on an expanding population: 'We know that labour was scarce in the early eighteenth century, and the stagnation of population aggravated this problem and contributed to the depression of both agricultural incomes and the demand for industrial goods'.[11] If there are unexploited economies of scale, growth will allow them to emerge and 'Verdoorn's Law', that is, an increase in productivity seems to follow from an increase in output, will come into play.[12]

Although a rising population may produce these favourable effects, it may also result in unfavourable consequences. These are likely to be apparent if some factor of scarcity is involved: if there is no more cultivated land to use; if, because of population growth, current demands reduce savings and so investment; if resources cannot be found for children's education and so on.[13]

It is hard to know how all these factors will balance out, particularly as they may have different short- and long-term effects. Historically, the evidence is uncertain, and other investigations do not throw a great deal of light on the question. Professor Thirlwall examined a cross-section of twenty-three less-developed countries and used econometric methods to see if the rate of growth of population was matched by the rate of growth of output.[14] The results were rather inconclusive suggesting that there was no close relation between the two, although from one equation it was possible to argue that the two kept pace, inferring that population increase did not have the effect of decreasing income per head. Thirlwall concludes that his data lend very little support to the notion that programmes for reduction of population growth will have much of an impact on the growth of output and output per capita. However, as he himself indicates, we must not conclude from such investigations with all their uncertainties of formulation, data quality and incompleteness that there is no need to control population growth in a number of countries.

When actual evidence is scarce or uncertain, one can resort to simulation. This is one use to which econometric models of the interaction between population movements and economic variables have been put. One of a number of such models is that constructed by Dr Stephen Enke, known as 'Tempo II'.[15] Like many other economic models, it assumes that the economy can be divided into two sectors: the traditional sector, which will eventually be phased out although it remains largely unchanged over the period covered by the model; and the modern sector, which expands as capital is invested in it and workers move from the traditional sector to find employment there. The growth of population affects the development of the economy in many interrelated ways, as shown by the model, but notably in reducing savings levels in the modern sector and in increasing the demands on government to provide for the needs of a rising population, for example, by spending on education instead of on directly productive services. The economy modelled is quite recognisable in its essentials as a developing country which has progressed some way from subsistence level (GDP per capita of $250 in the notional year 1975), as may be seen from Table 6.3 which presents a selection of Enke's statistics.

What would happen if such an economy is simulated over a period of thirty years terminating in the year 2005, first on the assumption that there is no family planning, and then on the assumption that a progressive programme of family planning, with rising unit costs, is introduced with the object of getting a family-planning acceptance rate of 50 per cent of eligible women (or their spouse) aged 14-49 in the modern sector by 1999? Obviously, assumptions of this nature can be varied greatly within

Table 6.3 Calculated effects of family planning, 1975-2005

	1975 for both projections	2005 with no family planning	2005 with family planning
Demographic variables			
Population (millions)	10.0	23.2	19.5
Age 0-14	4.3	10.0	6.9
Modern sector	4.0	15.5	12.0
Subsistence sector	6.0	7.7	7.5
Total births (thousands)	444.0	950.0	624.0
Crude birth rate (%)	4.4	4.1	3.2
Crude death rate (%)	1.6	1.3	1.3
Gross reproduction rate (%)			
Modern sector	2.90	2.64	1.32
Subsistence sector	3.12	3.1	3.12
Total dependency ratio (%)	86.9	86.8	65.3
Population growth rate (%)	2.8	2.8	1.9
Economic variables			
GDP per capita ($)	250.0	460.0	530.0
Modern sector	312.0	583.0	732.0
GDP ($billions)	2.50	10.67	10.30
Capital per capita ($)	357.0	837.0	1,027.0
GDP per capita growth rate (%)	1.3	2.6	3.0

Note: All dollar amounts are given in base year 1975 prices.
Source: Note 15.

the structure of a model and the assumptions that are made will depend on the personal choice or judgement of the model builder.

It may be seen from the demographic part of Table 6.3 that the effect of family planning is to reduce the projected size of population in 2005 from 23.2 million to 19.5 million, or by 16 per cent. Not a very great difference, it might be felt, but it has to be recognised that family-planning programmes, even if successfully designed, take a long time to be effective in controlling population movements. The effect of decreasing population growth on the overall GDP results is a slight *reduction* in the increase realised by 2005; the benefit of the reduction in fertility arises because a smaller population leaves fewer people to share what is produced, so that per capita income will be 15 per cent greater with family planning than without it. These beneficial effects, though not large, would of course increase as time went on and even more so if the family-planning programmes became more effective. Nevertheless, the improvement in living standards that results after thirty years, following the introduction of family planning, is quite small in relation to the increase that would in any case have materialised from improvements in technology and the growing importance of the modern sector. Three-quarters of the increase in per capita incomes by the year 2005 with family planning would have occurred without it, even though in this example the rate of population increase is assumed to fall from 2.6 per cent in 1975 to 1.9 per cent in the year 2005. Thus the effect of quite a substantial reduction in the rate of increase of the population is to leave the GDP largely unaffected in 2005 and to increase per capita income, as we have said, by only 15 per cent.

The results that Dr Enke derives from this model are of some help in understanding why it is possible to indicate that the rate of growth of population has little effect on the growth of output. There is perhaps less difference between Thirlwall's conclusions and Enke's simulation than may at first sight appear, and there is certainly little to suggest that growth in output and the rate of increase in population are closely related. Nevertheless, we cannot conclude that the growth of population in particular countries is not a crucial element in retarding the growth of income per capita. In short, generalisations relating population growth to economic development may often lead to erroneous conclusions.

Either of the views, that population does not affect growth rates or that it does, could be quite plausible, depending on the circumstances of the country in question. Imagine, for example, that there is some country with the smallest of modern sectors, so that for all practical purposes it is traditional in its economic behaviour. If the amount of capital employed were small and if land were in plentiful supply (as applies even today in parts of Africa), there is no reason to think that varying rates of population increase would necessarily have much effect on living standards or that output would not rise roughly in line with the increase in population. In fact, quite different rates of population increase could be associated with similar rates of increase in incomes. It need not necessarily follow either, in these circumstances, that a country with a rapid increase in population would have to increase production per head more slowly than one with a smaller rate of increase. It might be, for instance, that the country with a

more rapid rate of population increase was blessed with availability of under-utilised fertile soil while the other community was
not.

In a modern sector the relationship between the rate of population increase and the rate of increase in income might, of course,
be different. Progress would depend on increasing the amount of
capital per head and freeing resources for this purpose. In the
public sector of the Enke model referred to above, more spent on
education means less spent on capital accumulation; in the
private sector more people to employ means less capital per head
and so labour productivity increases less quickly.

As well as tracing the more important economic consequences
of population growth, some consideration needs to be given to
other consequences. Health is adversely affected by excessive
pregnancies; a life devoted to rearing large numbers of children
is very restrictive and has a significant effect on the contribution
that women can make to development in the widest sense. While
young entrants to employment contribute freshness and vigour,
they have to be trained and settled in their work, probably at some
net expense. Moreover, in countries without a plentiful supply of
land, job creation may lag behind the influx of workers; even when
land is available this is no guarantee that employment will be
sought in agriculture rather than in the towns. In many countries
migration from rural to urban surroundings creates great dislocation: available jobs are insufficient to give immediate employment; living conditions may be appalling and there may be strong
loss of community. Inexorably in the process large towns emerge
with many of the disadvantages of urban living; towns of 10
million people become all too common. It is estimated that by
2000, 44 per cent of people in the Third World will be living in
cities, compared with 17 per cent in 1950.[16]

POPULATION PLANNING AND POLICY

Should governments adopt population planning policies? In its
developing years, Europe managed without such policies, leaving
it to individuals to determine what happened to the birth rate. On
this matter governments, not surprisingly, are divided:

Thus around 1950 the Third World was almost unanimously against the
prevention of births or ignored it, with the same result. But slowly ideas

progressed and at the General Assembly of 1962 approximately a third of those countries voted in favour of contraception. The vote showed that the Catholic countries and all those influenced by Catholicism were against birth control while none of the protestant countries were.[17]

Not surprisingly there was a pronounced split in the views of Asia and Latin America with the former by and large in favour of contraception, and the latter against. The explanation for the difference in view was probably only partly religious; population density was almost certainly another factor. The change in view indicated the persistence of the Scandinavian countries who had first raised the issue in 1952 and returned to it again in 1965.[18] By 1978, thirty-five countries containing 77 per cent of the population of the developing world had adopted official policies to reduce population growth rates.[19] Nevertheless, we should remind ourselves that economic considerations are only some of many. The argument for economic intervention would rest on the assumption or fact that it may be profitable for the family to enlarge itself, but costly for the community at large.

Such considerations did not become pressing in European countries before the increase in population subsided; indeed, in so far as Europe was underpopulated in relation to the needs of industrialisation, as has sometimes been maintained, an expanding population was beneficial. When growth in population was no longer advantageous, the rate of growth was controlled not by government but by the independent actions of individuals themselves. It seemed as though the growth in income itself had the effect, directly or indirectly, of slowing the growth in population.[20] People wanted fewer children and were in a position to ensure that family numbers were limited to some degree. It might be supposed that the same sequence of events would transpire in the developing countries of today but there is no certainty of this happening. Social attitudes in the eighteenth and nineteenth centuries in Europe differed from those prevalent in Asia today. Even if this were not the case, the Asian birth rate would have to fall more quickly than it did in Europe if the increase in population were not to become intolerable. There is now also the danger in some cases that a poverty trap might operate; the birth rate might decline so slowly that the rate at which overall incomes would be increased would be too low for growth in real per capita incomes to exert a restraining power on population growth. Thus for some countries there may be no alternative to the use of government influence in trying to limit population growth.

It is one thing to adopt a policy, another to devise the measures to carry it into effect. It is possible that a mass-media campaign to reduce the birth rate in Britain would register some success, in the same way that such efforts to stop smoking seem to have shown some results over a fairly long period of time. But the possibility should not be overrated. The reverse, a campaign to increase the birth rate against personal inclinations, equally might not be expected to succeed, judging by pre-war attempts to do so. In developing countries it is difficult indeed to influence these matters for reasons that will become apparent. Before enlarging on these in the context of Bangladesh we briefly describe some of the family-planning policies adopted by India and China.

India

In the 1950s, India was the first developing country in the world to launch an official family-planning programme. There was no conscious effort to educate married couples in the need for family planning and it took almost a decade before an educational approach to creating awareness of family-planning methods was adopted. The scale of the task was daunting: in the 1970s it was hoped to reach 90 million couples and motivate half of them to adopt family planning. This involved the establishment of over 5,000 rural family-welfare planning centres, a formidable task reflecting the vast population of India. Sterilisation as well as the distribution of conventional contraceptives constituted a major part of the programme. Incentives for 'motivators' and doctors, and compensation for loss of time and cost of travel for those accepting family planning were also used to encourage the acceptance of a family-control programme.

Dr Banerji speaks very critically of the formulation of the family-planning programme in India, saying that it greatly overestimated the effectiveness of the 'motivators'.[21] What, he asks, can you hope to accomplish in preaching family planning to a mass of starving illiterates living in dilapidated huts and insanitary conditions, suffering from diseases and disabilities, and for whom life is an unending chain of misery, degradation and deprivation?

One lesson to be learnt from the Indian programme is that it is

extremely difficult to use personnel effectively. Banerji hazards
the estimate that in 1968-69 less than twenty-one sterilisations
and less than eight IUD insertions were done for every technical
person in the programme. In other respects the programme has
been open to criticism. In a study in Uttar Pradesh in 1965-66
referred to by Banerji, it was found that over 60 per cent of the
vasectomies could have no demographic effect on the population
since they were performed on persons whose wives were either 45
years of age or above, or because they were unmarried, widowed
or separated.

Later developments in India's family-planning policies are no
more encouraging. In 1976 family-planning programmes entered
a new phase. In practice, compulsory sterilisation was attempted
in Maharastria (one of the Indian states). Over 7 million sterilisations were carried out in the country as a whole. The revulsion
against this contributed to the downfall of Mrs Gandhi's government in 1977. The successor government, in turn replaced by a
new Mrs Gandhi government in 1980, did in fact continue major
aspects of the population policies of the mid-1970s, though with
less zeal than previously, particularly in terms of sterilisations.

It is not surprising, perhaps, that the census carried out in 1981
showed that the Indian population was still increasing almost as
fast as in the past at over 2 per cent per annum, a rate low by comparison with other developing countries but judged to be too high
when applied to a population of about 700 million.

China

Historically, the birth rate of China, as elsewhere, has been
dominated by traditional social attitudes. As in other countries
the death rate dropped with development in medical science, and
the population began to increase at about 2 per cent per annum.

Official policy towards population planning developed uncertainly and intermittently. Family planning was advocated as a
necessary service to the state with emphasis on the duty of the
individual to refrain from early marriage and to concentrate on
educational and other training for a full adult life.

As the long-term difficulties of China's economic circumstances became more apparent in the 1970s, the need for curbing
population growth gained wide political acceptance and much
more vigorous family-planning programmes were introduced

with strong elements of coercion as well as some incentives and disincentives. The birth rate fell from nearly forty per thousand in the mid-1960s to probably less than twenty in the late 1970s. For rural China as a whole, the total fertility rate appeared to have been reduced from 6.38 (children ever born) in 1970 to 3.04 in 1979, and in the case of Nanquan Commune from 5.18 to 1.23 over the same period.[22] Three-quarters of the change in fertility was ascribed to a reduction in age-specific marital fertility, the rest to late marriage.[23] The two-child norm gave place to the one-child pledge that married couples were pressed to adhere to in 1979, under pressure of person-to-person influence and with some benefits to those adhering.

If a policy along these lines succeeds in limiting average families to 1.5 children, it would have a very marked effect on the age composition of the population. From about one-third of the population being under 15 today, the proportion would drop to about one-half of that in thirty five years with a very large increase in the proportion of older people.[24]

Bangladesh

The picture that emerges from Bangladesh from a study of the past is of marked but not uninterrupted growth (see Table 6.4). The population has nearly quadrupled in one century since 1881, and more than doubled in three decades since 1951. The growth of population in Bangladesh as in other parts of the Indian sub-continent is essentially a modern phenomenon dating from the nineteenth century. In earlier times the area was probably under-populated; successive invaders saw it as a land of milk and honey where the population was small in relation to natural resources and available riches. Natural checks on excessive population growth have also occurred in the present century; the influenza epidemic after World War I at least partly explains why there was hardly any increase between 1911 and 1921; the famine of 1943 similarly explains the interruption of growth between 1941 and 1951; and the growth of population in recent years would have been greater had it not been for the 1971 War of Independence, followed by famine in 1974.

The age distribution of the population is characteristic of expanding populations. Forty per cent of the population is less than 15 years old and only 4 per cent 65 or over. For a developed

Table 6.4 Population of Bangladesh, 1881-1974

Recorded population (millions)		Illustrative figures of future population (millions)	
1881	24	1975	80
1891	27	1980	93
1901	29	1990	121
1911	32	2000	150
1921	33		
1931	36		
1941	42		
1951	42		
1961	51		
1974	77		

Source. Just Faaland and J. R. Parkinson, *Bangladesh: The Test Case for Development*, London, Hurst, 1976, p. 97

country the percentages would be more nearly equal to about 20 per cent in each case. Crude birth rates have declined in the present century from about 60 per thousand to about forty-five per thousand, and crude death rates from about fifty per thousand to less than twenty per thousand. The population is increasing by about 2.8 per cent at the present time.

What stands in the way of population control? Why is it so difficult and what can be done in spite of the difficulties to reduce the birth rate? Bangladesh, remember, is not like China; the social pressures that can be exerted on individuals are much less. First let us review some of the obstacles that have to be overcome:

The privations, all too evident in Bangladesh, are a part of life. Famine occurs at irregular but all too frequent intervals and thousands die. Nevertheless, over a period of years the supply of food (with the help of imports) has roughly kept pace with the growth of population.

Marriage is practically universal and at an early age; 50 per cent of women in the age group 12-14 are married to husbands who are somewhat, but not much older. With little contraceptive use the average number of children born is six to seven per woman.

The influence of religion on family planning in Bangladesh is not easy to assess. Neither Muslims nor Hindus are prevented from practising contraception; in fact, it is arguable that religious writings may support family planning. Yet, there is clearly some reluctance, even opposition, to accept family-planning programmes. The fact that most Muslim women in Bangladesh are in purdah (the custom of keeping women in seclusion) means that they are difficult to reach in campaigns for family planning.

The seclusion of women might be of less significance in respect of reproduction behaviour if the women (and their husbands) were in fact obtaining a satisfactory education; this, however, is not the case. Since education and family planning are related, as we have already seen, the effect on balance is to increase family size.

It is easy to assume that people in overpopulated countries would wish to have small families. This again is not generally the case. The people of Bangladesh seem to welcome large families. There is also the economic aspect. The welfare of old people depends on having sons to support them when they are no longer able to earn a living. With high death rates one son is not enough to ensure this. Therefore, in an effort to provide for old age, two or more sons may be sought, which, with prevailing death rates, implies a family size well in excess of four (surviving) children.

Another difficulty in getting acceptance of family planning lies in communications. There are many scattered villages in Bangladesh only partially linked by roads, tracks or water transport. It is time-consuming to meet people and try to influence them. Radio, and in due course even television, may help in this but with no great certainty of results from the effort to communicate.

Altogether, the impediments to an effective family-planning programme are so great as to give rise to despair in those so inclined. Yet somehow something must be accomplished. The population of Bangladesh, as we have projected it, will grow to 150 million by the year 2000 or very shortly thereafter. It will not have stopped increasing by that date and a hypothetical size of the population, when finally it might stabilise towards the end of the next century, may be of the order of 300 million, that is, four times the size of the population in 1975. In fact, we question whether the territory of Bangladesh will be capable of sustaining such a population. The Malthusian checks will operate long before the computer equations reach their zenith. If the forces of Malthusianism are to be defeated, effective government policies must operate to reduce the birth rate.

CONCLUSION

As we have seen, neither India, nor Bangladesh, nor as yet China definitively, have succeeded in controlling the growth of their populations. Some countries, however, have been fairly successful. In the island of Bali, the birth rate is thought to have fallen from forty per thousand in 1970 to twenty-seven in 1976 with the help of a well-developed government programme. In Taiwan, the birth rate fell to twenty-one per thousand, again using conventional methods. Measures to reduce population growth used in Singapore are of a different character, in that those having larger numbers of children are progressively penalised. Singapore has now reached an net reproduction rate of one, although because of the age structure the population will continue to increase well into the next century.[25]

Clearly, modernisation is the most powerful means for controlling population increases. High incomes, well-established education systems, and changed social norms are the major ingredients that history suggests can contain population growth without further interventions. Apart from the United States and the Soviet Union, there is scarcely an industrialised country that will add significantly to the world population in the next twenty or even fifty years. In populations of most developing countries, modernisation may not come about unless the reverse sequence of events can be imposed; lower population growth may be a precondition for ensuring modernisation in a reasonable time. What then can be attempted to contain population growth in countries where per capita income levels are, and will remain, a good deal lower than those prevailing in industrialised countries at a time when their birth rates declined so decisively? We suggest a short list of possible measures:

(1) the continued acceptance by government that it must seek to slow down and finally arrest population growth;
(2) propaganda measures, backed by valid analysis and argument, to convince individuals that they have a self-interest as well as a duty to limit their families;
(3) the encouragement of education with emphasis on social purpose and on opportunities for own advancement;
(4) legislation as well as education to discourage early marriage;

(5) the provision of contraceptives (and support services) when-ever family planning is impeded by means rather than motivation;
(6) a steady build-up of health care, with the objective of improv-ing health, reducing mortality, establishing channels for furnishing advice, and making a real option available for cou-ples to adopt family planning;
(7) the provision of trained personnel capable of influencing individuals to limit their families and disseminating informa-tion;
(8) the fullest possible preservation of existing traditions as well as the introduction of new measures of communal respon-sibility for the care of the aged.

It takes about ten minutes to write out the list above and it could be extended. Such a list is readily compiled from a study of existing schemes for family planning; for instance, most of the elements in the list have been incorporated into family planning measures attempted in India for many years. Yet success is far away. The scale of organisation that is needed for such pro-grammes is immense, the resistance to them is great, the dedica-tion of those engaged in them sometimes suspect, and conditions generally unpropitious. Some things can in the end be achieved only by moral and social coercion and China seems better able to exercise this than Bangladesh and India.

To sum up, the case for population-control programmes needs to be examined country by country. There are a number of coun-tries where we believe that it is most desirable, and probably essential, to try to limit population growth, if development is not to be severely impeded or brought to a standstill. Of these countries, Bangladesh is the clearest major example. It is densely populated; it is unable to produce an adequate and regular supply of food for its population; and few natural resources are available for exploita-tion. It is hard to see how material welfare can be increased if every advance is accompanied by a rapid increase in population. India, we feel, is also in some danger of being unable to accelerate development sufficiently to maintain the social fabric and escape the poverty trap without containment of the expansion of popula-tion. China, too, would be threatened if the reported successes in control of population growth were to prove only temporary. Other countries are not so threatened by population pressures. The

Sudan, Botswana and Mozambique, for example, ought to be able eventually to support considerably larger populations than they have at present. The population problem thus might appear to be centred in relatively few countries. Unfortunately, the countries that seem most prone to the pressures of population are amongst the most populous in the world. India, Bangladesh and China between them contribute almost half the world's population. The growth of population is a serious matter which cannot be ignored and needs to be brought under control by well-designed policy measures.

FURTHER READING

Robert H. Cassen, 'Population and Development: A Survey', *World Development*, Vol. 4 (1976), No. 10/11, pp. 785-830.

Roberto Cuca and Catherine S. Pierce, *Experiments in Family Planning: Lessons from the Developing World*, Baltimore, Md., Johns Hopkins Press, 1977.

Michael Drake *et al.*, *The Population Explosion: An Interdisciplinary Approval*, Milton Keynes, The Open University Press, 1971.

Stephen Enke, 'Reducing Fertility to Accelerate Development', *Economic Journal*, Vol. 84 (1974), June, pp. 349-66.

International Bank for Reconstruction and Development, *World Development Report 1984*, Oxford, Oxford University Press, 1984, pp. 51-185; Part II: *Population Change and Development*.

NOTES

1. This observation is based on figures contained in *World Bank Operations: Sectoral Programs and Policies*, Baltimore, Md., Johns Hopkins Press, 1977, p. 295.
2. For an economist's approach, see Richard A. Easterlin, 'An Economic Framework for Fertility Analysis', *Studies in Family Planning*, Vol. 6 (1975), pp. 54-63.
3. See J. C. Caldwell, 'The Mechanisms of Demographic Change in Historical Perspective', *Population Studies*, Vol. 35 (1981), No. 1, pp. 5-27, and 'Towards a Restatement of Demographic Transition Theory', *Population and Development Review*, Vol. 2 (1976), Nos. 2 and 3, pp. 321-66.
4. Dennis De Tray, 'Age of Marriage and Fertility', *Pakistan Development Review*, Vol. 16 (1977), No. 1, p. 96.
5. A somewhat similar study for Bangladesh gave much less conclusive results, illustrating the difficulty of isolating explanatory factors when primary variables play a major role in an economic model; see Ismail Sirageldin, M. Ali Khan, Farida Shah and Ayse Ariturk, 'Fertility Decisions and Desires in Bangladesh: An Econometric Investigation', *Bangladesh Development Studies*, Vol. 4 (1976), No. 3, pp. 329-50.

6. International Bank for Reconstruction and Development, *World Development Report 1984*, Oxford, Oxford University Press, 1984, p. 108.
7. For a much more detailed discussion, see Susan Hill Cochrane, *Fertility and Education*, Baltimore, Md., Johns Hopkins Press, 1979; World Bank Staff Occasional Papers, No. 26, particularly Table 6.1, p. 146.
8. See Ester Boserup, *Population and Technological Change*, Chicago, University of Chicago Press, 1981, pp. 144-57, Chapter 12, 'Sparse Population as Obstacle to Industrialisation'.
9. Gunnar Myrdal, *Population a Problem for Democracy*, Cambridge, Cambridge University Press, 1960, p. 26.
10. See, for example, Julian L. Simon, *The Economics of Population Growth*, Princeton, NJ, Princeton University Press, 1977, and Ester Boserup, *The Conditions of Agricultural Growth: The Economics of Agrarian Change under Population Pressure*, London, Allen & Unwin, 1965.
11. Phyllis Dean and W. A. Cole, *British Economic Growth*, Cambridge, Cambridge University Press, 1962, p. 96.
12. Peter J. Verdoorn, 'On an Empirical Law Governing the Productivity of Labour', *Econometrica*, Vol. 19 (1951), No. 2, pp. 209-10.
13. See Julian L. Simon, op. cit., Table 10-6, p. 232, for evidence that secondary education is reduced with higher birth and dependency rates.
14. A. P. Thirlwall, 'A Cross-Section Study of Population Growth and the Growth of Output and Per Capita Income in a Production Function Framework', *The Manchester School of Economic and Social Studies*, Vol. 40 (1972), No. 4, pp. 339-56. The percentage rates of growth of output and inputs were averaged over a number of years to reduce random fluctuations.
15. *Economic Journal*, Vol. 84 (1974), June. Other models include many variants of TEMPO associated with the General Electric Company and the International Labour Office's variants of BACHUE.
16. *World Development Forum*, Vol. 3 (1985), No. 7.
17. Alfred Sauvy, *General Theory of Population*, London, Weidenfeld & Nicolson, 1969, p. 424.
18. Louis B. Sohn in Just Faaland (ed.), *Population and the World Economy in the 21st Century*, London, Blackwell, 1982, pp. 241-4.
19. Bernard Berelson and Robert H. Haveman, 'On Allocating Resources for Fertility Reduction in Developing Countries', *Population Studies*, Vol. 34 (1980), No. 2, pp. 227-37.
20. This is, of course, just a shorthand for the many causes that may have led to decline. For a list of these, see Alfred Sauvy, op. cit., p. 363.
21. Dr Banerji, *Family Planning in India*, New Delhi, Peoples Publishing Home, 1971, p. 26 and the Epilogue.
22. See W. R. Lavely, 'The Rural Chinese Fertility Transition: A Report from Shifang Xian Sichuan', *Population Studies*, Vol. 38 (1984), No. 3, p. 383. The total fertility rates for 1979 were calculated on the basis of assumptions about age-specific marital fertility.
23. See *Intercom*, Vol. 9 (1981), No. 8.
24. Ibid.
25. See Malcolm Potts and Peter Selman, *Society and Fertility*, London, MacDonald & Evans, 1979, p. 331.

7 Work and welfare

In Chapter 2, we described the increased emphasis in recent years on development policies specifically designed to meet the needs of the poor. Such policies take a variety of forms and may be reflected in production patterns, efforts to change the distribution of income and to give support to low-income groups through subsidies and the provision of government services. We do not seek in this chapter to explore the whole gamut of policies that may favour the poor, but merely to examine three issues: the provision of employment, education and health care.

Employment is, of course, a means of improving access to goods and services, so contributing to welfare in a material way. In our view, however, it is much more than this. We believe that the state should recognise the need of individuals to have access to the means to support themselves, the opportunity to produce and earn a living, and should work towards this. But the value and importance of employment extends beyond this, for it provides an opportunity for individuals to take their place in society, to develop their potential and to establish themselves as human beings. We do not in this context confine employment to paid labour in industry, in commerce or services, for this would exclude much activity in the subsistence sector of the economy. We are concerned with people finding both a place in society and the opportunity to acquire the necessary material resources in order to attain improvement.

It is in something of the same context that we regard education. Without education, it is difficult to participate fully in the modern world; it is necessary for the development of the individual and it opens up opportunities of all kinds that might otherwise be inaccessible. In the early stages of economic development, this may amount to no more than an attempt to establish universal primary education with minimum provision for further education, but subsequently further provision is called for to take in more of the population.

The provision of health care is concerned with the rights and needs of individuals. It affects productivity, but even more the welfare of the individual by conferring some protection from illness and some opportunity to recover from it.

The policy issues concern the means to improve the situation. What, in practical terms, might government do to create employment of the quality desired, to provide education of suitable type, and use available resources for health care efficiently? Opportunities to do all these things are, in fact, severely limited and when resources are very inadequate it is particularly important to try to identify those policies that offer the best prospects of success.

The discussion in this chapter of certain social aspects of economic development and the importance of the welfare of the individual may serve as a reminder that measuring progress solely in terms of the rate of increase of real gross national product leaves many aspects of welfare ill considered. Services to self, the value of leisure, the (often frequent) dreariness of wage employment are not taken into the reckoning. Social indicators may provide useful information supplementary to that measured in terms of material welfare. It is not surprising, therefore, that there have been attempts to establish indices indicative of well-being using social indicators rather than those related to national income increase.[1] This is an interesting and sophisticated exercise. However, for the purpose of development and development planning, it may be sufficient to look at the more common indicators of social performance one by one, and to consider in each case whether performance can be improved and, if so, at what cost and with what sacrifices of other objectives.

EMPLOYMENT

In developed countries the concepts of employment and unemployment are fairly well differentiated in relation to a generally well-defined working day. In developing countries the distinction between the two is much more obscure. Many people are engaged in subsistence activities and are not employed in any formal sense. In rural areas, as we have seen, unemployment may be a reflection of the inability of the landless to lay their hands on the means of production, or of those with some land to secure sufficient of it for their needs and to work it productively.

Agricultural production may often be strongly seasonal in character, giving rise to fluctuating labour requirements, while leisure may figure more strongly in the preferences of those in developing countries (although not always) than in those imbued with the protestant ethic elsewhere.[2] Moreover, as we have seen, while it is often assumed that there is a plentiful supply of labour in developing countries, this is not always the case. Another complication is whether a job that is so poorly paid as not to provide an adequate diet for the employed himself and his dependants (often herself and her dependants) should be regarded as employment in any real sense. In a still wider setting, the term employment may be used to symbolise policies aimed at providing greater equality of opportunity within a country. It is with the object of devising programmes of this kind that the International Labour Office organised in the 1970s a series of so-called Comprehensive Employment Strategy Missions for a number of countries.[3] The term comprehensive indicates that the provision of employment opportunities should be interpreted widely. In this sense employment becomes one aspect of programmes designed to meet the basic needs of people: adequate amounts of food, basic housing, elementary health care and primary education. In fact, the term employment sometimes seems to be infinitely extendible to meet the aspirations of particular writers.

In many countries, unemployment is most visible in the towns. Potential workers move in from rural areas in quest of a job in circumstances where recruitment is by word of mouth and the connections of kith and kin, or regional or tribal affiliations. Many scratch a living as best they can in the so-called informal sector of the economy, carrying out non-agricultural activities making chairs or charcoal burners or a host of other things, or by providing simple services like selling drinking water to the thirsty in the street, or cleaning shoes. Yet another aspect of the need to earn a living is employment, mainly of women, for example, in the sweatshops of Bangkok, faced otherwise with the alternative of prostitution. It often takes time to find a job and many experience unemployment before they find work. Ironically, when attempts to measure unemployment in African towns were made in the 1970s, unemployment appears to have been no worse, and sometimes better, than is experienced in towns and areas within the United Kingdom in the 1980s. In Kenya in 1972, 11.5 per cent were unemployed in the three towns for which data were compiled and in Khartoum only about 5-6 per cent in 1974.[4] Such unemployment tends to fall on the young and uneducated, and on women.

There is no royal road to the creation of employment; however, it may be defined.[5] Maximum employment is not ensured by a simple tactic of attempting to increase output as quickly as possible. Output and employment are not synonymous and there may be some trade-off between them. Whether a reduction in output will be acceptable in order to yield more employment is a matter of judgement, including judgements about the welfare of those already in employment who might be made worse off. As Frances Stewart and Paul Streeten have argued, there may be circumstances where less in total, but more for the poor and less for the rich, may be preferred.[6] Nevertheless, in a developing country short of resources, a sceptical view should be taken of the virtues of sacrificing output in order to distribute opportunities more evenly. The search first of all should be directed to both having one's cake and eating it.

Table 7.1 shows a discouraging picture of employment prospects in Bangladesh. Others have taken a more optimistic view

Table 7.1 Employment by economic sector, unemployment and total labour force, 1975 and 2000 (million man-years)

	1975	2000
Employment in:		
Agriculture	15	20
Manufacturing	1	4
Commerce	1	2
Services	2	6
All other (including construction)	1	4
Total employment	20	36
Unemployment	8	20
Total labour force	28	56

Note: The figures for 1975 are rough estimates only, based on incomplete information. They must be considered only as indicative of the structure of occupations rather than absolute levels.

Source: Just Faaland and J. R. Parkinson, *Bangladesh: The Test Case for Development*, London, Hurst, 1976, p. 85.

but do not seem to have spelt out their assumptions in any detail. Often the underlying issue is the effect that the growth of domestic incomes in agriculture will have on rural activity of all kinds. How many new shopkeepers will be needed? What scope will there be for other service employment? Will rural industry greatly expand its activities? These are questions that must be posed but they are hard indeed to answer. The belief in the minds of the job seekers and planners alike, that jobs will be found, is sometimes no more than a matter of faith. In the developed countries, except for the 1930s and the last five or ten years, the flow of jobs has, by and large, kept up with population in spite of continuously recurring fears that the reverse would be the case. Despite the present high level of open unemployment in many industrialised countries, especially in Europe, the explicit and determined pursuit of employment-creating strategies may be decisive in such economies. The options in developing countries are clearly more limited.

By comparison with developed countries, capital is scarce in the developing world. Labour may seem to be plentiful although this is less easy to establish, as we have seen, and those seeking work are often unskilled, ill-educated and sometimes suffering from malnutrition. Nevertheless, it might be expected from elementary economic principles that production processes would combine more labour with a unit of capital. Specifically, it might be expected that different technical methods of production would be used, because some production processes are more labour-intensive than others. Another tentative conclusion is that goods that require a high proportion of labour to capital in their manufacture would be appropriate for production in less-developed countries. Yet none of these conclusions can be established with absolute certainty and general validity; indeed, there are circumstances in which they can be shown to be either ambiguous or untrue.[7]

A great deal of work has been done with regard to the use of alternative technologies that could be expected to match the availability of certain elements of production more closely. Some of the fiercest debates relate to agriculture. What techniques should be used in tilling the land? Should this, wherever possible, be done by manual labour, or is there scope for the use of machinery? In a free-market economy, decisions of this kind would be taken in response to market forces and to the variety of techniques available. In a less-developed country, market forces invariably operate less than completely and many decisions may be taken by those in government rather than by those who will actually be responsible for production.

Thus, as a generalisation for Bangladesh, for instance, the balance between the use of capital and labour lies very much in favour of using labour whenever possible; tractors or combine harvesters are not likely to commend themselves for ordinary purposes. Labour, however, cannot replace the use of fertilisers or even pesticides, which for this purpose may be regarded as capital. Similarly, capital invested in irrigation may be regarded as land-augmenting, thus extending a critically scarce reserve. As always there are exceptions. By permitting timely land preparation, the use of machinery may make an additional harvest possible. Sometimes only machinery can do the job. In the Sudan, cultivation of the clay plains stretching across the centre of the country simply cannot be undertaken by hoes! Similar considerations apply in the case of the production of irrigated crops. Cotton grown in the Gezira depends on the availability of water and this can be provided only by irrigation from the Niles. Such cultivation is expensive in the way of capital but it can be productive enough to justify the capital cost; raising water by hand in the Gezira, and directing it over very imperfectly levelled land without mechanical aid, could not function on the scale needed. In other respects there are strong arguments against the use of mechanised systems of cultivation, even in the Gezira. Cotton should be picked by hand rather than by imported machines because it creates employment opportunities for those in the traditional sector of the economy.

Sometimes employment is only one consideration affecting the choice of farming methods. In Mozambique the emerging system of agricultural organisation is dualistic. On the one hand, traditional labour-using agricultural production continues perforce; on the other, there are strong pressures to operate some very large state farms using advanced, capital-intensive agricultural practices. While this may not provide much in the way of employment opportunities, it is advocated as a means to ensure national food supplies and to increase exports, as well as conforming to a declared intention to modernise as an end itself.

In industrial operations also, the techniques adopted are seldom determined with an eye primarily to employment. There are a number of industrial processes that do not lend themselves to labour-intensive techniques. In Bangladesh the manufacture of fertiliser from natural gas is an operation that requires the latest techniques; if half a million tons or more of fertiliser are to be produced each year, there is really not much scope to economise on capital. In extraction of sugar from cane, it may pay handsomely to use machinery if extraction rates can be increased by one percentage point from 4 to 5 per cent of the gross weight of the cane. The same might also appear to be the case for the extraction of vegetable oils, although here a greater variety of technical alternatives present themselves.[8]

Efforts have been made to supplement traditional production methods by developing alternative or more appropriate technologies with the needs of particular developing countries in mind. These include the introduction of the canvas-sailed, Cretan-type windmill in Northern Ethiopia, and the introduction of rainwater-catchment tanks in Botswana, incorporating modern materials such as polythene or butyl rubber sheets (thus reducing expenditure on cement), and the installation of a lid to reduce evaporation. The design of basic housing for the new cityport of Tema in Ghana, and the introduction of a new method of egg-packing using local materials in the same country are other examples.[9]

Although efforts to develop appropriate technologies are interesting and valuable, their total impact on employment remains limited. Nevertheless, contribution of advanced technology in providing new opportunities for developing countries should not be lost sight of simply because some of it may be unsuitable. One of the problems is that the firms that use modern technology generally have little incentive to innovate and adapt rather than copy; it is much easier to stay with something that is known to work and with which everybody is familiar. Often firms using high technology are branches of multinational corporations concerned with dispensing standard products rather than adapting production methods to local situations. A notable exception of long standing is provided by the pilot plant established by the Philips Company at Utrecht in the Netherlands, which has set up more than a score of factories in developing countries for the production of small runs of electronic consumer goods.[10]

One aspect of using alternative technology lies in selecting the most appropriate from those available. Table 7.2 illustrates the range of choice amongst shirt-weaving techniques suitable for factory installation. It shows clearly that large amounts of labour can be saved by highly capital-intensive methods but, as discussed above, this may be quite inappropriate in a developing country which would do better to save on capital. If the amount of capital needed for the Sulzer operation were used to purchase Lancashire looms instead, nearly 7,000 thousand more jobs could be created and output could be more than quadrupled. Note that large factories will not necessarily have lower output-capital ratios than small ones. Note also that shift-working can be an important factor in economising on capital and is easier to adopt in larger firms. This, incidentally, is a major factor regulating the kind of technology that it is appropriate to consider: the more intensively machinery can be worked, the more likely it is to be economical to invest in capital equipment.

Howard Pack has made an interesting investigation of different techniques used by firms engaged in wheat-milling.[11] The proportions in which capital and labour were combined varied greatly. Some of the techniques could be shown to be totally inefficient since they required both more capital and more labour per ton of output than alternative methods. Amongst the techniques considered it proved possible to pick out two efficient but extreme cases, one requiring minimum labour per ton, the other minimum capital per ton. These 'frontier' cases were used in con-

Table 7.2 Aggregate effects of alternative weaving techniques

Technique applied	Requirements per 100 million sq. yds. per annum		Capital/ labour ratio	Investment funds saved using Lancashire technique
	(1) Man years	(2) Investment ($ millions)	(3) (2)/(1)	(4) ($ millions)
Lancashire	2,180	36	1,645	
Battery	1,110	72	6,545	36
Airjet	820	79	9,665	43
Sulzer	510	150	29,715	114

Source: Taken from Howard Pack, 'Policies to Encourage the Use of Intermediate Technology', in A. Robinson (ed.), *Appropriate Technology of Third World Development*, London, Macmillan, 1979.

junction with data on wages and capital costs to form a rough estimate of the elasticity of substitution between capital and labour. The elasticity of substitution is a measure of the extent to which the capital-labour ratios change in response to changes in the ratio of the price of capital to the price of labour. For grain-milling the elasticity turned out to be high, with a value of 3.7 (a 1 per cent shift in the unit cost of capital would lead to 3.7 per cent more labour being employed at a given cost of labour). Calculations of the elasticity of substitution for bicycles showed a low elasticity, but for paints, tyres, cotton textiles and woollen textiles the figure lay between 1 and 2.

If, as is sometimes argued, wage rates are higher in developing countries than the real scarcity of labour would justify, this would tend to inhibit employment in those industries for which the elasticity of substitution is appreciable. This has led to the suggestion put forward by—amongst others—Professor A. Qayum that subsidising the use of labour would increase employment.[12] The cost of the subsidy, he argued, could be met by taxing the increased returns to capital that would accrue from using a higher proportion of labour with it and from the increase in revenue from taxes on output and incomes which would be higher as the result of more employment. This interesting suggestion is not, however, a practicable solution for mass unemployment. It is very unlikely that the scheme proposed could be financially self-supporting.[13] Even if it were, there would be strong dangers of abuse and it would be hard to administer and police. It cannot really be recommended for developing countries, but there might be something to be said for trying to apply subsidies to labour use in developed countries, as has sometimes been done, where the operation might be self-supporting, unlike developing countries where, contrary to Professor Qayum's belief, net budgetary costs could be high.

The extent to which capital-intensive systems of production are used may depend on whether firms are large or small. Professor Gustav Ranis studied four Pakistani industries in Karachi in 1960 and came to the conclusion that in most cases small firms employed more labour per unit of capital than large ones.[14] Wages in small firms were lower than those paid in large firms and this may have led them to adopt more labour-intensive processes. With less capital per head, output per head is also less, but this may be an acceptable price to pay.

Clearly, in an ideal world, all possible technologies and combinations of large or small firms would have to be considered and cost-benefit relations established for all of them, using whatever shadow prices seem to be appropriate. Only then would it be possible to decide whether to establish large or small firms, or to use this or that technique. Rules of thumb like 'small is beautiful' or 'alternative technologies are needed' may at best be unhelpful and at worst deceptive, especially if they are applied without full knowledge of the social and economic conditions in which the productive operations will be carried out.

Policies to increase employment in rural and urban activities must take account of the technical, social and economic opportunities for substitution between production inputs, in particular substitution of labour for capital, as discussed above. Similarly, policies affecting the composition of output might be expected to have a significant effect on the amount of employment that can be offered by a less-developed country. In an open economy there could be significant effects on employment if the medium of international trade allowed the less-developed country to concentrate on producing those types of goods for which the labour content was inherently high. Developing countries often commence industrialisation with labour-using production operations such as the manufacture of textiles, or by undertaking assembly operations, and importing capital-intensive goods from developed countries. One consequence of this, it may be argued, would be that an export promotion strategy would be expected to be more conducive to the creation of employment than one based on import substitution. A study by Professor Anne Kreuger showed that the labour coefficients for a selection of developing countries did provide some evidence that exports were more labour-intensive than imports, although this was not universally true; for Indonesia, however, the labour content of exports was double that of imports.[15] The extent to which the tendency manifested itself could have been affected by factor price distortions; if wages in towns, for example, were inflated (for some of the reasons discussed earlier), this would have tended to reduce the comparative advantage of labour-intensive activity.

Even in a closed economy, however, the composition of output may be varied to some extent in labour-using directions. A great deal depends here on the extent to which government is prepared to try to intervene in the economy and establish particular patterns of demand and output. A major issue may be the distribution of income that it is intended to produce. Will a more equal distribution affect the use of labour favourably? It is often maintained that it will do so. Goods consumed by the poorer sections of the community may depend much more on indigenous resources than those consumed by the richer sections. The poor may also make fewer demands for imported goods which may constitute a bottleneck in promoting development. With demand deflected from imported goods, a more rapid increase in output may be generated and this will of itself be employment-generating.

One factor stressed in the ILO Comprehensive Employment Strategy reports referred to earlier was the contribution that the informal sector might make to employment promotion.[16] The informal sector of the economy is a most unfortunate term, apparently intended to distinguish a large and varied category of employment and means of livelihood from employment in agriculture, in government occupations, and in the large-scale industrial sector of the economy, where employees are deemed in some sense to be protected, fostered and approved. The informal sector is what remains: the roadside and empty-lot mechanics, the leather workers making bags for the tourist trade, the small furniture makers, those who recycle material of any description, those sitting on the verandas of houses in Dhaka making clothes, the casual dhobis of Islamabad taking in washing, the barber in the bazaar, the traders and hawkers in Khartoum, the prostitutes found everywhere, and the small boy, the self-appointed guardian of someone's car. Many of these people will fall by the wayside but some of them will gradually emerge as men of substance. A petty trader will graduate from possessing a tray with combs to sell to operating a *tabliya*, a compromise between a booth and a stall, then move to a more fixed and conspicuous place of work with a tin or wooden booth and, if all goes well, will eventually join the more formal sector with a permanent and respected place of operation. Those in the informal sector will set up their activities wherever they can. Shanty-town streets will grow on the sides of roads, in open spaces and wherever there is vacant land in the city. Obstruction to the flow of people and traffic may be the result and, with generally unsympathetic authorities, the places of work of these budding entrepreneurs may be demolished so that they have to start all over again.

The activities of the informal sector can make a sizeable contribution to the provision of employment opportunities. In the Khartoum area (including Omdurman) in 1974, over 5,000 informal enterprises were found by a household survey, conducted by the Comprehensive Employment Strategy Mission (CESM) of the ILO, to be engaged in manufacture, repair and construction in which no modern means of production were used. More than 1,000 of these were concerned with the manufacture of wood and about 2,000 with footwear and clothing, together providing jobs for nearly 10,000 people. Some had just begun business, but over 70 per cent had been established for six or more years. Expansion of their activities was held back mainly because of shortage of capital, although both demand for their products and the scarcity of raw materials and fuel were also restraining factors. These units of manufacture, repair and construction were, however, only some of the many small businesses that were conducted. In licensed service and commercial activities it was estimated that 30,000 people were employed, and in the transport sector about 6,000 people. With the addition of vendors and shoeshine boys, it was thought that the total of informal employment ranged between 50,000 and 60,000.

Government policies to expand this type of employment may start in the first instance most usefully and directly by refraining from official harassment and, more positively, by furnishing credit (a risky operation, however, as we have seen, and not easy to organise even with special institutions for the purpose). In short, while the informal sector can be recognised as an important source of employment, it is not easy to devise policies to encourage its expansion. Here, as always, expansion is also limited by the size of the market and this in turn by the favour shown to large-scale operations in the formal, government-recognised sectors.

In some instances it may not be possible to create employment opportunities in the traditional sectors of the economy on an adequate scale before it is overtaken by the growth of the modern sector. Botswana could be a case in point. In large parts of Botswana (as for the Sudan), it is not easy to see how cultivation can be much improved in the traditional sector of agriculture. Much of the soil is poor, the incidence of rainfall in many parts of the country is very uneven and irrigation an expensive solution even where it is possible. With great wealth being extracted in the mineral sector in Botswana, and the likelihood that there remains much more to come from beneath the Kalahari sands, the drift of those engaged in traditional agriculture to the towns is likely to continue and accelerate. If this were to be the case, the creation of jobs would turn much more on developing manufacturing activities associated with mineral extraction than on agricultural developments.

Recommendations that may seem most likely to have a significant impact on employment will not always do so immediately or easily. There are few short cuts; in the Sudan, as elsewhere, employment creation is very much a question of developing a country in its entirety and this cannot really be done by a separate strategy directed only at the creation of employment opportunities. For mixed economies the objective of employment strategies is likely to be a modest one aimed to ease the situation rather than transform it.

The communes organised by China appear to have been much more effective than rural institutions elsewhere in creating employment in the countryside. Norman Macrae, describing the situation as it was in 1977, attributed this to village Keynesianism:

The communes achieve rural full employment by giving every able-bodied member–plus most of the feeble-bodied grandmas–a job during the crop off-season, either in the quite sizeable enterprises run by the communes or in the small enterprises run by the commune subdivisions called brigades.[17]

The Keynesian aspects included not only protectionism but also, and more important, the creation of a money supply in the form of work points entitling the worker to a share in the proceeds of economic activity, in part determined by their contribution to it. This underlines one of the difficulties encountered when public works are considered as a means to increase employment in a mixed economy: it is simply impossible to raise the finance on the scale needed and it may be hard to secure the participation of those who consider it beneath them to engage in manual toil. Since in such countries there is no ground organisation ready and waiting to put employment policies into effect, efforts to create employment as a community endeavour are cumbersome to organise and tend to be of an *ad hoc* or of a once-and-for-all nature. The benefits from such endeavours also tend to be unevenly distributed, while when land is communally owned this can in principle be avoided.

The commune in China is reported to have been a powerful force for diversification of activity first within the agricultural sector and then by means of small industries based on local raw materials, including sugar, rice and flour mills, brick and cement manufacture, spinning, weaving and garment production. More-over, the linkage effects within a commune are considerable and lead not only, for example, to the repair of agricultural machinery but even to manufacturing some items. The incentive to carry out such activities is high and the assured supply they create is par-ticularly valuable. The diversification of activity creates pressure to train labour and to acquire new skills. Education and training can be geared to the needs of the commune, as they must be in a system which does not allow much mobility between the rural areas and the towns, or even within the rural area itself.

The adaptation of technology appeared to be progressive in the early days of communal activities, using in the most primitive conditions whatever materials came to hand or could be found on the waste heaps. Motor-vehicle lamps made from leftover materials, screws made from steel wire salvaged from dumps, ball-bearings produced with metal from broken cooking pans using hand-operated presses, diversification from raincoat repair to electronics, and the domestic production of iron, steel and fertiliser–these were just some of the ways of getting going. But with relentless pressure to increase output, to find new markets and develop new products, more sophisticated and capital-using methods of production gradually replaced primitive and later intermediate technology.[18]

This ability to stimulate progressive development was again in evidence from 1978 when a production responsibility system for agriculture was introduced. With this system a contractual rela-tionship is established between the commune and a group of farmers, a household or an individual, which specifies the amount of land to be cultivated and the amount of produce to be delivered, as well as financial contributions. The response to this change was impressive. Output in agriculture rose rapidly and with it a more efficient use of the rural work-force emerged that made about one-third of the workers redundant. The reaction to this was to stimulate employment in livestock breeding, com-merce, handcrafts, construction and other occupations. The increase in rural output generated further demand for consumer goods, putting pressure on supplies.[19]

The possibilities sketched above call to mind the entrepreneurial activities attributed to the leaders of the industrial revolution. Enterprising people are not confined to China. Energetic industrialists operating on a small scale are to be found everywhere in the informal sector of mixed as well as communist economies: in Chittagong in Bangladesh, producing coach bolts with small furnaces, sledgehammers and hand-operated dies with two or three workers employed, or, on a larger scale, repairing diesel engines, pumps or anything easily copied with the use of primitive tools; in the tribal arms factories of the North West Frontier in Pakistan, where any hand-held arm could be reproduced down to the registration number of the weapon serving as the model. The abilities are always there but the environment in which they can flourish is not so easily found.

Perhaps the worst setting of all for the creation of employment in small industry is in the mixed, controlled economy where not only has the private entrepreneur all too often to struggle against the shackles of government control, with little benefit from it, but where also the stimulus and enterprise of communal organisation are absent.

EDUCATION

In the 1950s and 1960s, economists directed attention to the profitability of investing in the enhancement of human capabilities and performance. Money spent on improving health or providing education began to be looked at from the point of view of an investment, to be gauged like any other investment in relation to the return expected from it and its opportunity cost.

The costs of different types of education in the form of expenditure on teachers' salaries, buildings, equipment, etc., including the loss of earnings that education often implies, can usually be measured in a rough-and-ready way. The increase in earning power as a result of education is more difficult to assess. It is necessary to take account of the extent of unemployment, in so far as it affects earnings, if a true picture of rewards and benefits is to be obtained and to give attention to the participation rates in the labour-force of various categories of worker. Educated married women, for example, may be more inclined to participate in the labour-force than those without education and this has to be allowed for. In most cases it is likely that individuals will take too little account of the possibility that a job will not be obtained, or that there will be periods of unemployment; thus the rate of return expected may tend to be higher than that actually obtained if jobs are hard to come by, or a decision is taken subsequently not to work.

These features have to be accounted for if a realistic rate of return on expenditure is to be arrived at. In a study carried out for 1967-68 for West Malaysia, Mr O. D. Hoerr attempted to do so by using multiple regression techniques to establish an econometric relationship between years of schooling or other forms of education and income as revealed by household surveys.[20] Table 7.3 below shows the cumulative and the marginal rates of return to different types of education derived. The term 'net' signifies that a deduction from earnings has been made to take account of the effect of being either voluntarily or involuntarily unemployed. The gross private return is calculated without making this deduction because it is felt that when individuals decide to incur the cost of education they will assume, perhaps optimistically, that they will not be affected by unemployment and will wish to work. In the case of the private rate of return, no allowance is made for the cost of education since this is frequently met by the state rather than the individual, and for the same reason no allowance is made for educational costs incurred in respect of those who fail

Table 7.3 Internal rates of return to education, West Malaysia, 1967-68 (percentages)

	Net social return		Net private return		Gross private return	
	Cumulative	Marginal	Cumulative	Marginal	Cumulative	Marginal
Primary	8.2	8.2	12.9	12.9	29.5	29.5
Forms I-II	11.9	15.6	17.0	21.1	45.5	61.5
Forms III-IV	13.6	15.3	17.6	18.9	52.0	65.0
Sixth form	13.2	12.8	17.1	15.6	52.8	55.3
University	9.5	5.8	16.0	11.4	49.7	37.2
Teacher training*	9.6	6.0	23.6	49.8	n.a.	n.a.

* As compared with the sixth form.

Source: O. D. Hoerr, 'Education, Income and Equity in Malaysia', *Economic Development and Cultural Change*, Vol. 21 (1973), No. 2, pp. 247-73.

to complete their courses. The distinction between the cumulative and the marginal rate of return is of some significance. In order to reach higher levels of education it is necessary to pass through the preceding stages and very often it is the returns on the total educational programme that should be considered. In practice, the nature of the decision may be more fragmented; proceeding to the next stage of education will be conditional to some extent on accomplishment of the preparatory stage and at this point the decision will be more closely related to marginal rates of return.

As shown in the table, the social rate of return of primary education is not very high, secondary education yields well (here the marginal rate of return is relevant when primary education is compulsory), while the marginal rate of return on university education and teacher training is low. The gross rates of return, as they appear to private individuals, are all quite high, particularly if marginal rates of return are considered. This is because in the calculation of private benefits the only cost that has to be met is that of loss of earnings during the period of education.

It is evident that with private rates of return as high as appears from the table, parents are likely to exert great pressure to secure higher education for their children; this is a common phenomenon in the developing world. It is also possible to understand why cheating in examinations in some countries is part of the struggle to get preferment. If the full costs of education had to be met, private rates of return would be much less and there would be less pressure to expand the education system. The high returns on education as viewed from the private standpoint will continue only so long as people of the required educational attainments are scarce. It may not require a large increase in the number of secondary school leavers for scarcity to disappear. When this happens the minimum educational standards needed for jobs of different types tend to be pushed up, thus erecting a further barrier of a wasteful kind to entry into certain positions, and leading to further pressures to increase educational provision, even though this may not really be needed. We return to the issue of the so-called upward push in a later section. The study by O. D. Hoerr is only one of many that have been carried out for developing countries at various times.[21] As might be expected there are wide differences between countries and generalisations should be made with great care.

Any investment in education and training may not always be of full benefit to the country concerned, at least not as measured in the studies referred to above. The outflow of economists from developing countries to international organisations, and, at another level, the movement of cooks or drivers from Bangladesh, and skilled workers from the Sudan to the prosperous Middle East are reminders of this.[22] In recent years this kind of migration, particularly but not exclusively to the Middle East, has been massive, amounting to hundreds of thousands of persons from Pakistan and Bangladesh. In addition to those from other countries, one major result has been that remittances by these migrants add up to a very large item in the home country's balance of payments and even in relation to its gross national income, reflecting very large private as well as national benefits.

Calculations of the rate of return from different types of education can tell us something about the kind of facilities that should be provided for education and training but they do not take us very far. It is hard to say what types of manpower are likely to be in demand, what their supply should be, and how these requirements can be related to the provision of educational and training facilities. Nevertheless, policies have to be formulated for educational development, for the provision of training, and for the necessary institutions for carrying out such programmes, and these policies have to be established or expanded and provided with resources. This may be most important for those sectors that require large amounts of resources, such as medical education and other forms of higher education and training. This has led to attempts to look at the whole question of supply and demand of different types of labour in a systematic manner, in short, to try to establish manpower planning, perhaps using an existing economic plan as a basis for working out requirements. In order to do this, some knowledge is needed of manpower requirements in relation to the output or activity in each of the sectors concerned; for example, how many extension workers would be needed to impart the knowledge necessary for the adoption of new agricultural techniques on the scale envisaged? The requirements for skills of different kinds could then be matched against the capacity of education and training facilities, and this in turn against the number of teachers that would be needed to man them and the institutions available to train them. This is essentially what manpower planning is about. In more sophisticated planning models, calculations of this kind might be incorporated into a computer model and a number of them have been devised for this purpose.

We remain at one and the same time sceptical about what can be accomplished by manpower planning and very much aware of the damage that can be caused to a development programme if the manpower needed to run it cannot be provided. This may point to the need to have a flexible approach at least to training that can be accomplished in a fairly short time by providing training programmes as a particular need becomes evident or can be foreseen. In other cases, training may respond in relation to evident shortages or oversupply. Where long training periods are involved, estimates of future needs will have to be prepared in order to furnish some guide to the need for training programmes.

In relation to GNP, even primary education is a significant cost. To provide universal primary education in a country such as Bangladesh might well take 15 per cent of the government's budget.[23] It is doubtful if the commitment of 15 per cent or more of the budget to primary education would be nationally acceptable or economically justified in the face of other needs, particularly if attendance is irregular, or less than complete, or if drop-out rates are high, as is often the case. It might even be argued for instance, in the light of O. D. Hoerr's study, that more resources should have been put into secondary education where the rate of return on resources appeared to be higher than in primary education, but this is not, of course, the only consideration.

The cost of secondary education is much greater per pupil per year than that of primary schools. The recurrent yearly cost per student in university education is probably of the order of 100 times that of primary education.[24] The steep rise in the cost of education, as a student moves from primary education through secondary to tertiary and university education, has considerable bearing on the educational strategy that can be followed. The private interest is clear: to strive after every educational advantage that can be taken as a means of obtaining a remunerative job. Many fail at the educational hurdles they encounter. Every successive step is achieved at progressively greater cost to the state, and after a point the marginal social return from higher education will almost certainly diminish steeply. One effect of the upward push is that each stage of education is regarded as a step to the next, and insufficient attention is given to the needs of those who will terminate their studies at one stage or another. This also requires a different curriculum, an issue to which we now turn.

We draw on the proposals of the ILO CESM to the Sudan to illustrate some facets of educational policy. The report observed:

There is no suggestion that primary students–the level at which most will terminate–are being prepared for futures as farmers, to become men and women who might develop the resources of their area ... It is not with any sense of irony that the children come out of their thatch sleeping huts, cook their breakfast, and then settle down to read, in the *Oxford Reader for Africa*, Book 4; ...

Even nowadays in some distant countries wild men still live in caves and in little huts among trees of the forest. In those parts of the world men do not wear clothes like ours. They hardly have any clothes at all. They do not eat food like ours and they live hard and dangerous lives, just like the ancient men of long ago.[25]

The above quotations illustrate the need to look at curricula critically–not only, may we add, in developing countries. Efforts to adapt education to the needs of people who will not receive much of it have led to a variety of suggestions. In the case of the Sudan, the most important of these was the recognition that each type of education should be considered to be an end in itself and not just a stepping-stone to further education. Thus it was proposed for primary education that, in addition to literacy and numeracy, national consciousness and some familiarity with the local environment should be taught. It was suggested that this programme of basic education should be followed by two or three years of prevocational training for those who wished to attend.

A sharp reduction in secondary education was proposed by the CESM because it was felt that vocational training could be better given on the job than in the classroom, and that the object of higher education should be related to the growth of modern-sector jobs. The pared-down secondary system would then have served as a conduit to higher education.

The proposals for higher education followed a similar emphasis: a reduced rate of expansion in which mathematics and science received preference; and opposition to the establishment of new universities. In total the proposals may be summed up as attempting to gear the educational system to the needs of the nation and to make it efficient in its use of resources. These major proposals were flanked by others, such as packages for adults geared to basic needs: education related to production, nutrition, sanitation and personal health. In this way it was hoped to form a bridge between the modern and the traditional sector of the economy.

The proposals put forward by the Mission were not well liked by those responsible for education in the Sudan. More than a single report was needed to reduce the force of the upwards push and university education continued to be expanded. Perhaps it was unrealistic to expect that it would not be. Those in political power are also those with an interest in securing educational opportunities for people like themselves. In this respect the diversification of educational resources to tertiary education is a factor making for inequality in the distribution of income. To some extent, increased educational opportunities at early stages of education may help to redress the balance. Using regression analysis, Dr M. A. Ahluwalia has suggested that increasing the primary school enrolment rate appears to improve the income share of the poorest 40 per cent of the population, while increasing the secondary school enrolment rate improves the position of the middle 40 per cent in the income distribution.[26]

Formal education in schools and other institutions is only one way to attain useful knowledge. For those who have had little or no education in their youth, attempts may be made to provide educational opportunities suitable to their needs. In this, Mozambique gives a lead. Literacy can be taught in the work-place as well as in educational buildings. It can be taught after working hours to quarry workers sitting round their teacher in a circle in the open air before the sun sinks below the horizon, or anywhere else where the minimum of instruction and materials need be provided. Again, as many know and have experienced, in rich and poor countries alike, doing a job and continuing to attend classes in the evening is one way of extending one's qualifications. In Mozambique, there are too few people with even limited education for them to be spared from work for full-time studies and they have to combine the two. Again in Mozambique, the party cadres are also instruments of political and other forms of education. In Bangladesh, efforts have been made to use cooperatives as a source of educational opportunity. Organisational efforts of a high order are necessary to promote informal education. Botswana provides an example of what such organisation entails. One approach there has been to try to use farms and workshops attached to schools as a means of providing technical training, accustoming pupils to productive work, and giving them a sight of opportunities for technical improvement. Another model has involved the establishment of so-called brigades. These are work groups acting both as centres of training in skills and productive enterprises and of general education. Skilled craftsmen are all too scarce in most developing countries and the brigades have demonstrated their capacity to train good artisans as well as to impart farming skills. While such developments may succeed in making education more responsive to community needs, they are not necessarily cheap to run and often depend on initiatives supported by public or private agencies providing external assistance and enthusiasm. Even so, about 70 per cent of the money needed to operate the brigades in Botswana came from their own resources.[27]

While informal education may greatly extend people's knowledge in a variety of ways, it cannot be expected to provide for high technical skills, the training of most types of teachers and the many specialised staff that modern life requires. Medical schools, teacher training colleges, engineering colleges and numerous other specialised institutions have to be created. For the higher specialities it may be necessary to rely on training abroad, although there is much to be said for developing domestic institutions to replace foreign instruction when this is practicable. Domestic courses may be more cheaply run. Foreign courses widen the experience of the students undertaking them, but they sometimes impart alien standards and values as well, and they may lead to a brain drain.

HEALTH

Mortality rates are much higher in low- than in high-income countries, as Table 7.4 illustrates. Perhaps the most striking thing about the table is the increase in life expectancy since 1960, not only in the rich countries but in those of low income as well. In China, life expectancy is now reported to be 67 and in India 55. Income is only one (and not necessarily the most important) determinant of longevity. Amongst the poorest countries expectation of life in 1982 varied from 36 in Afghanistan to 69 in Sri Lanka. Medical provision is only one aspect of this. The number of people per physician in 1980 varied from 3,480 in Pakistan to 58,490 in Ethiopia, to take but one indicator of health care. In Sri

Table 7.4 Life expectancy and child death rates, 1960 and 1982

	Life expectancy at birth		Child death rates (per thousand of age group 1-4)	
	1960	1982	1960	1982
Low-income countries (excluding China and India)	42	51	31	19
China	41	67	26	7
India	42	55	26	11
Middle-income countries	51	60	23	10
Industrialised market economies	70	75	2	0.5

Source: Based on *World Development Reports* of the World Bank.

Lanka it was 7,170, much more unfavourable than in 1960, when it was 4,490, although since then expectation of life has risen.

Historically, prevention of disease by improvement of nutrition, by immunisation and by public health measures can be seen to have been of great importance. In the developing countries, too, prevention is much better than cure, not least because it is cheaper to carry out in the initial stages of improving health care. It is also effective, as shown by results achieved from the institution and expansion of a service of 'barefoot doctors' in China and elsewhere, or from investments to improve the water supply or sanitation.

The socially orientated policies of Sri Lanka, particularly up to the mid-1970s, illustrate what can be done for a country with a per capita income of $320 (at 1982 prices) when primary education is almost universally provided, health services are available at nominal cost and food is subsidised to ensure an adequate diet. It may be worthwhile sacrificing some growth potential if such benefits can be conferred.

Infant mortality rates (children aged under 1) are ten or less per thousand in industrialised market economies, compared with over two hundred in some low-income countries. The reasons for these differences are not so much lack of medical specialised care as the results of poor diet and living in an uncontrolled environment. The most widespread diseases in developing countries are probably those transmitted by human faeces. These include intestinal parasitic and infectious diarrhoeal diseases as well as poliomyelitis, typhoid and cholera. Infants are particularly prone to die from diarrhoeal diseases and often because oral rehydration is not practised.[28] Intestinal parasitic diseases are more likely to be debilitating than a cause of death, but are very common. Airborne diseases are probably the second major disease group and include the usual childhood diseases as well as meningitis. Such diseases are spread by living in close contact with infected people and poor housing conditions greatly increase their impact.

Vector-borne diseases are less widespread than the other categories mentioned above but are significant in various parts of the world. The most widespread of these diseases are malaria, trypanosomiasis (sleeping sickness), Chagas' disease (a variety of sleeping sickness), onchocerciasis (river blindness) and schistosomiasis (bilharzia).[29]

To a greater or lesser extent these diseases can be controlled by environmental measures. The faecally transmitted diseases can be controlled by taking sanitary measures and providing a safe water supply. The introduction of pit latrines, provided that they are properly maintained and, even more important, are used, may serve to deal with infection from human excreta. The provision of safe water supplies can be much more expensive but no less necessary if health is to be maintained. In many cases, relatively simple measures are capable, if strictly observed, of reducing the transmission of diseases by faeces and a contaminated water supply.[30]

For many diseases, as is well known, it is possible to reduce their impact and to prevent them spreading by providing immunisation, sometimes in advance of infection, or sometimes by *ad hoc* measures to deal with epidemics. Smallpox has now been eliminated by immunisation and public health measures. Not all diseases are responsive to relatively simple preventive or curative measures and the incidence of some of them may be extended by development activities, as occurs with bilharzia. The snail, the vector transmitting the disease, thrives in slow-moving water, and irrigation systems therefore greatly increase the opportunity for it to spread its effects. Onchocerciasis, of which the vector is the simulium fly, may increase when dams with turbulent water near sluice gates are constructed, for it thrives in swift-running water.

Control of the various diseases mentioned can be expected to improve living standards indirectly, in addition to its effects on well-being. As we have seen in the discussion of population issues, the high birth rate of the less-developed countries is, in some measure, the consequence of high infant mortality. If the latter were reduced, experience shows that the birth rate might also fall, at least after a time. This in turn would be beneficial for the health of women, for recurrent child-bearing has adverse effects on the mother's health.

The incidence of disease also impairs the work of those affected by it. Unfit people might seek less demanding jobs, work shorter hours and produce less. Curiously, not all these effects seem to manifest themselves. A study by Robert E. Baldwin shows that the incidence of schistosomiasis was significantly associated with lower earnings on piece rates, amounting to about 30 per cent of average earnings for men and 15 per cent for women.[31] Earnings, however, were less affected; sufferers tended to work longer in the week so that the effect of the disease was to reduce leisure rather than income. In other ways, ill health is wasteful of resources. Parasitic worms, intestinal infections and fevers make heavier demands on nutrition and so are costly in this respect.

The first lesson to learn is that environmental health care should take precedence over other medical provisions. The most cost-efficient measures are likely to be those aimed at the prevention of disease rather than its cure. This is not to say that there should be no hospitals, but that building more of them should not be seen as the main solution to improving health care in developing countries. As always there will be pressures on the part of the medical profession and authorities to provide the advanced facilities that are needed at the boundaries of medical science, and there will be a need also to train doctors; both of these require hospital research and teaching facilities.

The justification for attempting to use paramedics lies not so much in the fact that they are less costly to train and so may be provided quickly and in greater numbers than fully trained medical practitioners, as in the fact that there are simple measures that can be carried out to improve health out of all proportion to their cost. Sanitation and the provision of clean water is something that can be carried out by planners, engineers and plumbers; it does not need a doctor to effect such improvements once the ground rules for supply, construction and use have been worked out.

Apart from the relatively simple measures advocated above, nutrition can make a signficant improvement in health. This is likely to be more costly than the provision of privies or even clean water. Nevertheless, in some cases a modest supplementation of diet, including perhaps a meal a day in schools, could succeed in bringing nutritional standards to a higher level. Here the general development of the country overlaps with the needs of health care.

FURTHER READING

Philip H. Coombs and Manzoor Ahmed, *Attacking Rural Poverty: How Nonformal Education Can Help*, Baltimore, Md., Johns Hopkins Press, 1974.

E. Costa, 'Maximising Employment in Labour-Intensive Development Programmes', *International Development Review*, Vol. 108 (1973), No. 5, pp. 371-94.

International Bank for Reconstruction and Development, *World Development Report 1980*, Oxford, Oxford University Press, 1980, Chapter 5: 'Human Development Issues and Policies', pp. 46-70.

International Labour Office, *Growth, Employment and Equity. A Comprehensive Employment Strategy for the Sudan*. Report of the ILO/UNDP Employment Mission 1975, ILO, 1976, Summary and Main Recommendations, pp. XVII-XXX.

Thomas G. Rawski, *Economic Growth and Employment in China*, Oxford, Oxford University Press, 1979.

Paul Streeten *et al.*, *First Things First: Meeting Basic Human Needs in the Developing Countries*, Oxford, Oxford University Press, 1981.

NOTES

1. For an innovative experiment of measurement in this field, pioneered by Dudley Seers, see Henry Lucas, *Life Expectancy as an Integrating Concept for Social and Demographic Data*, OECD Development Centre, 1985.

2. Gunnar Myrdal, *Asian Drama. An Inquiry into the Poverty of Nations*, London, Allen Lane, 1968, 3 vols; Volume II: Chapter 2, in particular pp. 1019-27, and Chapter 5.

3. See, for example, *Growth, Employment and Equity: A Comprehensive Strategy for the Sudan*. Report of the ILO/UNDP Employment Mission 1975, ILO, 1976.

4. Data drawn from *Employment, Income and Equality: A Strategy for Increasing Productive Employment in Keyna*, ILO, 1972, p. 59, and *Growth, Employment and Equity*, op. cit., Table 67, p. 313.

5. For an indication of some of the dimensions of the problem in the case of

Bangladesh, see Just Faaland and J. R. Parkinson, *Bangladesh: The Test Case for Development*, London, Hurst, 1976, p. 83.

6. Frances Stewart and Paul Streeten, 'Conflicts between Output and Employment', *Oxford Economic Papers*, Vol. 23 (1971), No. 2, pp. 145-68.

7. For a discussion of the underlying theory, including the Heckscher-Ohlin theory of international trade, see, for example, Bo Södersten, *International Economics*, 2nd edn., London, Macmillan, 1980, or other similar textbooks.

8. Sohail J. Malik, 'A Note on the Edible Oil Milling Sector Output, Value-added and Employment', *Pakistan Development Review*, Vol. 16 (1977), No. 4, pp. 449-63.

9. See P. D. Dunn, *Appropriate Technology*, London, Macmillan, 1978, pp. 3-17.

10. J. C. Ramaer, 'The Choice of Appropriate Technology by a Multinational Corporation: A Case Study of Messrs. Philips, Eindhoven', in Austin Robinson (ed.), *Appropriate Technologies for Third World Development*, London, Macmillan, 1979, pp. 239-45.

11. Howard Pack, 'The Employment-Output Trade-Off in LDC's', *Oxford Economic Papers*, Vol. 26 (1974), No. 3, pp. 388-404.

12. Abdul Qayum, *Theory and Policy of Accounting Prices*, Amsterdam, North Holland, 1960.

13. Professor Qayum worked with a Cobb-Douglas function as a means to estimate the effects of a subsidy on output, employment and taxation. The coefficients used, however, were more related to the conditions of developed than developing countries and changing them to more appropriate values affects the results appreciably. It may also be wondered whether the products manufactured by appropriate techniques are always fully substitutable with more mechanised systems of manufacture and whether those responsible for the choice of technique would be responsive to a reduction in the cost of labour.

14. G. Ranis, 'Production Functions, Market Imperfections and Economic Development', *Economic Journal*, Vol. 72 (1962), June, pp. 344-54.

15. See Anne O. Kreuger, 'Trade Strategies and Employment in Developing Countries', *Finance and Development*, Vol. 21 (1984), No. 2, pp. 23-26, and the same author, *Trade and Employment in Developing Countries, Volume 3: Syntheses and Conclusions*, Chicago, University of Chicago Press, 1983.

16. This injection of thought is generally ascribed to the mission to Kenya led by Professor Hans Singer.

17. *Economist*, 31 December 1977.

18. See Wilfred Burchett and Rewi Alley, *China, the Quality of Life*, Harmondsworth, Middx., Pelican, 1976.

19. See Luc De Wulf, 'Economic Reform in China', *Finance and Development*, Vol. 22 (1985), No. 1, pp. 8-11

20. O. D. Hoerr, 'Education, Income and Equity in Malaysia', *Economic Development and Cultural Change*, Vol. 21 (1973), No. 2, pp. 247-73. Note that this method is likely to encounter a number of technical snags including collinearity. It is also possible that omitted variables will have the effect of exaggerating the effects of education on earnings.

21. See George Psacharopoulos, 'Returns to Education: An Updated International Comparison', in Timothy King (ed.), *Education and Income*, World Bank, 1980, pp. 73-109. World Bank Staff Working Paper, No. 402.

22. There are, of course, some benefits to the providing country through emigrants' remittances and sometimes the return of more experienced workers, but the inflow of money may also be spent in wasteful ways as is said to be occurring in Bangladesh at the present time.

23. See Nurul Islam, *Development Strategy of Bangladesh*, Oxford, Pergamon Press, 1978, p. 74. If classes consist of forty pupils, perhaps 2 per cent of the total labour-force would be needed as teachers. Including some other costs, this might involve the expenditure of, say, 3 per cent of GDP or if government expenditure were 20 per cent of GDP, about 15 per cent of government expenditure.

24. A. F. A. Husain, *Educational Development and Reform in Bangladesh*, Chr. Michelsen Institute, 1978. DERAP Working Paper, A 106, Table XII, p. 268.

25. *Growth, Employment and Equity*, op. cit., p. 400.

26. See 'Income Inequality: Some Dimensions of the Problem', in Hollis Chenery *et al.*, *Redistribution with Growth*, Oxford, Oxford University Press, 1974, p. 17.

27. For an account see Patrick Van Rensburg, 'Education versus Exploitation', *Guardian*, 18 March 1981, p. 8.

28. For further details, see Part I in James P. Grant, *The State of the World's Children 1984*, published for UNICEF by Oxford University Press, 1983.

29. See the World Bank's *The Assault on World Poverty*, Baltimore, Md., Johns Hopkins Press, 1975, p. 353.

30. It should be pointed out that there are many pitfalls in attempting to improve water supplies and many ancillary measures that need to be taken, such as ensuring that pure water does not get contaminated after it is drawn. Evaluating the results of providing improved water supplies is a highly complicated business. See Sandy Cairncross *et al.*, *Evaluation for Village Water Supply Planning*, London, John Wiley, 1980.

31. Robert E. Baldwin and Burton A. Weisbrod, 'Disease and Labor Productivity', *Economic Development and Cultural Change*, Vol. 22 (1974), No. 3, pp. 414-35.

8 International development policy

Each developing and developed country has its own interest in international trade and economic relations and in devising national policies that will enable it to make the best use, as it sees it, of its opportunities. International transactions imply interdependence between countries and sets of countries, which extend from the movement of goods and services to aid and capital flows, with accompanying indebtedness, and even further to the transfer of technology and to the migration of labour and of whole populations. We shall deal only with some selected aspects of international trade and finance. In principle, such transactions could take place without any formal international framework of agreement to guide them. However, experience has shown, particularly in the 1930s, that without adequate international understanding, international transactions are constrained and differences of interests between countries are more than usually hard to resolve.

Thus over time and in response to need, various international agreements have been reached about how international transactions should be conducted and certain rules have been established to which countries are expected to adhere. These rules are not sacrosanct but are amended, often under pressure and reluctantly, to meet changing needs and in response to the representation of groups who feel themselves to be adversely affected by them. Interest here centres on what may be the differing needs of developed and developing countries. Certainly in the last decade the developing countries have felt that the rules discriminated against them and have campaigned, largely unsuccessfully, for changes in them.

The rules are, of course, closely related to the institutions, particularly those of the United Nations and affiliated bodies, that are established to operate them, to exercise surveillance and to provide a forum for discussions, as well as to consider modifications as they may be required. Different interests may see such institutions as favouring or obstructing their cause and one way to influence the situation may be to set up new bodies to govern international relations.

In this chapter we are concerned with instances where the needs of developing and developed countries both coincide and differ, and also with the inadequacy of international machinery for supervision, regulation and revision to deal with all the problems that arise in a rapidly changing world. The events of the last decade have shown the increasing interdependence of the developed and developing world and the need to make adjustments to preserve an effective working system. In surveying events, we are particularly concerned with the interests of the developing countries in world trade.

We start the discussion by considering some aspects of the patterns of trade and finance, such as the dependence of many developing countries on exports of primary products, although others are rapidly becoming major exporters of manufactures. To this end we present in a series of tables a selection of data characterising the current and changing position of developing countries in world trade and finance. This provides a basis for consideration of the kind of international arrangements for trade and payments that many developing countries would like to see. The discussion is broadened later to consider some aspects of the operations of transnational corporations, which play such a large part in economic operations and particularly in international exchanges. Finally, we try to peer a little into the future to see whether world resources are adequate to sustain development on the scale needed and how the developing countries may fare.

THE STATISTICAL STRUCTURE OF TRADE AND FINANCE

It is necessary to know something about the structure of the trade of developing countries in order to understand where their interests lie in the world trading and payments system. We set out some background statistical information below as a prelude to a discussion of salient features.

Expansion of world trade can exercise a major influence on the opportunities for developing countries to expand their economies. Table 8.1 shows how the quantum of their exports has increased since 1938 and contrasts it with the exports of the developed market economies. As we have seen, many discussions about the policies appropriate for the developing countries to follow have turned on what was happening, or assumed to happen, to their terms of trade. Some rather crude figures are given in Table 8.2 to show how complex and varied the movements have been over a long period. An allied issue, on which we have refrained from presenting detailed facts, is the extent to which prices of primary products fluctuate. Monthly fluctuations are in fact quite considerable; calculations by UNCTAD show that, in the period 1972-83, the monthly price of sugar (an extreme case) varied on average as much as 50 per cent from its trend. For other commodities such as coffee, cocoa, copra and coconut oil the extent of the fluctuation was over 30 per cent. Fluctuations for many other commodities were less marked, varying typically from 10 to 20 per cent.

Table 8.1 Quantum of visible exports of developing and developed countries in selected years (1980=100)

	Developing market economy countries	Developed market economy countries
1938	(32)	(10)
1950	(34)	(13)
1955	(39)	(18)
1960	49	24
1965	65	34
1970	100	54
1975	90	73
1980	100	100
1981	94	102
1982	88	101
1983	89	102

Source: UNCTAD, *Handbook of International Trade and Development Statistics 1984*, and *United Nations Statistical Yearbook*, various editions. The series have been adjusted to put them on base 1980=100. Figures in parentheses are to be regarded as orders of magnitudes.

Table 8.2 Terms of trade in selected years (1980=100)

	Developing countries			Developed market economy countries
	All developing countries	Major petroleum exporters	Other developing countries	
1938	(41)			(123)
1950	(58)			(112)
1955	(57)			(112)
1960	51	22	120	117
1965	45	20	115	120
1970	42	19	125	122
1975	79	60	129	109
1980	100	100	100	100
1981	107	117	92	98
1982	103	115	98	100
1983	98	103	91	101

Source: As for Table 8.1.

The geographical distribution of trade is important in giving some indication of the countries, or blocs, that are most involved with the developing countries and therefore most likely to be concerned in negotiations with them about trading conditions. Table 8.3 provides some indication of the network of world trade as it appeared in 1982. Attention is often centred on visible trade in commodities to the exclusion of service transactions. However, the latter are of increasing importance in world trade. Table 8.4 illustrates this by giving figures for three countries, Bangladesh, Botswana and the Sudan. Finally, the net flow of financial resources to developing countries is a matter of great importance both from the point of view of providing resources for them and in relation to the debt issue. Table 8.5 shows the magnitude and nature of these flows over a number of years, distinguishing between grant aid, commercial and other flows.

SALIENT FEATURES OF TRADE AND FINANCE FLOWS

Exports of the developed countries are now roughly ten times their 1938 level as against only three times for developing countries. This is partly due to the fact that exports of manufactures

Table 8.3 Trade of developing countries in 1982 (in billions of US$ equivalents)

Exporting countries	World total	Exports to developed market economies					Exports to socialist countries	Exports to developing countries
		Total	EEC and EFTA	Japan	USA	Other countries		
OPEC	225	163	71	48	30	14	3	59
Other developing countries	255	159	55	24	66	14	16	79
All developing countries combined	481	323	127	72	97	27	18	138

Importing countries	World total	Imports from developed market economies					Imports from socialist countries	Imports from developing countries
		Total	EEC and EFTA	Japan	USA	Other		
OPEC	144	111	61	22	20	8	8	24
Other developing countries	318	180	68	40	55	18	24	114
All developing countries combined	462	292	129	62	75	26	33	138

Note: (1) The details of the table may not add to the totals because of the effects of rounding. (2) The classification of countries followed here is that of UNCTAD with China included in the tabulations as a socialist rather than a developing country. This makes rather little difference to the picture emerging from the statistics in the table.

Source: UNCTAD, *Handbook of International Trade and Development Statistics, 1984 Supplement,* pp. 62–4.

Table 8.4 Illustrations of importance of service payments in 1983 (in million units of IMF Special Drawing Rights–SDR–in 1983 approximately equal to US$1.00)

	Bangladesh	Botswana	Sudan
Merchandise exports	677	603	482
Emigrants' remittances, etc.	614	45	230
Merchandise imports	−1938	−571	−657
Investment income payments	−110	−118	−214

Source: International Monetary fund, *Balance of Payments Statistics Yearbook 1984*, Vol. 35.

have increased very much more rapidly than exports of primary products. In 1955, exports of manufactured goods accounted for only about 5 per cent of developing countries' total exports, compared with over 50 per cent for developed market countries. In 1913, primary products, excluding fuel, accounted for almost 60 per cent of world trade; in 1980, this had shrunk to 25 per cent. Although the OPEC countries increased the value of their oil exports after prices were raised in the 1970s, the volume of their exports fell. As a result of changes in market shares and price relationships the composition of world trade has been changing rapidly and appreciably. In 1980, manufactures accounted for nearly 70 per cent of world trade, excluding fuel, and over 50 per cent when fuel is included.

For many poor developing countries exports of manufactures are now very important; more than half of the exports of Bangladesh, India, China and Pakistan, for example, consist of manufactures. Other countries were very differently placed. Amongst the low-income countries, fuels, minerals, metals, and other primary commodities accounted in 1980 for over 90 per cent of the export receipts of Ethiopia, Malawi, Somalia, Niger and Madagascar, and over 60 per cent of export receipts for Nepal, Burkina Fasso, Tanzania, Central African Republic, Sri Lanka, Togo and Kenya. Other, wealthier countries also were highly dependent on exports of primary products.

Countries heavily dependent on exports of manufactures

Table 8.5 The net flow of financial resources from DAC countries and multilateral agencies

Net disbursements at current prices and exchange rates	1970	1975	1980	1981	1982	1983
			($billion)			
I. Official development assistance	6.9	13.8	27.3	25.5	27.7	27.5
1. Bilateral grants and grant-like flows of which:	3.3	6.3	14.1	13.2	13.4	14.1
technical cooperation	1.5	2.9	5.5	5.2	5.4	5.8
2. Bilateral loans at concessional terms	2.4	3.5	4.0	5.0	5.0	5.8
3. Contributions to multilateral institutions of which:	1.3	4.0	9.2	7.3	9.3	8.9
UN	0.4	1.2	2.2	2.2	2.3	2.2
EEC	0.2	0.7	1.6	1.6	1.4	1.4
IDA	0.6	1.3	3.1	2.4	2.8	3.1
Regional development banks	0.1	0.4	1.7	0.8	1.6	1.6
II. Other official flows	1.1	3.9	5.3	6.6	7.4	5.0
1. Bilateral	0.8	3.8	5.4	6.5	7.4	4.9
2. Multilateral	0.3	0.1	−0.1	0.1	−	0.1
III. Private flows	7.0	25.7	40.4	57.2	46.4	34.3
1. Direct investment	3.7	10.3	10.1	15.4	10.2	6.3
2. Bilateral portfolio	0.7	9.3	17.3	27.5	23.7	17.5
3. Export credits	2.2	3.5	11.5	10.5	7.3	5.2
IV. Grants by private voluntary agencies	0.9	1.3	2.4	2.0	2.3	2.3
V. Total net flows	15.9	44.8	75.3	91.4	83.9	69.1

Note on terms:
Official development assistance, which in the context of the table is synonymous with aid, is provided by the official sector, designed to promote economic development and welfare in the recipient country and given on concessional terms defined as at least a 25 per cent grant element.[1]
Bilateral flows are direct from a donor to a recipient country.
Multilateral flows are channelled via an international organisation, e.g. the World Bank.
Direct investment e.g. by foreign companies, includes reinvested earnings.
Portfolio investment includes bank loans as well as other loans or purchase of securities.
Export credits amount to loans from exports to importers in developing countries; they are often rather expensive forms of credit.
Source: OECD, *Development Co-operation. Efforts and Policies of the Members of the Development Assistance Committee, 1984 Review*, OECD, 1984.

clearly have an interest in extending their markets for those products by whatever means they have in their power, whereas countries much more heavily dependent on exports of primary products are more likely to look for international measures designed to strengthen the markets for their products and protect them against adverse trading conditions. All countries have an interest in improving their terms of trade but, as is evident from the above description of the composition of exports, an improvement for exporters of mainly primary products or fuels may affect other developing countries adversely. Exporters of manufactures will benefit from a rise in the price of such goods, which again may be to the disadvantage of other developing countries. Thus it is becoming much less revealing to enquire how the terms of trade for developing countries as a group have been changing than it was some decades ago when developing countries could be regarded typically as exporters of primary products and importers of manufactures. Table 8.2 must be read with this in mind.

The terms of trade of the industrialised countries have worsened since 1938, reflecting, in particular, the increase in the price of oil imposed in 1973 and subsequently. This factor also affects the developing countries but differentially. Since 1960 the oil-exporting developing countries have seen their terms of trade improve nearly fivefold, while over the same period the terms of trade of the non-oil-exporting developing countries have deteriorated by about one-quarter. Even so, it is possible that their terms of trade have not changed greatly by comparison with 1938, judging by estimated movements between 1938 and 1960 for developing countries as a group.

The net effect of changes in the volume and prices of internationally traded goods was that in 1982 the developed market economy countries had more than 60 per cent of world trade and the developing countries about 25 per cent; the developed, centrally planned economies account for less than 10 per cent of world trade. None of these proportions is very different from 1955 although they have fluctuated in intermediate years. Nevertheless, the figures conceal divergent trends between the oil-exporting and other developing countries. Between 1955 and 1982, the share of the former in world exports rose from 8 to 14 per cent while that of the others fell from 17 to 12 per cent.

Exports of OPEC go, in large measure, to developed market economies, but other developing countries are also supplied with

substantial amounts of petroleum. The exports of other developing countries are very similarly divided. OPEC is also supplied
predominantly from the developed market economies. The other
developing countries are less dependent on this source, partly
because of their imports from OPEC.

Developing countries clearly have an interest in increasing
their receipts from service activities such as transport, banking,
insurance and tourism, and this is likely to lead them to seek
maximum access to such activities in world markets. For Bangladesh and the Sudan, private unregulated transfers (mainly workers' remittances from abroad) are a major contribution to
revenues. Here again there is likely to be concern about continued
access to employment in other countries.

Over the years private flows of funds have generally been
greater than official flows, but in 1983 private flows diminished
reflecting the effects of the debt crisis. The advantage of official
flows is that they are generally provided on better terms than
private financing, but their amount is less than the total capital
inflow required. In total, the resource flows amount to about 4 per
cent of the gross national product of the developing countries but
there is a great deal of variation from country to country.

There can be no doubt about the importance of the operation of
transnational corporations in developing countries but statistical
assessments are hard to come. It is, however, generally assumed
that most direct investment in developing countries is carried out
by transnational corporations. Table 8.5 gives some indication of
the magnitude of such flows (say $10-15 billion per year), but it is
unavoidably incomplete since part of the loans from banks in
DAC countries goes to the support of the transnationals and they
may borrow locally also. The flow of private investment has been
widely spread, but developing countries in Latin America may
have received one-third of total world-wide foreign investment in
the years 1969-76 and sizeable amounts have been invested in
Asia.[2]

The United States has been the major investor: in 1971, of total
direct foreign investments at that time, over 50 per cent was in
their hands, followed by 15 per cent for the United Kingdom and
5 per cent for France.[3] Since then, the role of Japan has become
increasingly important, as has that of some medium-income
developing countries, including even India. It should not be
assumed that all such investment goes to manufacturing. At the

end of the 1960s, about one-third was in this sector and about the same in petroleum with the rest more widely spread.[4] Of the manufacturing concerns, many of the affiliates of the United States' transnationals exist as important suppliers to that country.[5] Interestingly, multinational corporations are now in evidence in some countries of the Third World, notably India, Hong Kong, Argentina and Brazil.[6]

DEVELOPING COUNTRIES IN THE WORLD ECONOMIC SYSTEM

The facts analysed above can be used to identify some of the interests of the developing countries in improving their position in the world's trading system. As we have seen, the market for manufactures is an expanding one and the developing countries have an interest in increasing their share of it. Their present share in the apparent consumption of manufactures in 1980 in the eleven major industrial countries is only about 3 per cent, although for clothing, footwear and leather products the share is over 13 per cent, and as a percentage of imports the proportions are obviously much greater.[7]

It appears that the terms of trade of developing countries have not changed greatly on balance over the last thirty years. More favourable terms of trade would, of course, improve their position.[8] Developing countries may be helped to get more remunerative prices for their manufactured exports to the industrialised countries, in some cases, by reducing import duties on them, but the scope for this may be limited. Moreover, at the present time, developed countries have sought to limit imports from developing countries by imposing non-tariff barriers. About 15 per cent of EEC imports, 13 per cent of those of the United States, and 19 per cent of those of Japan appeared to be affected by this in 1983.[9]

For exports of primary products, however, ways may be sought through commodity agreements to establish some monopolistic edge on markets, while at the same time reducing fluctuations in price. This was one of the objectives of developing countries when they attempted to persuade the industrial countries that a new international economic order was needed. Before we consider the nature of the desired international order, we briefly examine the existing order and the circumstances in which it emerged.

The 1930s proved to be a very testing time for international economic cooperation and showed up many weaknesses of the system then in operation. As World War II neared its close, plans were prepared for new institutions and international arrangements designed to improve cooperation between countries in the economic sphere. It was hoped that these would provide monetary stability, encourage the operation of the world's economy at a high level, facilitate growth in the industrialised countries and contribute to the development of the Third World. Within this framework, the principle of removing restrictions on trade between countries gained acceptance as one means of promoting an efficient use of the world's resources.

In many major essentials the structure of international economic relations devised at that time remains to this day, although significant changes took place in the early 1970s. Two of the principal international institutions that were established, the International Bank for Reconstruction and Development (IBRD or the World Bank) and the International Monetary Fund (IMF or the Fund) are still with us. The third institution proposed, the International Trade Organisation, never materialised and the role of international regulation of trade was taken by other international institutions, mainly through the acceptance of the General Agreement on Trade and Tariffs (GATT) in 1947. This was supplemented in 1964 by the UN Conference on Trade and Development (UNCTAD). This was in response to the dissatisfaction of the developing countries with GATT, which was and so far remains an organisation mainly for trade of, and between, industrialised countries. UNCTAD I marked the beginning of the Group of (initially) seventy-seven developing countries, which was to be regarded by the developed countries as a pressure group designed to represent the interests of the Third World.

When the role of GATT was formulated there was some recognition that the developing countries would be likely to encounter balance of payments difficulties and that they would wish to protect their industries by maintaining tariffs and other restrictions on imports. As time went on, it became apparent that it was not enough to focus on import replacement, and that it would be necessary to consider export promotion and, therefore, for the developed countries to eliminate or reduce barriers to trade which affected exports of special interest to the developing world. In practice, the concessions made over the years by developed countries were not insubstantial; of particular importance was the

1970 agreement to establish a Generalised System of Tariff Preferences (GSP) in favour of developing countries' exports. Yet the GSP did not add very much very quickly. Thus, according to estimates by the UNCTAD secretariat, only 13.4 per cent of the dutiable imports in 1976 into EEC and ten other preference-giving countries did in fact receive preferential treatment.[10]

Although, as we have seen, some concessions were made to the needs of the developing countries, they became increasingly dissatisfied with the slow rate of progress. The increase in world trade, as our figures show, had been less marked in its effects on the developing countries and the concessions made to encourage the exports of the developing countries were regarded as inadequate. While some developing countries had done well, the low-income countries seemed to be falling further and further behind. To the developing countries there seemed to be a maldistribution of economic power in the world system. The search for a new economic order began within the framework of the non-aligned countries and the Group of 77 which, as time went on, became an organised force in other fora in addition to UNCTAD and increased the weight of its membership. The developed countries opposed this movement and gradually reduced it to ineffectiveness. Nevertheless, it is important to understand how the issues came to be discussed and the underlying reasons that led the developing countries to feel that they were being taken advantage of.

The international monetary order imposed at Bretton Woods broke down in the early 1970s and a considerable further shock was given to it by the large increases in oil prices in 1973 and then again in the late 1970s. The advantages secured by an enforced price increase for one primary product kindled the imagination of the developing countries and led them to call for a Special Session of the United Nations General Assembly on Problems of Raw Materials and Development, which took place in 1974.

The demand of the developing countries for a new international economic order, as embodied in resolutions adopted by the Special Session of the General Assembly in 1974 and 1975, are wide-ranging. They include:

1. changes in the power structure to achieve equity and social justice and introduce more democratic processes of international decision taking;

2. control and regulation of activities of transnational corporations in investment, technology, production and trade;
3. greater participation of the developing countries in the processing, marketing and distribution of their primary products and in trade-related activities such as shipping and insurance;
4. improvement in the access of the developing countries to the markets of the developed countries and for special and more favourable treatment for developing countries;
5. new efforts on the part of developed countries to facilitate industrialisation of the developing countries;
6. proposals for managed cooperation between developing countries.

Basically, the new economic order calls for a system of preference in favour of developing countries on as large a scale as the developed countries might be prepared to concede. The justification for such demands may be put in humanitarian terms but they may also be revealingly put in their historical context, as Sir Arthur Lewis has done.[11] This not only gives insights into how the present international division of labour emerged; it also permits some reflections on what the future may hold. Lewis argues that a precondition of industrialisation in a closed economy is the existence of an efficient agricultural sector which can provide both the surplus food and raw materials needed by the industrial sector and the markets needed by entrepreneurs for their industrial products. (A suitable investment climate is another precondition for capital accumulation.) This, not colonial suppression, explains why the industrial revolution did not catch on in other countries. As Western countries industrialised, it became an article of faith that they had a comparative advantage in industrial production, while what is now the so-called developing world was assumed to be well equipped for agricultural and raw material production. Yet, in absolute terms, agricultural productivity in Britain around 1900 was high, as Lewis observes: 'In Britain, which was the biggest single source of European migration, the yield of wheat by 1900 was 1600lbs per acre, as against the tropical yields of grain of 700lbs per acre.'

Since the Europeans had better equipment than did the tropical inhabitants, output per man was much greater. Living standards were correspondingly higher. The reverse was true in India and China; an unlimited supply of labour, ready to move anywhere for a shilling a day, kept wages down. It was not possible for the tropical countries to escape from the unfavourable terms of trade they experienced by increasing productivity and exporting more, for this only caused the terms of trade to decline. In mineral production, low wages meant high profits for foreign investors. The West was thus at great advantage in its trading pattern, drawing on cheap supplies of primary products, earning a high income in manufacturing, benefiting from economies of scale and large markets and generating a surplus for investment. As Lewis puts it: 'The market price gave the Nigerian for his peanuts a 700lbs of grain per acre level of living, and the Australian for his wool a 1600lbs per acre level of living . . . because these were the respective amounts of food that their cousins could produce on the family farms.'

Why then, asks Lewis, did the Third World countries not set up their own factories? Partly because of foreign dominance in trade, banking and insurance where good profits were to be had; partly because consumers in the Third World grew to prefer the products of the West, for example, wheat to yams and cement to local building materials; and exports tended to buy imports, not domestic products. In these circumstances, material progress was determined above all by the pace of industrialisation. If industrialisation is so important for the development of countries, the abolition of restrictions on imports of manufactured goods by the North is much more important than anything that can happen in the commodities area.

Sir Arthur Lewis's analysis provides some of the intellectual underpinning needed for attempts to encourage the exports of manufactures from the developing countries. What is being advocated is a considerable reversal in the degree of the world division of labour between industry and agriculture. The process will be gradual and directed to achieving a shift in emphasis. The Third World is not destined to become the exclusive workshop of the world, or the North the supplier of the world's food, but if living standards are to be raised in the Third World, industrialisation must of necessity play a large part and the search for markets will intensify so long as there is advantage to be gained from trade.

The force of Sir Arthur Lewis's argument is directed to the need of the developing countries to secure markets for their exports. This, of course, is one of their objectives, but they have also (perhaps mistakenly) made great efforts to improve the conditions on which they sell their primary products. The reasons why the developing countries proposed commodity stabilisation schemes may seem to be self-evident: many of them are highly dependent on commodities subject to fluctuating prices for export revenues and in other ways. Yet it should not be taken for granted that this will necessarily have markedly harmful effect without further examination of the likely consequences. A country experiencing fluctuation in export receipts will find that in some years it is very short of foreign exchange. Budgeting for imports could be troublesome with an irregular and fluctuating income. It need not be so if it is possible to keep substantial amounts of foreign exchange in reserve and, up to a point, this might be the best course to follow. Yet the building of reserves reduces the scope for increased domestic development effort or other forms of economic activity. An alternative might be to rely on the IMF for temporary assistance. The evidence seems to be that fluctuations in commodity prices are not a source of major difficulties for the less developed countries, certainly not large enough to justify international action on a grand scale to moderate commodity fluctuations.[12] Many of the effects of fluctuations can be absorbed. In the most favourable case they will affect only the activities of multinational corporations which absorb fluctuations in income in their profit figures (most of which is sent abroad), rather than in the employment that they offer or in the terms of the economic benefits they yield in the host country. More normally, fluctuations will be absorbed by a series of small adjustments and are smoothed over time as a result of government action and the use of reserves.

The arguments advanced above may have weakened the case for commodity stabilisation presented by the developing countries. The proposals were in any case vigorously opposed by most developed countries and even a greatly watered-down scheme for commodity stabilisation has not so far got off the ground. Experience of commodity schemes at the international level in the past shows that it is difficult to get agreement between producers and consumers and that agreements, when reached, are very hard to sustain.[13] By the end of 1985, only two commodity agreements, cocoa and rubber, survived; the tin agreement had collapsed and the OPEC countries had lost their ability to control prices.

Doubts on theoretical grounds may also be cast as to whether it is in the best interests of producers of primary products to establish price stabilisation schemes if no more than this is attempted. Whether receipts from the production of commodities are increased or decreased by price stabilisation depends on the conditions of supply and demand of the products in question; these may not, even generally, favour developing countries exporting primary products. Since this conclusion is not intuitively obvious, Appendix 4 shows on simple assumptions what conditions have to be met if benefits are to be obtained.

THE EFFECTS OF FOREIGN AID

It might seem that any flow of additional resources to developing countries would be beneficial, but this view is not without its challengers. If the inflow serves to relieve an import bottleneck it may be of much greater value than the actual amount, measured against the totality of available resources, might suggest. An inflow equivalent to 4 per cent of the gross national product may amount to no more than one year's growth in output once development has built up momentum. In the early years of development the inflow may, however, have the effect of filling two gaps that would otherwise tend to constrain growth: the import gap and the savings gap. Development makes considerable demands on imported goods and services and it may not be possible to increase export earning power sufficiently rapidly to meet this need. One consequence is that an inflow of resources may have very much greater impact on development than the amount of the inflow. Supposing that the import content of capital investment is 30 per cent, then $30 of imports would make it possible to undertake $100 of investment, the additional $70 of resources being provided domestically. This assumes, however, that domestic savings are sufficient to finance the additional investment. If this is not the case, then the imported resources can be used instead of domestic savings, effectively covering the savings gap. When this is the case, the effects of the inflow of resources will not be as great as they would be if it were possible to combine domestic resources with them.

In the 1950s and 1960s, an inflow of foreign resources was seen largely as a way to increase domestic investment. Ideally, this would not only result in an increase in income but would also help to produce commodities or services that would provide the means to service the inflow of capital by increasing exports or enabling imports to be reduced, so lessening demands on foreign exchange. Thus aid tended to be given for productive projects which might be concentrated on the provision of infrastructure (typically transport or public utility services), which otherwise might have been difficult to finance. Capital is still provided for such things but gradually it was realised that in some cases there was also a need for the provision of imported raw materials and other inputs, which could be processed but could not be paid for out of the country's limited foreign exchange resources. As a result, commodity aid emerged as an important element in the assistance given to some countries, including Bangladesh. In the 1970s, a further shift in emphasis took place when aid agencies became disillusioned about the effects that aid was having on development. It was argued, for example, that too much weight had been given to industrialisation and too little to the rural sector of the economy and agriculture. In the process, it was contended, the rich had grown richer and the poor perhaps even poorer in some instances, although not, it appears, as a general case.[14] The remedy proposed was to switch aid to the neglected areas in an attempt to make it more beneficial to the poor. In all this the providers of aid were inclined to try to influence the economic policies of the recipient countries in the direction of the donor countries' and agencies' thinking.

Thus the wrong use of aid was looked upon as an unfavourable influence on development by those concerned with the welfare of the poor. Others were inclined to consider it as harmful in nearly every way it might be used. Prominent among these is Professor Lord Bauer, a forceful writer. Bauer criticises the use of aid unmercifully:[15]

advocates of aid encourage the unfounded belief that the prime requisite of development can be had for nothing . . .[16]

the suggestion that foreign aid is indispensable for the development of the recipients implies that the progress of persons and groups depends on external forces.[17]

Many recipient governments pursue courses of action which patently reduce the level of income or retard its increase . . . The flow of unconditional aid supports . . . such policies.[18]

Foreign aid has probably affected adversely the market opportunities, and therefore the material position and development prospects, of many aid recipients.[19]

Foreign aid appears to be summed up by Bauer as a process by which poor people in rich countries help rich people in poor countries.[20]

Bauer's manifold strictures have not been without an echo amongst econometrically minded economists. One issue that they raised was simply whether an inflow of aid actually had the effect of increasing the rate of investment. This relates to the original intention of aid to increase productive capacity rather than subsequent attempts to direct it to improving the situation of the poor. Of course, aid is not intended in all cases to increase the rate of investment. Food aid is a case in point, being palpably given in famine and hunger conditions with the intention of increasing consumption. Even in different circumstances it is not to be expected that an influx of aid will be concentrated entirely on supplementing investment; any increase in resources is likely to be used for consumption as well as investment, in accord with normal economic principles. Nevertheless, some of the economic relationships did seem to suggest that the effects on investment were rather small.

Table 8.6, assembled by Professor Gustav Papanek shows the results of some studies of the effects of aid on investment or savings.[21] The first study, for example, by Griffin and Enos, suggests that an increase in foreign inflows of $1 would reduce savings by $0.73. Papanek shows, however, that the statistical work on which the conclusions are based is defective in a number of respects. For instance, a country experiencing famine might benefit from an increase in imports of food grains provided under aid programmes. In national-income-accounting conventions, the inflow of aid is regarded as foreign-financed investment in the country concerned and this is deducted from the total of investment in the country to give that part of the investment financed domestically. Since food aid is not likely to increase investment in the country (as it is destined for consumption), the statistical effect is to show a reduction in domestic savings. Hence it is concluded that aid reduces savings. There are other reasons also why the conclusions may be defective statistically, to which Papanek draws attention.

Table 8.6 The effect of resource inflows on savings or
investment

	No. of observations	Time series or cross-country	Savings or investment	Effect of foreign inflows on savings or investment
Griffin and Enos	32	C	S	−0.73
Rahman	31	C	S	−0.25
Areskoug	22	T	I*	+0.40*
Weisskopf	38	T	S	−0.23†
Chenery (JPE)	16	T	S	+0.64 to −1.15‡
Chenery (EDR 148)	90	C	S	−0.49
Chenery (EDR 148)	90	C	I*	+0.11*

  * Since savings in all calculations are defined as investment minus foreign inflows, an 0.40 increase in investment is equivalent to an 0.60 decrease in savings and vice versa.
  † According to Weisskopf, this is a minimum estimate and the reduction in savings is probably greater.
  ‡ Twelve out of twenty-six countries show a negative relationship.
  Source: Gustav F. Papanek, 'The Effect of Aid and Other Resource Transfers on Savings and Growth in Less Developed Countries', *Economic Journal*, Vol. 82 (1972), September, p. 937.

The theme is taken up again by Papanek in a later publication in which he draws attention to the differences that emerge if calculations of the kind described above are carried out in constant rather than current prices.[22] Nevertheless, it may be reasonable to suppose that aid does not generally result in a completely corresponding increase in investment; instead it may lead to a relaxation of government austerity policies and to some easing of the pressures to raise resources for development.

The effectiveness of aid must also be considered from the point of view of the composition of donor countries' aid and also to some extent in relation to multilateral aid. Aid from donors is frequently tied to the purchase of goods from the aid-providing country. To the recipient country such goods may be worth less than the goods that they would have bought had they been free to use the aid for purchases of other things elsewhere in the world. The administrative costs of donors may also be met out of the funds set aside for aid and these may therefore give a misleading impression of the totals that are available for use in the recipient country.

Most donors restrict the purposes for which they are prepared to give aid. It may be that these are not those that the recipient countries themselves would wish to promote or extend. If, however, such purposes figure in the programmes of the recipients, aid may be used to finance them, thus freeing the country's own resources for other uses. If this is not the case, the aid may still be accepted because it will be of some benefit, although not so much as it would have been, in the eyes of the country receiving it, had it been available for other purposes. In some cases, if, for example, it is not ideologically acceptable, it is likely to be refused.

There are considerable dangers in countries becoming too dependent on aid. Aid or some forms of aid may be withdrawn and may be difficult to replace. Moreover, aid does give countries and multilateral agencies the opportunity to exercise considerable influence on the policies of the recipient countries–an opportunity which is hard to resist. Some of these have been described elsewhere and the negotiations over the debts incurred by a number of Latin American countries in the 1980s amply illustrate the power of international financial forces to interfere in the affairs of debtor countries.[23]

In the 1970s, many developing countries acquired debts to international lenders that were to prove far beyond their capacity to pay. In total amounts, the most serious cases were those of Latin American countries, Argentina, Brazil, Mexico and Venezuela, but many other countries were involved too. In 1984 alone, the debts of thirty-four countries had to be renegotiated. The IMF recipe for situations in which countries are unable to meet their immediate financial obligations is essentially concerned with applying a 'realistic' exchange rate, controlling bank credit and the government deficit, with accompanying measures to control incomes and reduce inflation.[24] These measures may, in fact, greatly improve the situation in some cases. Helmut Reisen has analysed the course of adjustment to disequilibria in twelve countries and finds that price adjustments can have the effect of correcting disequilibria in the balance of payments by encouraging the production of tradable goods, mobilising savings and discouraging capital flight.[25]

To correct the debt situations in these ways is costly in terms of lost output and carries with it dangers of social unrest. Moreover, it does nothing to encourage creditors to make their own adjustments to facilitate debt servicing by increasing imports, seeking to reduce interest rates (which in the early 1980s were high), and providing means to reduce the debt burden itself on a sufficient scale.

As we have seen, aid and resource inflows come from both bilateral and multilateral sources. Some part of the bilateral flows is related to previous colonialist affiliations; political considerations also play a part; and sometimes also the desire to propagate the social and moral convictions of the countries offering aid. The Scandinavian countries, for example, have provided aid with the express intention of helping the downtrodden and the poor. It should not be supposed that multilateral agencies are free of political or other considerations of the same kind. Their policies are dictated by the countries which provide them with money, although they frequently develop a pattern of their own with their own particular ethos and predilections.

The most important multilateral institution in relation to the transfer of resources to developing countries is the World Bank. Its affiliates, the International Development Association (concerned with, virtually, extending grants to poor countries) and the International Finance Corporation (concerned with the provision of capital to the private sector of the economies), disperses about $12 billion per year at the present time. It is in a position of considerable power because, in addition to providing its own funds, it exercises a great deal of influence over the policies of other countries and agencies engaged in channelling funds to developing countries. It is also a centre of great knowledge and experience about the process of development and is staffed with very competent people. It frequently organises consortia of donors assisting a particular country and convenes meetings of those concerned to oversee the aid programmes, to discuss the progress of the country concerned and its policies and, incidentally, to attempt to mobilise the aid that it is judged to need.

The International Monetary Fund has a different function from that of the World Bank, that of dealing with short-term problems of liquidity, mainly in relation to the balance of payments. In recent years, its activities have gone far beyond that and most particularly in relation to those medium-income countries experiencing serious debt problems; thus the IMF has increasingly provided medium-term finance of a varied nature. In addition, it has mobilised loans and support from banks in many countries. In this respect the activities of the IMF are becoming closer to those of the World Bank, although the bulk of the assistance that has been given has concentrated on the activities of medium-income countries.

Many other international organisations are engaged in channelling resources to developing countries: regional development banks such as the Asian Development Bank, banks with special interests such as the International Fund for Agricultural Development, as well as a host of United Nations organisations and institutions concentrating on children, health, culture and many other special interests. The full list is a very long one.

Very many countries benefit from official development assistance and funds channelled through international agencies. Once on the aid list, countries tend to remain there. A more selective approach might be preferable in that it would concentrate a greater proportion of resources on particularly difficult cases. India and China, for example, with savings amounting to 20 and 30 per cent of their gross domestic products and with a definite export potential, might sensibly be largely excluded, and most middle-income countries would fall into the same category. If this were done, and a much more discriminating approach adopted, it would be possible to increase the effort to help deeply impoverished countries in Africa and elsewhere.

TRANSNATIONAL CORPORATIONS AND FOREIGN INVESTMENT

Trade and aid are only two of the ways in which developing and developed countries interact. In the last ten to twenty years, increasing attention and criticism have been directed at the operations of the transnational corporations (TNCs). Although transnational corporations might be regarded as a powerful instrument for modernisation of developing countries, the discussion of their operations has often been conducted in an atmosphere of antagonism and distrust, reflecting fear of exploitation by an overwhelming economic force, which to some extent eludes national control and makes it impossible to ensure that the resources and powers of such corporations are used for the benefit of the countries in which they operate, and not just in the interests of the corporations themselves.[26]

Since investment is very much at the heart of economic development it may seem strange at first glance that the activities of the transnational corporations should be the subject of attack. Absence of competition and the opportunity to charge monopoly prices is often an important factor, as there is seldom sufficient room in the market for manufactured products for more than a handful, sometimes only one or two, of producers. It may also be feared that if multinationals once gain a foothold in a developing country, they will expand their activities into other areas where they have expertise and so increase their hold on the economy. Criticism may be easily overdone. It should not be assumed from such strictures that branches of multinationals contribute less well to the economies in which they operate than indigenous firms of comparable size and standing.

Lall and Streeten, examining the performance of a sample of multinationals operating in Kenya, Jamaica, India, Iran, Columbia and Malaysia, found that they did not appear to have higher capital output ratios than other firms, that their capital to labour ratios were smaller and the extent to which they financed themselves from abroad higher.[27] They did appear to have adverse effects on the balance of payments, but these were not greater than those arising from the operations of other types of company, although it might have been that foreign control tended to limit exports to areas not supplied from other companies operated by parent companies. Similarly, they did not appear to make higher demands on imports. The extent to which royalty payments from subsidiaries to parent companies could be justified proved difficult to judge, although in some cases they were certainly considered to be excessive.

A matter of concern, the incidence of transfer payments on prices and profits, could not be investigated satisfactorily in most cases. It is extremely hard to establish whether the prices at which products (and services) are transferred from one firm to another within a group are close to the prices that could be secured in a competitive market. But Lall and Streeten suggest that for pharmaceutical firms operating in Columbia evidence of overpricing was strong.[28] Clearly there is considerable scope for the manipulation of transfer prices with the intention perhaps of justifying excessive charges for locally manufactured products based on imported inputs, or of transferring profits to countries where taxes were low. Transfer pricing can also serve as a vehicle to move money from one country to another and as a means to circumvent exchange controls. It is known, for example, that during the period 1966-75 over one-third of the sales of majority-owned affiliates of United States' companies were to the parent corporation.[29]

Attempts to appraise the social effects of multinational corporation activities using shadow prices suggested that their operations were undesirable from the national point of view; but again there did not seem to be very much difference in this respect between the multinational and other firms.

Standing behind all these criticisms voiced against transnationals is the thought that they are a law unto themselves concerned exclusively with private gains without regard for social considerations and that they constitute a state without a state. Moreover, they represent a powerful foreign influence–often with colonial overtones–in socially, politically and culturally vulnerable developing countries. While recurrent criticism of this nature has served to convey exactly these impressions and has been drawn on by the Group of 77 to reinforce their case for reform, there is in the literature a relative absence of defence of the activities of the transnationals in relation to the development of the Third World. Transnationals can be a powerful force in accelerating development in the Third World if their potentiality is properly exploited and directed.

Efforts have been made to suggest codes of conduct for transnational corporations aimed at outlawing a variety of objectionable actions evident in past history. Thus, transnational corporations should refrain from political intervention in the countries in which they operate and recognise a country's right to ownership of its natural resources. Other suggestions include the acceptance of local control, the need to contribute to the balance of payments of the country concerned and to limit calls on available domestic finance.

It has also been suggested that the issue of transfer pricing might be dealt with by reference to the principle of 'arm's length pricing', which means the acceptance of prices that would have been obtained in a market of independent sellers and buyers. Similarly, it has been proposed that issues of taxation should be dealt with through inter-governmental agreements and that problems of restrictive practices should be dealt with by compulsory disclosures of such practices, backed up by international agreements on enforcement. Clearly, today's world of international production, trade and finance is far from providing the institutions and means, not to speak of the political will, effectively to control and direct the operations of TNCs in these and other respects.

Control to restrain excesses and negative aspects of TNCs may indeed be needed, but so is action to ensure that the maximum benefit is derived for the host country from the positive elements of the operations of TNCs. Here, perhaps, the most important is the role of the TNC as a conduit for the transfer of technology.

The training and conditions of employment of labour is another issue. The demands of trade unions in developed countries, that their members should not be subject to competition from cheap labour overseas, are reinforced and provided with moralistic underpinnings by the arguments of other pressure groups, that TNCs should offer wages in host countries that do not smack of exploitation. From an economic point of view in the developing country itself, the determination of an appropriate level of wage rates would need to reflect–*inter alia*–an assessment of the employment opportunities that might be lost if higher than local labour market wages were to be paid by TNCs.[30]

Attempts to subject transnational corporations to intensive regulation by the countries in which they are prepared to invest may well prove to be counter-productive and lead to wider adoption of new forms of international investment less beneficial to the receiving countries. *Direct investment* with full control of production facilities is only one form of investment in developing (or other) countries.[31] Alternatives include *joint ventures* between a foreign firm and business interests in the country where development takes place; *licensing arrangements* for the use of technologies; *franchising*, whereby licensing, technical assistance, know-how, local exclusivity, trade marks and management assistance may be provided in return for a fee, royalties and compliance with corporate regulations; *management contracts*, by which the foreign company manages, trains and perhaps hands over to local managers in due course; *turnkey contracts*, in which a contractor provides a complete production unit and hands it over in a fully operational state; *product in hand*, in which the contractor's task is completed only when the turnkey installation is completely operational with local personnel operating it; *production-sharing*, used notably in the petroleum industry whereby the output is divided between corporation and company; and *international sub-contracting*, whereby a multinational firm places orders with a sub-contractor in a developing country.

All these arrangements may appear to offer advantages to the developing country in that they secure increased or total participation in the activity in question and hence apparent independence from outside influences. In this, such arrangements may prove to be deceptive in their assumed advantages and harmful in their effects. Algeria is a case in point. During the period 1966-71, almost all foreign firms were nationalised and foreign, private, direct investment effectively ruled out. Algeria's state industries, however, still needed to be able to draw on the services and expertise of foreign firms to extend productive facilities. This was arranged by placing contracts for the provision and installation of plant and equipment and extending this to turnkey and product-in-hand contracts. Even when major manufacturers were involved, technology and initial production management were usually supplied to the engineering firms establishing the plants. Through these arrangements, the provision of capital could be local, with the provision of know-how from one foreign company, and that of equipment from another engineering group. Thus the services normally provided by an investing firm were divided amongst a variety of participants.

With such arrangements, it may be difficult to ensure that what is received is up to date, efficient, well managed and capable of finding markets abroad if these are required. Guarantees may be asked for, but those furnished are likely to be well within the capabilities of the plants and not necessarily in line with the state of the art. Access to the most modern technologies may well be protectively restricted by firms that might have been prepared to utilise them if they had been in control. Risk resides with those who operate the plants rather than those who supplied them and might have operated them if different conditions for investment had been offered. Training may prove to be inadequate and obtaining spares needed to keep the plant in operation difficult.

If it is accepted that much greater industrialisation of the Third World is desirable, the transnational corporations might be looked at in a more positive manner, as a means of accomplishing this industrialisation, rather than as something that must be feared and fought, controlled and regulated. The experience of

Korea and Taiwan may point the way to effective industrialisation with transnational corporations playing a major role. The experience of Malaysia in recent years may also be worth considering for countries with the capabilities to buy up multinational corporations by effective take-over bids. However, the financial requirements for such exercises are undoubtedly beyond the resources of all but a few developing countries. It may well prove to be a very long time before codes for the conduct, operation and participation of transnational corporations are devised and even longer before any such codes can be put into operation.

What can the developing countries do in the meantime? It may be worthwhile to recognise that, in appropriate instances, transnationals can make a contribution to development that local companies cannot. When this is the case, satisfactory terms for the participation of the transnational corporation have to be negotiated by the government concerned so that there may be mutual understanding of what is needed. To take a telling example, though not necessarily a typical one because of that, the arrangements entered into between Botswana and the De Beers company for the mining and sales of diamonds have made a very considerable contribution to the development of Botswana. It was not necessary to have codes for international action to achieve a mutually satisfactory agreement in this case; even if such codes had existed, they might have been found to be deficient or irrelevant for this particular agreement. The proposition that the activities of transnational corporations are harmful to developing countries is not sustainable in general, but circumspection in particular cases is certainly called for. Neither in principle nor in practice is there any reason why transnational corporations should not contribute well to the progress of developing countries, but suitable arrangements must be negotiated with them. The fact that small is supposed to be beautiful should not be allowed to hide the fact that big may be dynamic.

LOOKING TO THE FUTURE

In the early 1970s there was a fear that the development effort was failing. Growth, it was thought, was slow and the gains, such as they were, inequitably divided. Looking back, it may be seen that these perceptions were over-pessimistic. Progress was being made but it was very uneven. Some countries stagnated and per capita incomes fell, while in others progress was slow or intermittent (see Table 1.3). Amongst the low-income countries, China attained a rapid rate of growth and Sri Lanka, progressing more slowly, succceded in providing for basic needs in spite of low production. In many other countries, extreme poverty persisted for large numbers of individuals, and there may have been about half a billion seriously undernourished people in the world, including at times many who were starving. Human affairs seldom meet the aspirations of caring people and it is likely to be half a century or more before the worst consequences of poverty can be eliminated. The impatient will say this is too long to wait, but students of history may well compare progress in the last forty or so years favourably with other periods of time and look forward to better things to come.

Growth of output has been surprisingly high in some areas of the world, as Table 8.7 shows, but output in other areas has declined, reducing the average for developing countries as a whole quite significantly. It appears that the low-income countries have managed to insulate themselves with some success from the slow growth rates of the developed countries in recent years.

Table 8.7 Growth of GDP per capita, 1960-95 (average annual percentage change)

Country group	1960-73	1973-80	1980-85	1985-95 High	Low
Industrial countries	3.9	2.1	1.8	3.7	2.0
Developing countries	3.6	3.4	0.9	3.5	2.7
Low-income countries	3.3	3.0	4.0	3.4	2.7
Asia	3.6	3.4	4.5	3.7	3.0
Africa	1.2	−0.1	−1.7	−0.1	−0.5
Middle-income oil-importers	3.8	3.3	−0.2	3.6	2.6
Major exporters of manufactures	4.3	3.7	0.1	4.4	3.3
Other countries	2.5	2.1	−1.0	1.5	1.0
Middle-income oil-exporters	3.5	3.1	0.8	2.7	2.0

Source: International Bank for Reconstruction and Development, *World Development Report 1985*, Oxford, Oxford University Press, 1985, p. 138.

Growth in output at a little less than 5 per cent per annum may provide for an increase in per capita income of about 2.5 per cent per annum. At this rate, per capita income doubles from its present average of about $300 to $600 in a little less than thirty years. For Asian countries the situation is better than average, reflecting the very poor performance in the African continent, where the increase in GDP has been insufficient to sustain the increase in population of about 3 per cent per annum. The slow rate of growth of middle-income countries since 1980 reflects, amongst other things, retrenchment in an effort to service the burden of debt they have accumulated. The slow rate of increase in the industrial market economies suggests that the developing countries will gradually catch up with them and that the stronger of the developing countries may overtake the weaker industrial countries in the not too distant future.

Another aspect of these disparate movements in output is the need to concentrate attention more on the plight of the African nations. They will have to seek most of their remedies themselves, but other countries may be able to assist in providing an increased flow of aid, helping to diversify production, increase agricultural output and improve the flow of trade by reducing barriers to their exports.

In these and other ways the economies of the developed and developing worlds are linked. Each of them, as we have seen, depends for export markets on the other. A high rate of growth in one area will tend to increase output in other areas through the growth of trade. In this respect also the growth of population in the developing world will tend to expand the markets of the industrial countries. But in other respects it may be harmful. How long will it take to arrest the growth of the world's population? Can food production be expanded sufficiently to provide for a greatly enlarged world population and can the resources be mobilised to do so? It may also be asked whether the supply of primary products and energy can be increased to support greatly expanded economic activity involving not only many more people but better-off ones as well. Some of the answers to these questions have been indicated by a series of studies.[32]

The population of the world is currently growing at about 1.7 per cent per annum, but there are very great differences between the more-developed and the less-developed regions and between the countries within them. The more-developed countries are experiencing a population increase of about 0.7 per cent per annum against about 2 per cent for the developing regions; the difference would be much greater if it were not for the much-reduced rate of growth in China's population. Nevertheless, there are signs of a general reduction in the rate of population increase in other developing countries, at least outside Africa. These trends have led Leon Tabah to suppose that the population of the world will move from its present total of some 5 billion to about 8 billion by the year 2025, finally perhaps stabilising somewhere between 8 and 14 billion.[33]

Could a population of this magnitude be fed? The answer is almost certainly yes, although whether the measures necessary to ensure this can be taken is uncertain. Detailed surveys of the earth's agricultural potential suggest that it would be possible to crop about one-quarter of its non-ice surface, say 3 billion hectares, and that this could be extended by irrigation and multiple cropping and further greatly extended if it were possible to find ways to cultivate the humid tropics, bringing the cultivable area to about 5 billion hectares. Without using the humid tropics, and assuming cereal yields only half that of the American corn belt, about 35 billion people could be fed at an average of 2,350 calories per day. This is using existing techniques: much greater yields than that assumed could almost certainly be obtained with existing techniques, and even more so if further advances were made, as may well seem likely. If the world's population could be contained at 10 billion or little more, and if the land could be used more productively than assumed, a very adequate diet for all could be produced.

The needs of the various areas of the world, however, are imperfectly matched with agricultural potential. Further computations suggest that at present developing countries would need to import about 250 million tons of foodgrains by 2030 from countries such as America that could produce a surplus, that is, about twice to two and a half times the present level of imports. Dependence on this scale might not be acceptable. Finally, if potential, rather than present, performance were to become operative, there would be no need for Africa to be suffering the present shortage of food.

The reason for studying economic development is to find ways of improving the position of impoverished people. There is no reason to be pessimistic about the existence of the material resources to do this, if population can be contained, but there must be concern about the ability of societies to mobilize themselves effectively to accomplish it. This is why it is so important to identify and implement such policies as are likely to provide for and hasten the progress of the poor. For many of them, inevitably, life will be short and miserable, for many others improvement will come but slowly, and recent history has demonstrated that there will be setbacks as well as gains. The time-span for the elimination of poverty is longer than might be thought from an apparent shortening of Rostow's stages of economic growth; perhaps a century or more must pass before the standard of life in backward countries can approach that of developed countries today. But in recent economic history it is also possible to see how—through determined and persistent domestic effort and adjustment to the changing international economic opportunities—some developing countries have emerged to growing affluence.

FURTHER READING

Just Faaland (ed.), *Population and the World Economy in the 21st Century*, London, Blackwell, 1982.
Robert Findlay, 'Trade and Development: Theory and Asian Experience', *Asian Development Review*, Vol. 2 (1984), No. 2, pp. 23-42.
W. Arthur Lewis, *The Evolution of the International Order*, Princeton, NJ, Princeton University Press, 1978.
Gustav F. Papanek, 'The Effect of Aid and Other Resource Transfers on Savings and Growth in Less Developed Countries', *Economic Journal*, Vol. 82 (1972), September, pp. 934-50.

NOTES

1. The grant element is obtained by calculating the total present value of all repayments (capital and interest) by discounting (in 1984) at a conventional 10 per cent, deducting this total from the amount borrowed, and then expressing the result as a percentage of the sum borrowed. No repayment, no interest, gives a grant element of 100 per cent; borrowing at 10 per cent results in a grant element of zero.
2. See Isaiah Frank, *Foreign Enterprise in Developing Countries*, Baltimore, Md., Johns Hopkins Press, 1980, Table 5, p. 19.
3. United Nations, Department of Economic and Social Affairs, *Multinational Corporations in World Development*, New York, 1973, Table 12, p. 148.

4. Ibid., p. 150.
5. See, Gerald K. Helleiner, *Intra-Firm Trade and the Developing Countries*, London, Macmillan, 1981, p. 19, quoting from William K. Chung, 'Sales by Majority-Owned Foreign Affiliates of US Companies 1975', *Surveys of Current Business*, Vol. 57 (1981), No. 2.
6. For an account, see Sanjaya Lall *et al.*, *The New Multinationals: the Spread of Third World Enterprises*, London, John Wiley, 1983.
7. International Bank for Reconstruction and Development, *World Development Report*, 1982, Oxford, Oxford University Press, 1982, Table 2.7, p. 14.
8. Note that for trade deficit countries, as with most developing countries, unchanged terms of trade, measured as a ratio of price indexes of exports and imports, at ever-increasing world market price levels result in an expanding trade-gap to be financed by capital import and foreign aid.
9. International Bank for Reconstruction and Development, *World Development Report 1984*, Oxford, Oxford University Press, 1984, Table 2.5, p. 18.
10. See Stein Rossen, *Notes on Rules and Mechanisms Governing International Economic Relations*, Chr. Michelsen Institute, 1981, DERAP Publication, 127.
11. Arthur W. Lewis, *The Evolution of the International Economic Order*, Princeton, NJ, Princeton University Press, 1978, pp. 14-19.
12. Some studies have gone so far as to suggest that the effects of fluctuations could be beneficial in some cases. It seems from the studies of Odin Knudsen and Andrew Parnes, (*Trade Instability and Economic Development*, London, Allen & Unwin, 1966, p. 112) that instability of income does have the effect, noted by Friedman in his permanent income theory, of increasing savings; it also appears from this study and that of Alasdair I. MacBean [*Export Instability and Economic Development*, London, Allen & Unwin, 1966, p. 112) that instability may be associated with higher investment ratios. Nevertheless, in a country such as Zambia faced with a ten year slump in the copper market, the effects can be very severe.
13. The tin agreement, now in a total state of collapse, is considered to have reduced instability in prices to only a marginal degree; the stock of 20,000 tons was never adequate and the price ceiling was frequently breached.[a] Fluctuations in the price of coffee over the period 1964-72 when an agreement was in operation were at least 50 per cent greater than for the non-agreement period 1950-63.[b] Large amounts of money are involved if stabilisation is to be brought about. To have held copper prices within a band of +15 to −15 per cent of long-run equilibrium levels between 1955 and 1974 would have required a maximum copper stock valued at over $3 billion in 1977 prices.[c]
   (a) Gordon W. Smith and George R. Schink, 'The International Tin Agreement: A Reassessemnt', *Economic Journal*, Vol. 86 (1976), December, p. 715-28.
   (b) Alasdair I. MacBean, 'Commodity Prices in a New International Order', in Arjun Sengupta (ed.), *Commodities Finance and Trade*, London, Frances Pinter, 1980, p. 63.
   (c) Alasdair I. MacBean, ibid., p. 63.
14. See, for example, Robert S. McNamara, *Address to the Board of Governors*, The World Bank, Washington DC, 29 September, 1972; and Irma Adelman and

Cynthia Taft Morris, *Economic Growth and Social Equity in Developing Countries*, Stanford, Calif., Stanford University Press, 1973, p. 179.

15. The quotations are taken from P. T. Bauer, *Dissent on Development*, student edn, London, Weidenfeld & Nicolson, 1976.
16. Ibid., p. 100.
17. Ibid., p. 101.
18. Ibid., p. 101.
19. Ibid., p. 102.
20. Ibid., p. 115.
21. Gustav F. Papanek, 'The Effect of Aid and Other Resource Transfers on Savings and Growth in Less Developed Countries', *Economic Journal*, Vol. 82 (1972), September, p. 937.
22. Gustav F. Papanek, 'Aid, Growth and Equity in Southern Asia', in Jack R. Parkinson (ed.), *Poverty and Aid*, London, Blackwell, 1983, pp. 169-82.
23. Just Faaland (ed.), *Aid and Influence*, London, Macmillan, 1981.
24. For a much-quoted recipe, see Cheryl Payer, 'The IMF in the 1980s: What Has It Learned: What Have We Learned About It?', *Third World Affairs 1985*, Third World Foundation, 1985, pp. 1-9.
25. See 'Disequilibrium Prices and External Debt: An Empirical Analysis for 1978-1984', in *Europe and Latin America in the World Economy*, Yale Center for International and Area Studies, 1985.
26. For a full-blooded condemnation of 'colonial' exploitation by transnational corporations, see Louis Turner, *Multinational Companies and the Third World*, London, Allen Lane, 1973, pp. 17-44, Chapter 2, 'The Bad Old Days of Naked Force'. The size of some corporations is commensurate with that of the national income of small or even medium-sized developing countries.
27. Sanjaya Lall and Paul Streeten, *Foreign Investment, Transnationals and Developing Countries*, London, Macmillan, 1977, Chapters 8-10.
28. Ibid., p. 153.
29. Gerald G. Helleiner, *Intra-Firm Trade and the Developing Countries*, London, Macmillan, 1981, p. 19, quoting from William K. Chung, 'Sales by Majority-Owned Foreign Affiliates of US Companies 1975', *Survey of Current Business*, Vol. 57 (1977), No. 2.
30. Attempts to outline codes for the behaviour of TNCs are often extended to take in other objectives related, on the side of the host country, to such issues as consumer protection and disclosure of information and, on the side of the TNCs, to guarantee against expropriation without adequate compensation. The issues involved in the formulation of a code of conduct are discussed in *Transnational Corporations*, Centre on Transnational Corporations, United Nations, 1976, E/C.10/17, 20 July, 1976.
31. The discussion draws on Charles Oman, *New Forms of International Investment in Developing Countries*, OECD, 1984.
32. For example, those contained in Just Faaland (ed.), *Population and the World Economy in the 21st Century*, London, Blackwell, 1982, which are drawn upon in this discussion.
33. Ibid., p. 230.

Appendices

APPENDIX 1: CORRECTING DOMESTIC PRICE DISTORTIONS
BY TARIFFS OR SUBSIDIES

The argument and presentation in this appendix, as in
Appendix 2, draws heavily on an article by Harry G. Johnson,
'Tariffs and Economic Development, Some Theoretical Issues',
published in the *Journal of Development Studies*, Vol. 1 (1964),
No. 1, pp. 3-30.

Suppose that wages in a domestic industry competing with
imports are artifically high so that output is less than it would be
without this distortion and imports correspondingly greater. If it
is required to correct this without attacking directly the root cause
of the distortion, the artifically-high wage level, should it be done
by imposing a tariff on competing imports or by subsidising the
use of labour? Welfare considerations suggest that the subsidy
would be the better choice. A proof of this is derived from
Figure A1.

In the diagram SS would be the domestic supply curve if there
were no distortion in costs. S^1S^1 is the supply curve after taking
account of such distortions. The line drawn at the height P_f is the
foreign supply curve with infinite elasticity. If there were no
distortion, the minimum cost supply curve would be compounded
from the domestic supply curve S to E and the foreign supply
curve (imports) from E to F. With distortion this becomes S^1 to G
and G to F. The demand curve is DD. Without distortion on the
supply side, the optimal home output would be Q_2, to which
would be added foreign supply (imports) $Q_4 - Q_2$. With distortion
in domestic costs, home output would be Q_1 and imports $Q_4 - Q_1$.
In both cases consumption would be Q_4 if an appropriate tariff
equivalent to a proportion d of the foreign supply price were
imposed, the new total supply curve would become S_1 to H and H
to I if supply distortion obtains. This would have the effect of

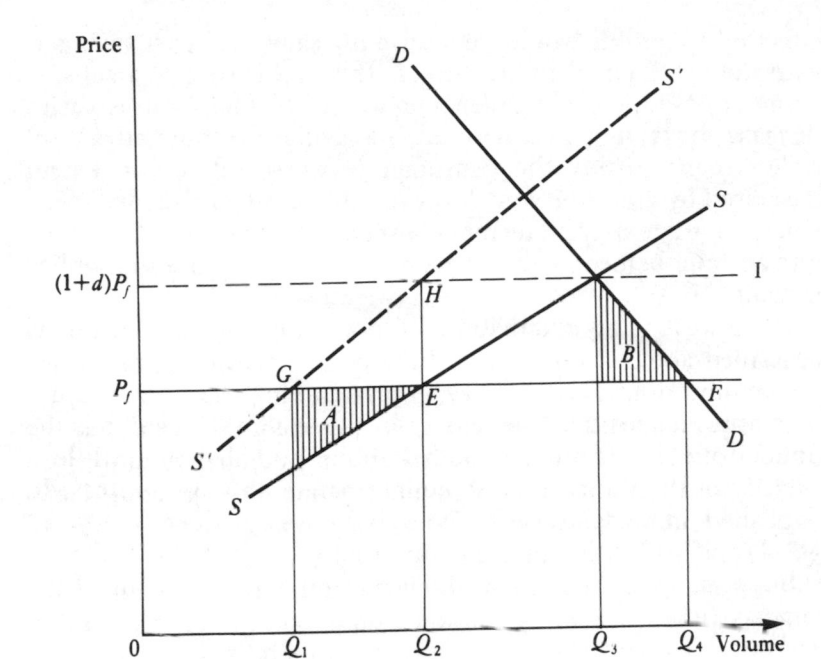

Figure A1 Effects of tax and subsidy intervention

giving domestic output Q_2 (as it would be without distortion and without the tariff) and total demand of Q_3, with the foreign supply now amounting to $Q_3 - Q_2$. In the process there is a saving of domestic production cost of A, equal to the area A, because the real (undistorted) cost of production domestically is less than the foreign supply price. However, the price to the consumer will be increased and he will reduce his purchases by $Q_4 - Q_3$, so incurring a net loss equivalent to the area B. (Note that the loss to the consumer from the imposition of the tax is assumed to be balanced by the receipts of the state and the producer). Area A may be greater or less than area B and so it is possible that the imposition of a tariff will result in net gain or loss.

If, as an alternative to the tariff, it were decided to subsidise the domestic producer so as to lower his distorted cost sufficiently to give him the same sales, Q_2, again as he would have had without distortion, the producer will have to be paid a subsidy of $d \times Q_2$. (Here the cost of the subsidy to the state is assumed to be balanced by the receipt of the subsidy by the producer.) One effect of doing this would be to give the same real cost saving as with the tariff, equal to the area A. But in this case of a subsidy being imposed, the consumer is no worse off. This contrasts with the case above: in both cases there is a saving of A, but with a tariff rather than subsidy the consumer is worse off to the extent measured by area B. (Note, however, that as in any 'second-best' situation, there may be further consequences that would be taken into account before weighing the pros and cons of different policy measures.)

If, however, in a situation of domestic cost distortion as described above the purpose of the policy measure is to reduce the amount of imports, it is appropriate to impose a tariff rather than apply a subsidy. The reason for this is that the tariff has the double effect of reducing both imports and demand, while a subsidy of the same amount would operate only on imports. In Figure A1, imports would be reduced from the amount $Q_4 - Q_1$ to $Q_3 - Q_2$ if a tariff is imposed, and from $Q_4 - Q_1$ to $Q_4 - Q_2$ if a subsidy is used, that is, a difference of $Q_4 - Q_3$ in favour of the tariff.

APPENDIX 2: EFFECTS OF UNIFORM AND DIFFERENTIAL DUTIES

An administrator, faced with a demand to rationalise import duties imposed for protection purposes, might well start by arguing that price relativities would be least disturbed if the same rate of duty were imposed on all classes of goods. Unfortunately for this simple judgement, it may be shown that, given different elasticities of supply and demand for the various commodities imported, welfare will be increased if duties are tailor-made for the demand-and-supply conditions applying to each commodity. In short, for a given amount of protection, duties should vary in order to maximise welfare. A proof of this is given below using Figure A2, which is similar to Figure A1.

The analysis starts with considering the effects of applying a uniform tariff on the two goods depicted, one on the left and the other on the right. Note that the left-hand part of the diagram is drawn as though looking in a mirror; the demand curve slopes down to the left and the supply curve rises also the left. In order to make it possible to compare the two sides of the diagram, the units of quantity in each case are those worth, say, £1 at world market prices.

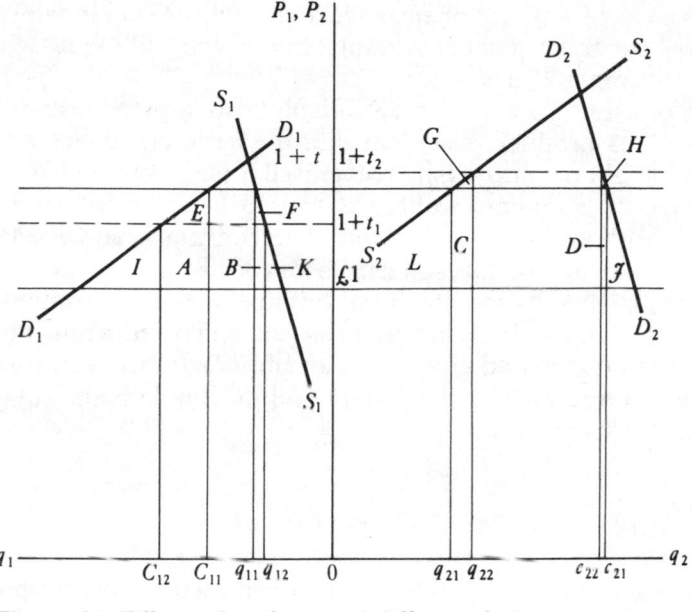

Figure A2 Effects of uniform and different duties

The effect of the uniform tariff (t) is to cause a loss in welfare from reduced consumption for the left-hand side of $I + A + E$ (after allowing for tariff receipts) and for the right-hand side of J (again after allowing for tax receipts). In each case there will be an excess cost of production above the cost at which the products could be imported. This is $F + B + K$ for the left-hand side commodity and L for the right-hand side commodity. Thus, the total cost or loss resulting from the imposition of the tariff is

$$I + A + E + J + F + B + K + L$$

Now suppose that the tariffs imposed are not uniform but equal to t_1 for the left-hand side and t_2 for the right-hand side, the rates being chosen so as to keep the total value of imports the same. The loss is now:

$$I + D + J + H + K + L + C + G$$

The difference between these two situations is:

$$A + E - (D + H) + F + B - (C + G)$$

This may be positive or negative and from the way in which the curves are drawn a net gain results from having different tariffs on the two commodities.

In practice it is clearly very difficult to attempt to measure consumers' or producer's surplus, but the basic argument outlined above might be more easily recognised if put in other terms. Less damage to economic welfare is caused by imposing duties on goods with an inelastic demand. The consumer pays the tax on what is consumed, thus suffering a loss of consumers' surplus, but this is matched by the receipt of revenue by the government; and since demand is inelastic there is not much reduction in consumption that would give rise to an additional loss of consumers' surplus unrequited by the receipt of duty. Similarly the supply of goods is elastic.

APPENDIX 3: EFFECTIVE PROTECTION

Tariffs on imported goods, whether imposed for the purpose of raising revenue or for other reasons, confer protection on domestic producers of those goods. In so far as the purpose of imposing a tariff is not to produce differential effects, but rather to raise revenue, it has to be considered how the tariff structure may be organised so as to provide equal treatment to different industries, so that one or more of them are not given favourable treatment at the expense of the others. At first sight, an approximate answer might seem to be to impose a uniform tariff, although, as we have seen, this will not have the effect of maximising welfare when the effects on consumers' and producers' surplus are taken into consideration. In practice, tariffs are unlikely to be imposed at uniform rates and we may need to establish what effects this will have on the protection afforded to the different industries.

It would be wrong to assume that the degree of protection afforded should be measured by the nominal rate of the tariff imposed. A 20 per cent tariff on the import of bicycles does not necessarily imply that the domestic producers of bicycles are protected to this extent. How much protection is given to them will also depend, amongst other things, on whether the materials they use are also subject to import duties, which has the effect of raising their prices above the world level. In assessing the extent to which industries are protected, we need to know what the degree of protection is on the value that they add. This is best worked out with reference to an international standard for comparison. To this end we may use, as a measure of effective protection, the difference in value added when calculated in, respectively, domestic and international prices, divided by the value added at international prices.

An illustration may show how this works. Suppose a finished manufactured commodity is imported for $100 and competes with a similar domestic product. In a freely functioning market and with an import duty of 20 per cent, it would sell for the equivalent of not more than $120 assuming that some imports take place. Suppose also that domestic production of the commodity requires $20 of imported raw materials subject to a duty of 10 per cent. Then the value added by the foreign manufacturer would be $80 while the value added by the domestic producer would be $98 (120-22). Thus effective protection would be (98-80)/80 or 22.5 per cent. If the exchange rate corresponds to the value of the domestic currency in competitive conditions, estimating effective protection is thus straightforward in principle. But if, for example, imports are restricted by controls and so are scarce, domestic prices may exceed the landed cost of the imports plus any duties imposed. This in effect would give an additional degree of protection which would have to be taken into account. Some results from calculating effective protection for Pakistan in 1963-64 are shown below in Table A1. Here the figures given for nominal protection refer simply to the rates given in the official

Table A1 Nominal and effective production in Pakistan, 1963-64

	Average nominal tariff protection	Effective tariff protection
Industries producing primarily:		
Consumption goods	78	477
Intermediate goods	29	22
Investment and related goods	31	43

Source: Bela Balassa *et al.*, *The Structure of Protection in Developing Countries*, Baltimore, Md., Johns Hopkins Press, 1971.

tariff schedule. As for the effective tariff protection rates, there are various measures, depending on whether imports are considered to be 'scarce', that is, commanding a premium over landed cost plus duties, and whether domestically produced intermediate goods are integrated within an industrial sector or not. The definition used here is that of Balassa and assumes that imports were not scarce. It should be noted that the different concepts give very different measures of effective protection, varying in the case of silk from 626 to 9,900. Clearly, the figures have to be interpreted with the utmost care.

It is clear from the table that the two measures of protection differ markedly. It is possible for effective protection to be negative as well as positive, for instance, when raw materials used in industry are subjected to greater rates of duty than the finished product. It may also happen that calculations of effective protection can show that value added, when measured in international prices, may turn out to be negative. This was true for sugar in the 1960s for Pakistan because the price of the cane was greatly in excess of the world price. It may also occur when parts of motor vehicles are imported for assembly at a price in excess of the world price for an assembled vehicle. Something similar may sometimes arise, or nearly arise, when manufacture for export is subsidised by one device or another, which was the case for cotton in Pakistan in the 1960s.

The variations in the degree of protection is evident, that is, Table A1 shows clear evidence of distorted price signals. The effects of such distortions can be serious as maintained by the World Bank in *World Development Report 1983*, particularly in chapter 6.

APPENDIX 4: THE EFFECTS ON REVENUE OF PRICE STABILISA-
TION

It appears that if instability is caused by the demand curve shifting, price stabilisation reduces the revenues of the exporting country; if however, instability is caused by shifts in the supply curve, the reverse applies. The simplest models to illustrate the various issues involved have been developed in terms of straight line supply-and-demand curves as presented in Figures A3 and A4. One such model has been prepared by the World Bank and

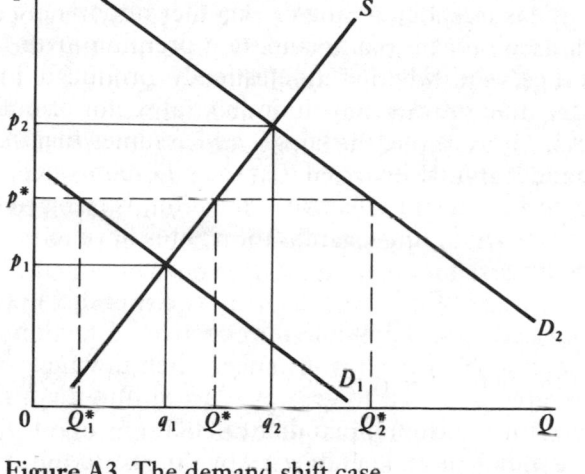

Figure A3 The demand shift case

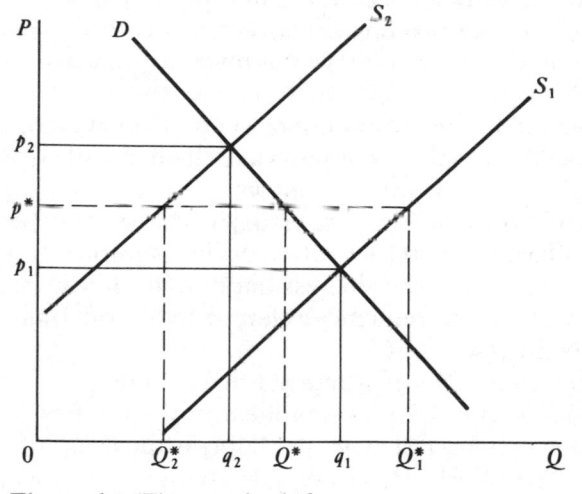

Figure A4 The supply shift case

published as an article by Ezriel M. Brook, Enzo R. Grilli and Jean L. Waelbroeck as World Bank Staff Working Paper No. 262 on *Commodity Price Stabilization and the Developing Countries*.

For the purposes of the argument, assume that there are instantaneous reactions of supply and demand to price changes and that shifts in the state of supply and demand can be represented by parallel movements of the supply or demand curves, whichever may be under consideration. A price level midway between the prices determined by the alternative positions of the curves is taken to represent the price stabilisation position P*. The form of the model may readily be discerned from the two figures. In Figure A3, for example, the supply curve remains stationary and the demand curve shifts from D_1D_1 to D_2D_2 respectively. The question to be answered is, will the revenue received when the curves shift without price stabilisation being applied be greater or less than the revenue than would have been obtained with stabilisation? In terms of Figure A3 this may be expressed in the following form:

$$(Op_1 \times Oq_1) + (Op_2 \times Oq_2) \geqslant 2 \times (Op^* \times Oq^*)$$

where the two parentheses on the left represent the export revenue without price stabilisation in the two respective market situations, and the parenthesis on the right represents the revenue that would have been received if the price had been stabilised. (Since we consider two unstabilised cases we need to multiply the latter expression by 2 to make the revenue comparison comparable.)

The second figure carries out the same kind of comparison but in this case the supply curve shifts and the demand curve remains the same. The results are as follows: if the demand curve shifts, price stabilisation reduces revenue; if the supply curve shifts, price stabilisation increases revenues. For a formal proof of these propositions based on the assumption of linear supply and demand curves, the reader is referred to World Bank Working Paper No. 262 (see above).

The determination of whether price stabilisation is beneficial to developing countries as suppliers now becomes a matter of determining whether demand or supply is the cause of price fluctuations. The World Bank analysis attempted to ascertain this, but the method used was technically defective. Nevertheless, it may be said that there does not appear to be convincing evidence that commodity stabilisation will generally enhance the position of the developing countries, given their import and export patterns. Some of these issues are treated in a paper by D. T. Nguyen, 'The Effects of Partial Price Stabilisation on Export Earnings Instability and Level', in Arjun Sengupta, (ed.), *Commodities, Finance and Trade*, London, Frances Pinter, 1980.

Index

FAALAND, J. & PARKINSON, J. R — Political economy of dev'